ROSCOMMON

D0869337

Roscommon

The Irish Revolution, 1912–23

John Burke

FOUR COURTS PRESS

Set in 10.5 on 12.5 point Ehrhardt for
FOUR COURTS PRESS LTD
7 Malpas Street, Dublin 8, Ireland
www.fourcourtspress.ie
and in North America for
FOUR COURTS PRESS
c/o IPG, 814 N. Franklin St, Chicago, IL 60610.

A catalogue record for this title
is available from the British Library.

ISBN 978–1–84682–807–2

Printed in England
by CPI Antony Rowe, Chippenham, Wilts.

Contents

Illustrations

Credits

Illustrations 1: Eugene Daly; 2, 28: Jim Ganly; 3: John Burke; 4: *Roscommon Messenger*, 29 November 1913 (image adjustments by Clair O'Reilly); 5, 6, 21, 23, 27: Albert Siggins; 7, 12: Richie Farrell; 8, 9, 10, 13, 16, 17, 19, 26: Getty Images; 11, 20: Liam Byrne; 14, 15, 18, 32: National Library of Ireland; 22, 25: Aidan Heavey Library, Athlone; 24: May Moran; 29, 30, 31: Ó Dulacháin Collection

MAPS

Abbreviations

AOH	Ancient Order of Hibernians
APJ	*Aberdeen Press and Journal*
ASU	Active Service Unit
ATIRA	Anti-Treaty Irish Republican Army
BMH	Bureau of Military History
BNL	*Belfast News Letter*
BT	*Belfast Telegraph*
BWT	*Ballymena Weekly Telegraph*
CDB	Congested Districts Board
CI	County Inspector, RIC
CMA	Competent Military Authority
CO	Colonial Office, TNA
DC	*Dundee Courier*
DDE	*Dublin Daily Express*
DÉLG	Dáil Éireann Local Government Department
DET	*Dublin Evening Telegraph*
DH	*The Daily Herald*
DI	District Inspector, RIC
DJ	*Derry Journal*
DORA	Defence of the Realm Act
EPG	*Exeter and Plymouth Gazette*
FJ	*Freeman's Journal*
GAA	Gaelic Athletic Association
GE	*Gloucestershire Echo*
GHQ	General Headquarters, IRA
Hansard	House of Commons debates
HC	Head Constable, RIC
IC	*Irish Citizen*
IFS	Irish Free State
IFU	Irish Farmers' Union
IG	Inspector General, RIC
II	*Irish Independent*
IMA	Irish Military Archives
INL	Irish Nation League
INV	Irish National Volunteers
IPP	Irish Parliamentary Party
IRA	Irish Republican Army
IRB	Irish Republican Brotherhood

IT	*Irish Times*
ITGWU	Irish Transport and General Workers' Union
IV	*Irish Volunteer*
JP	Justice of the Peace
LGB	Local Government Board
LS	*Londonderry Sentinel*
MP	Member of Parliament
MS	Manuscript
MSPC	Military Service Pensions Collection
MVF	Midland Volunteer Force
NAI	National Archives of Ireland
NLI	National Library of Ireland
NW	*Northern Whig*
OC	Officer commanding
RAEC	Roscommon Associated Estates Committee
RDC	Rural District Council
RH	*Roscommon Herald*
RIC	Royal Irish Constabulary
RJ	*Roscommon Journal*
RM	*Roscommon Messenger*
ROIA	Restoration of Order in Ireland Act
RTC	Roscommon Town Commissioners
SD	*Strokestown Democrat*
SDT	*Sheffield Daily Telegraph*
SF	Sinn Féin
TD	Teachta Dála
TG	*The Globe*
TNA	The National Archives, London
TS	*The Scotsman*
TTL	Town Tenants' League
UCDA	University College Dublin Archives
UIL	United Irish League
UVF	Ulster Volunteer Force
WFJ	*Weekly Freeman's Journal*
WI	*Westmeath Independent*
WIT	*Weekly Irish Times*
WN	*Western Nationalist*
WO	War Office, TNA
WS	Witness statement to Bureau of Military History
YPLI	*Yorkshire Post and Leeds Intelligencer*

Acknowledgments

I was invited to contribute to the Irish Revolution series in 2013. I never imagined that it would be over seven years before it was ready for publication! As ever, an undertaking such as this is never really a solo project.

I would like to thank the members of the County Roscommon Archaeological and Historical Society for all of their assistance. It is heartening to meet so many people who have such an interest in their own area; they will keep the old stories alive. Specifically, I would like to thank Mary O'Connell, Marian Harlow, Albert Siggins, May Moran and Jim Ganly for their help with sourcing images for the book. Thanks also to Liam Byrne for providing not only some quality images, but for putting me in contact with Conor Dullahan, who selflessly consented to providing further illustrations. Thanks also to two retired librarians, Richie Farrell of Roscommon and Gearóid O'Brien of Athlone, for their help in sourcing pictures of important people and events. Many thanks to Paul Davis of Getty Images for his help in securing the use of many high-quality images of events and personalities that influenced Roscommon's experience of the revolutionary period. Also, a belated thanks to Brendan and Vicky McGowan. Their inclusion here will hopefully right a previous omission!

I would also like to extend my gratitude to the staff at the Roscommon County Library in Roscommon town, the staff at the James Hardiman Library at the National University of Ireland Galway and the staff at University College Dublin Archives. I am very grateful to the staff at the National Archives of Ireland and the National Library of Ireland who, even during lockdown, responded promptly to all my queries. I would like to both thank and congratulate the Irish Military Archives for their assistance and their work in rendering so many important records of the Irish Revolution even more accessible. Similarly, the archivists and staff at The National Archives at Kew in Britain have realised great advances in making their vast archive that bit easier to trawl.

To the series editors, Dr Daithí Ó Corráin and Professor Mary Ann Lyons, I extend both thanks and apologies. Often progress was neither as I hoped or forecast. Thanks also to the series cartographer, Dr Mike Brennan, for the expertly rendered maps.

To my two (conscripted) proof readers, Drs Conor and Helen Burke, your assistance was essential in helping me identify the flaws that I could no longer see. I will reward your efforts by calling on your skills again in the future!

To my parents, John and Carmel, and my sisters, Stephanie and Suzanne, I would like to confirm my love and thanks. It was difficult for you to know when to ask about the book and when not to; you navigated that minefield expertly!

My most heartfelt thanks goes to my loving wife, Clair, and my two beautiful girls, Isabelle and Aoife. I began this project before either were born; it will be a pleasure to devote more time to them now that it is completed.

The Irish Revolution, 1912–23 series

Since the turn of the century, a growing number of scholars have been actively researching this seminal period in modern Irish history. More recently, propelled by the increasing availability of new archival material, this endeavour has intensified. This series brings together for the first time the various strands of this exciting and fresh scholarship within a nuanced interpretative framework, making available concise, accessible, scholarly studies of the Irish Revolution experience at a local level to a wide audience.

The approach adopted is both thematic and chronological, addressing the key developments and major issues that occurred at a county level during the tumultuous 1912–23 period. Beginning with an overview of the social, economic and political milieu in the county in 1912, each volume assesses the strength of the home rule movement and unionism, as well as levels of labour and feminist activism. The genesis and organization of paramilitarism from 1913 are traced; responses to the outbreak of the First World War and its impact on politics at a county level are explored; and the significance of the 1916 Rising is assessed. The varying fortunes of constitutional and separatist nationalism are examined. The local experience of the War of Independence, reaction to the truce and Anglo-Irish Treaty and the course and consequences of the Civil War are subject to detailed examination and analysis. The result is a compelling account of life in Ireland in this formative era.

Mary Ann Lyons
Department of History
Maynooth University

Daithí Ó Corráin
School of History & Geography
Dublin City University

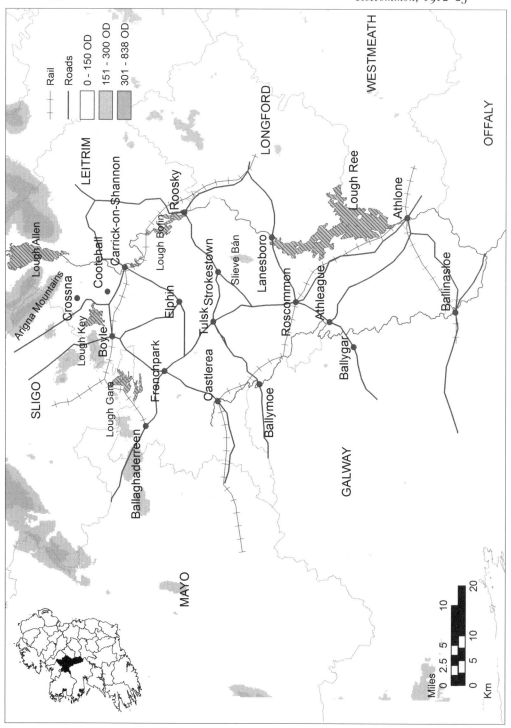

1 Places mentioned in the text

1 County Roscommon in 1912

Sitting at his typewriter in January 1922, J.P. Hayden, the former Irish Parliamentary Party (IPP) MP for Roscommon South, must have looked bewildered as he finished composing an editorial for his *Roscommon Messenger*: 'the present settlement ... would have satisfied the people at any time since the passage of the Act of Union'.[1] He referred to the Anglo-Irish Treaty that ended the Irish War of Independence. As he recalled the adulation he enjoyed while the inferior 1914 home rule act was being drafted, his difficulty comprehending the politics of 1922 was understandable. How could a man so central to Roscommon's political life in 1912 be so peripheral just ten years later? In part, it was because from 1912 Hayden and his colleagues focused on high politics rather than the personal and local concerns that drove political activism at county level. In Roscommon, they neglected the fight for the land. The preceding thirty years proved that land was the one issue that could motivate Roscommon people to engage in agitation on a quasi-revolutionary scale. Roscommon supported the IPP when MPs like Hayden campaigned alongside their constituents, secured beneficial land acts and kept land at the heart of their policies. Indeed, when the IPP held the balance of power at Westminster after the 1910 general election and sought a third home rule bill, support in Roscommon was not so much for the measure of self-government as for home rule's potential to deliver land equity. Hayden's relegation was also the result of developments that were beyond the IPP's control. With the First World War, the home rule act was suspended and land agitation stalled. People in Roscommon chafed at IPP calls for patience and became increasingly receptive to advanced nationalist arguments that the IPP was favouring the empire over Ireland. Growing anger was amplified by efforts to promote army enlistment, the British reaction to the 1916 Easter Rising and moves to partition Ireland. As this book will show, when people in Roscommon began to align themselves with a new political movement, Sinn Féin (SF), and elected the first MP supported by that party in 1917, land was never far from their minds. Certainly, many in Roscommon wished to break with Britain. Thousands marched in support of the republic, voted for representatives who pursued it and assisted the minority who took up arms and fought for it. However, land was the only issue that inspired hundreds to engage in large-scale violent conflict throughout the War of Independence (1919–21). When the Anglo-Irish Treaty was signed, the majority in Roscommon accepted the settlement given that it would end the violence and more quickly address inequity in land distribution and other socio-economic concerns. The minority who did not were driven by republican ideology rather than the localism that defined Roscommon politics.

In 1912 Roscommon was the eleventh-largest county in Ireland and third largest in Connacht. Defined in the east and north-east by the River Shannon and on the south and south-west by the River Suck (see map 1), the county's boundaries enclosed expansive lowlands across the bulk of its land area with limited upland regions only in north Roscommon. Bordering six other counties – Counties Galway, Mayo, Sligo, Leitrim, Westmeath and Longford – ensured that Roscommon was not only a destination but a thoroughfare for many travellers. In 1912 it was served by an extensive road network and three railway routes. The Midland Great Western Railway managed all lines in Roscommon. Two entered Athlone in the south from Dublin. One went north-west to Ballinlough via Roscommon town and Castlerea and then west into Mayo. The other went directly west to Ballinasloe and from there to Galway. A third line in the north of the county ran from Mayo into Ballaghaderreen and from there to Boyle via Kilfree junction. It exited the county at Carrick-on-Shannon, extending eastwards towards Broadstone in Dublin (see map 1).

The Local Government Act (1898) reformed the constitution, responsibilities and jurisdictions of the bodies that administered each county's affairs. Subordinate to Roscommon County Council were the rural district councils (RDC). The smallest of these retained the names of administrative centres outside of the county: Athlone No. 2, Ballinasloe No. 2 and Carrick-on-Shannon No. 2 (see map 2). Boards of guardians operated at Roscommon, Castlerea, Strokestown and Boyle. They were responsible for managing workhouses and related relief programmes for the poor. The towns of Roscommon and Boyle each also hosted a board of town commissioners. The expanded franchise that resulted from a provision in the 1898 Act ensured that all of these bodies were controlled by supporters of Ireland's dominant nationalist party, the IPP.

In the early 1910s, Roscommon was still experiencing population decline that began during the Great Famine. Between 1901 and 1911 its population fell by 7,835 people to 93,956. Not since 1821 had the number dropped below 100,000. The dominant religion was Roman Catholicism (97.6 per cent).[2] Protestant Episcopalians numbered just 1,887 (two per cent) and were concentrated in north Roscommon.[3] All denominations experienced declining numbers since the turn of the century. The most dramatic decline occurred in rural areas encircling Castlerea, Roscommon town, Strokestown, Athlone and Boyle. In general, there was no growth in these urban areas. Only Boyle, the largest town with 2,691 citizens, witnessed modest growth which equalled roughly twenty per cent of the decline in its rural hinterland. The county town, Roscommon, lagged behind Boyle, its population (1,858) having declined since 1901. With small populations in Ballaghaderreen (1,317), Castlerea (1,224), Strokestown (801) and Elphin (649), County Roscommon had the second-highest rurality rate in Ireland at 90.9 per cent, just behind Leitrim.[4]

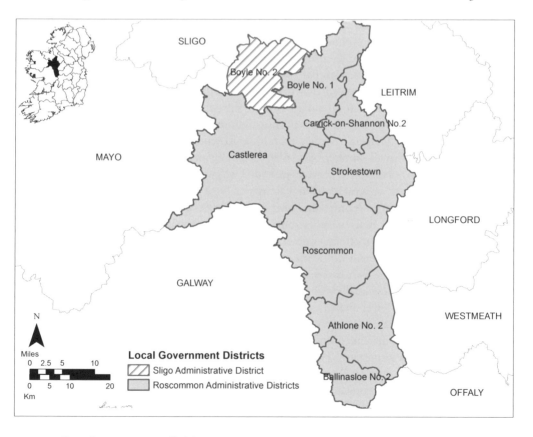

2 Local government divisions

Population decline was in part the result of emigration. Between 1891 and 1911, Roscommon experienced the sixth-highest emigration rate in Ireland. During the decade to 1911, 11,000 people left the county.[5] Tellingly, although there was an overall fall-off in the average numbers leaving since 1901, there was an upward trend from 1908 to 1912.[6] Similar patterns in other western counties suggested that those leaving in 1912 had no intention of returning. Of the 747 Roscommon people who emigrated – mainly young, single and almost evenly split between the sexes – all bar four went to North America.[7]

A major reason for this emigration was unemployment. In Roscommon, just over 28,500 people were employed in agriculture, an unappealing sector given disputes over land and pay. Regions bordering the towns were unemployment black spots.[8] In 1912 'industry' employed only 4,522 people, and even then, this number included tailors, blacksmiths, thatchers and chemists. The Arigna mines in the north, considered by the county's Royal Irish Constabulary (RIC) county inspector (CI), G.B. Rutledge, to be the only good employer 'off the land', had a mere forty-three coal miners in 1911.[9] General labouring was the next most common occupation for men (at just over 1,450). While many may have been hired to assist with ancillary mining activities, road maintenance and similar projects, the majority worked on farms. Underemployment ensured that Roscommon's decades-old tradition of supplying seasonal migrant labour to Britain was still a necessity in 1912. Only Mayo and Donegal supplied proportionately more individuals, with similarly circumstanced Galway roughly matching Roscommon's contribution. The comparatively small number of women in employment were also mostly working on farms. Domestic service provided employment for 1,100, the next highest number of females. The vast majority of people, some 57,000, were categorized as in indefinite or non-productive occupations, a category that included not only housewives, young children, pensioners and the infirm, but also many younger men and women for whom finding sustained employment was a challenge. Small numbers of the more prosperous classes operated in the larger towns, which had fewer than 550 shop owners, merchants and publicans. The professional classes of doctors, police, teachers, clergy and solicitors numbered fewer than 1,100.[10]

Unlike Galway, Sligo or Westmeath, which had large towns, Roscommon's commercial life depended on agriculture. The vagaries of farming were therefore especially important. The county was dominated by farmsteads and since the nineteenth century Roscommon was a premier region for cattle fattening. Pastoral farming occupied more than five times the acreage of crop farming by 1912, the more lucrative animal industry ensuring that great prosperity was available to those with the means to increase their herds and acres. The consequences for their less able neighbours were obvious.[11] Although in 1912 sheep still dominated, cattle numbers in Roscommon had increased in line with the national trend since 1903. Large number of pigs and horses were also recorded, together with various species of fowl.[12] The most popular crops grown in the decreasing acreage under tillage acres were potatoes – champion potatoes specifically – followed by oats, turnips, beetroot and cabbage.[13]

Legislation enacted in the three decades prior to 1912 had seen the emergence of numerous peasant proprietors in Roscommon. Indeed, fractious relations in Roscommon on the county's largest estate, that of Lord de Freyne of Frenchpark, helped shape the 1903 Land Act under which many tenants became proprietors. Decades of animus on the estate fed anger that manifested as a nationally significant rent strike between 1901 and 1903.[14] By 1912 inequity in access to land was reduced due to the land acts of 1903 and 1909, yet there were still ample grounds for agrarian agitation. Letting season, the period from April to July, was the most volatile time. The main target of disgruntled and small tenant farmers were graziers, however, rather than gentry landlords. Graziers bought and hoarded vast tracts of land to increase their livestock numbers.

Often, they leased land to other part-time graziers. In 1911 a total of 373 of these lessees, most often merchants and publicans, were recorded as 'jobbing' in land – using it as a secondary occupation.[15] One of the most popular methods for persuading graziers to sell was the cattle drive. The first 'drive' in Ireland in the twentieth century was staged in 1906 at Tonlagee, just outside Roscommon town. The premise was to drive all livestock off the contested lands, frequently scattering the animals across many square miles. This inconvenience could prove costly for the targeted parties, not only because of financial loss due to lost or dead stock and labour expended, but also because of local opprobrium and ostracism. The practice was so widespread in Roscommon during 1907–8, the period of the 'ranch war', that the county recorded the highest number of farms or acres unlet as a result.[16] The level of disturbance was unmatched in the twentieth century according to the RIC and they petitioned for the county to be proclaimed under the 1887 Criminal Law and Procedure Act. Police numbers increased by almost fifty per cent as reports of escalating intimidation of landowners led to revolvers being purchased by both sides.[17] However, news of a forthcoming land bill in 1909 caused the agitation to abate and police numbers were reduced towards the end of 1908.[18] The 1909 Land Act did not facilitate the change desired by the agitators though, and by 1912 Roscommon remained proclaimed alongside only Galway and Clare. Indeed, it still hosted one of the very few 'protection posts' in Ireland at Ardkeenagh, near Tulsk, where members of the RIC maintained constant watch over a particular property/landowner. In 1912 fourteen of the thirty-one criminal proceedings for 'unlawful assembly' linked to land agitation pertained to Roscommon, the highest figure in Ireland.[19]

A significant reason for this unsatiated land hunger was the slow rate of land transfer by the Congested Districts Board (CDB). From its inception in 1891, the CDB had identified most of Roscommon for land redistribution and congestion relief. To this end, large tracts had been purchased by the CDB in the twenty years prior to 1912. While sales increased markedly with the 1903 Land Act, larger holdings of over 200 acres were bought at a relatively slow rate.[20] The largest sale occurred in 1906, when Lord de Freyne eventually agreed terms for 30,000 acres. Other larger landowners engaged with the CDB in greater numbers as 1912 approached. For example, 1911 saw the Wills-Sandford estate in Castlerea union vesting 1,200 acres and the Pakenham-Mahon estate in Strokestown union selling 8,600 acres.[21] Returns in the aftermath of the 1909 Land Act, when all of Roscommon was placed under the CDB's remit, indicate large reductions in the number of tenants and a concomitant increase in ownership. In 1908 just over 8,400 people were tenants. In 1912 there were just under 5,000.[22] The rate of transfer was also increasing. The reduction in tenants from 1911–12 ran at a fifth in that year alone. This compared favourably with the 1908–11 figure of twenty-five per cent over three years.[23] While the trend had positive aspects and it was noted that Roscommon had the highest average valuation of lands in Connacht at £14 (the Connacht average was £11 and the national £19), continued issues around access to sufficient land in some areas generated unrest.[24]

A précis of the information presented across six of the seven union areas in County Roscommon is instructive. Statistics for the Boyle, Carrick-on-Shannon, Strokestown, Roscommon, Athlone and Ballinasloe unions show that holdings of less than twenty acres constituted the majority of farms, just over 8,700, and supported the most people, 31,000. The established trend was for the number living on the smallest farms of less than ten acres to reduce quite markedly, with related, though not equal, increases in ownership of larger holdings. In all cases, those on the smallest plots were outnumbered by those on farms of ten to fifteen acres and, in the case of Carrick-on-Shannon, those on plots of fifteen to twenty acres constituted the greatest number overall, a sign of improving distribution given the number of farms involved.

Castlerea union presented a different picture, however. There, some 3,118 ten-acre farms catered for 11,802 people, a cohort that was not only the largest in that union, but one that outnumbered the cumulative total of people similarly circumstanced across all six other union regions. Castlerea union also had 7,346 people living on 870 plots of ten to fifteen acres, making it the only union in which this cohort was outnumbered by those on smaller holdings. The percentage of people on larger plots of fifteen to twenty acres in Castlerea when presented as a proportion of those on the plots of less than fifteen acres was exceptionally low in comparison to the other unions: 12.6 per cent in Castlerea, jumping to 31.5 per cent in Boyle, between 46 and 50 per cent in Athlone, Ballinasloe, Roscommon and Strokestown, with the Carrick-on-Shannon figure standing at 59.4 per cent.[25] The mid-Roscommon region, Castlerea union, was the only part of the county that reflected some of the land problems seen further west in counties such as Mayo, Galway and Donegal, where large tracts of poor land were common and those living on them sought better ground. Like those counties, the potential for agrarian strife was strong in 1912.

Roscommon's urban areas also exhibited contrasting fortunes. While population decline in Roscommon town indicated difficulties, in certain respects it was better circumstanced than other towns in the county. For instance, it had only ten single-room tenements, the lowest number of any settlement with a population over 500. The greatest concentration of poor accommodation was in Ballaghaderreen which had hundreds resident in seventy-two tenements, a number only slightly higher than the more populous Boyle which reported sixty-seven.[26] Branches of the Town Tenants League (TTL), a body that sought better conditions and rights for those renting homes, had been established in most of the towns during the decade prior to 1912. However, of the five noted in 1911, just those at Elphin and Castlerea were active.[27] The county town was also exceptional in hosting more merchants than any other, including Boyle, whose greater population was in part due to the presence of 150 British army men and their dependants.[28] Roscommon town was well presented with the new Harrison hall in its centre and the large and ornate Roman Catholic Sacred Heart church, a building considered so grand by the Conservative pictorial *The Bystander* that it deemed Irish claims of penury to be disingenuous.[29] The same magazine described the town as a picture of prosperity on market day, something replicated in Boyle, Strokestown, Castlerea and Ballaghaderreen.

Throughout the history of Irish land agitation, disgruntled small farmers combined to prosecute their cause. By 1912 their most prominent organization was the United Irish League (UIL). Formed in January 1898 in County Mayo, the first branches in Roscommon were founded late the same year.[30] By 1901, the year after the UIL became the constituency organization for the IPP, Roscommon had fifty-one branches with 5,500 members.[31] The opposition of the bishop of Elphin, John Clancy, to the intimidation of landowners slowed organization during 1902 when the de Freyne rent strike raged, but could not subdue the movement.[32] Peaks in activity preceded the introduction of the 1903 and 1909 Land Acts, which themselves then undermined interest in the UIL; by 1911 only eighteen of the fifty-four branches noted in police reports were affiliated with the UIL national directory.[33] Unsurprisingly, the most active branches were those in mid-Roscommon. Organizers appointed by the national directory of the UIL, such as Boyle auctioneer John Keaveny, regularly undertook tours to imbue greater vitality.[34] The UIL was strongest in north Roscommon where T.J. Devine, a county councillor, store owner and auctioneer, chaired an active executive from Boyle. Despite being chaired by political potentate John Fitzgibbon MP, the south Roscommon UIL executive was much less active. This created space for Canon Thomas Cummins of Roscommon town to form the Roscommon Associated Estates Committee (RAEC) in 1911. Cummins had shunned the UIL for refusing to follow his suggestion for county council candidates in 1911.[35] He instead used his influence to render the town's apathetic UIL and TTL branches largely redundant and moved to secure the 'sale of all of the estates in and adjacent to the town of Roscommon'. The RAEC enjoyed some success by 1912, the canon's association being essential.[36]

As shown in map 3, Roscommon was divided into two parliamentary constituencies. James Joseph O'Kelly represented Roscommon North. During his early political career, he was a significant figure in the Irish Republican Brotherhood (IRB). He first represented the constituency for the IPP in 1885, but lost the seat in 1892. He regained it 1895 and held it until his death in 1916. Suffering poor health from 1900, O'Kelly's final public appearance in Roscommon was at Elphin in 1902. By 1910 he was profoundly compromised physically and largely inactive politically.[37] As will be seen in chapter 4, the

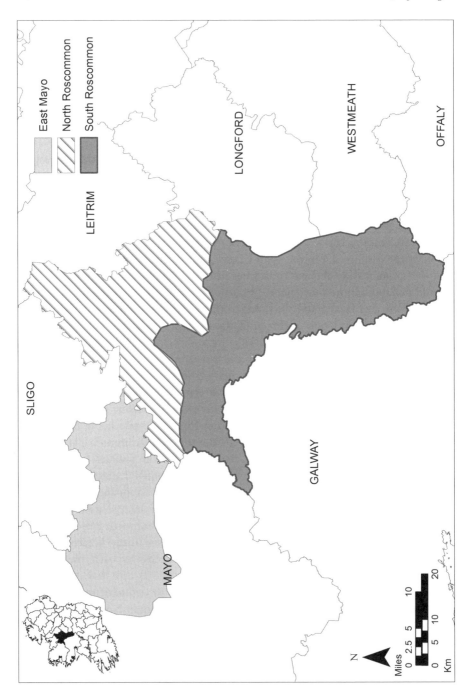

3 Parliamentary constituencies in 1910 and 1918

election occasioned by his death had profound consequences for Roscommon and for Ireland.

In Roscommon South the MP was J.P. Hayden, a close friend of IPP leader John Redmond. Hayden gained the seat in 1897 after the premature death of his brother Luke and was subsequently returned unopposed. He was a militant land agitator during the first decade of the twentieth century. He gained much kudos for this from the UIL faithful, although he did waver somewhat when the letting of lands affected his family members.[38] A supporter of the Gaelic Athletic Association (GAA), by 1912 he had shifted his political focus to the greater prize of home rule. While Hayden devoted much time to his own constituency, it was in Mullingar, County Westmeath, that he was more likely to be found. There he spent much energy attending to his newspaper, the *Westmeath Examiner*, and battling with the independent MP Laurence Ginnell, a former ally in the ranch war, by then turned arch-enemy.

John Fitzgibbon, MP for Mayo South, also had exceptional influence in Roscommon. His power base was Castlerea town, where he owned a large provisions store and held the chairmanships of the board of guardians and RDC alongside that of the county council. Deemed in some quarters to be the leading nationalist politician in the province after IPP deputy leader John Dillon of Ballaghaderreen, Fitzgibbon supported the UIL and the inchoate labour movement in both Roscommon and Mayo.[39] By 1912, like Hayden, he had abandoned militant agrarian agitation. This was in part due to being gifted an uncontested parliamentary seat in 1910 and being rebuked by Prime Minister Asquith for promoting land agitation.[40] After extensive lobbying, Fitzgibbon gained a position on the CDB in 1910. While he claimed that he did so to accelerate the pace of the board's work in mid-Roscommon, he was justifiably accused of using the position to further his own interests, especially in connection with the Wills-Sandford estate.[41] Given his chairmanships and Hayden's Westmeath duties, Fitzgibbon was the most influential politician in Roscommon.

While both Hayden's and Fitzgibbon's association with the UIL had ensured that it was the pre-eminent grassroots organization in Roscommon in the first decade of the twentieth century, it faced a challenger of sorts in the Ancient Order of Hibernians (AOH). Ostensibly considered a counterbalance to the unionist Orange Order, the AOH reached Roscommon in 1904; the county's small unionist population reduced the urgency for AOH formation felt by nationalists elsewhere. Recognizing its potential, Jasper Tully, then MP for Leitrim South, used his Boyle newspaper, the *Roscommon Herald*, to promote the order.[42] In 1905, when the IPP's third in command, Joe Devlin, assumed control of the AOH, it adopted the subtitle Board of Erin to differentiate it from other Hibernian groups and began to expand rapidly in the north and west of Ireland. Roscommon had ten 'active and prosperous' divi-

sions by 1906.[43] Stating that UIL membership was expected of brethren, the
AOH did little to impose itself during the agrarian agitation of 1907–8, yet its
orientation made it clear to the CI that it was 'really a party to the parliamentary movement'.[44] In May 1911 the AOH opened its most southerly
Roscommon division at Athlone where Hayden targeted younger members.[45]
After the order had become an approved body under the 1911 Insurance Act,
membership grew further. There were twenty-three divisions in Roscommon
in 1912. These were mostly in the north where Strokestown auctioneer
George O'Reilly maintained his presidency of the AOH county executive,
with T.J. Devine as vice president. Both men strengthened the alliance
between the order and the UIL, ensuring that the two organizations were not
competitors, as they were, for example, in County Clare.[46]

Roscommon also had a disparate, if intermittently influential, labour
movement by 1912. Support for the unionization of general workers was
demonstrated in 1898, when labourers' representative John McGreevy gained
a seat on the Roscommon RDC.[47] McGreevy used his success as a springboard to assist in establishing a Labour League in Roscommon in March
1899, and set about agitating for improved conditions for workers.[48] Unlike
the AOH, the Labour League attracted the enmity of the *Herald* and gained
limited support in other local newspapers. This ensured that labour in
Roscommon had a difficult time furthering its cause. It was not until the
county led the way in promoting the direct (as opposed to contract) labour
system for roads maintenance that greater union-like consolidation occurred.
This began in earnest from 1906 through the expansion of the Irish Land and
Labour League in the county, with at least ten branches agitating for direct
labour to become the local default. In this they had the support of
Fitzgibbon.[49] After effective mobilization and significant success, especially in
Castlerea, labour activists turned their attention to issues such as labourers'
houses and wage rates. Although league branches had halved by 1911, they
were assisted by a number of short-lived trade and labour associations that
emerged in Castlerea, Roscommon and Strokestown.[50] The introduction of the
national Irish Transport and General Workers' Union (ITGWU) to neighbouring Sligo in 1911 had little effect on the labour movement in Roscommon
which struggled to exert a sustained influence in 1912.[51]

Given its policies after its emergence in 1905, it was not surprising that
when labour made headway in Roscommon, SF policy was also discussed.
Ostensibly promoting Irish political autonomy along with Irish goods and
industry, the potential of the policy prompted labour activist Tom Egan to
establish a SF branch in Castlerea in June 1907.[52] That others also saw potential in SF was illustrated by an unseemly incident at the unveiling of a Michael
Davitt portrait in the county council chambers the following October. Showing
more continuity between labour activism and SF, John McGreevy delivered a

pro-SF, anti-IPP speech that led John Fitzgibbon to wrestle him to the door. The intervention of McGreevy supporters Michael Finlay and George Geraghty, both members of the Roscommon Town Commissioners (RTC) and local AOH division, caused J.P. Hayden to enter the fray. A serious tussle ensued, one punctuated by personal insults.[53] In the aftermath, the pro-IPP *Roscommon Messenger* (*Messenger*) devoted two editorials to criticizing SF policy, while the North Roscommon UIL executive warned members that SF was just another factionist group: 'the old enemy in a new boat'.[54] The CI was unconcerned by the interest in SF. According to his reductive view, each man 'is playing his own little game, the source of which is often his own little shop or personal interest'.[55] He dismissed SF's growth in Roscommon town since those involved were 'simply labourers who disapprove of the attitude towards labour of Hayden and Fitzgibbon'.[56] His observation that SF support was insubstantial was accurate. The CI largely omitted SF from his reports during the summer of 1908, with the vagaries of a short-lived branch in Athlone during 1909 typifying the poor fortunes of provincial SF in Ireland up to 1912.[57] In a final comment on early SF in Roscommon, he suggested: 'the favourable opportunity for this party has not yet arrived'.[58] With the exception of McGreevy, most of those involved reconciled themselves to the IPP's position given its productive efforts for home rule.[59]

A unique feature of SF (seen in the Athlone branch) was the admission of women. Neither the UIL nor AOH allowed women enter directly, with the latter catering for them only by way of adjunct auxiliary divisions. Unionist women in Roscommon also had no representative group. Overt displays of political organization among women in the county were largely absent, something bemoaned in the *Irish Citizen*, the newspaper of the Irish Women's Franchise League.[60] One obstacle to organization from 1913 was Jasper Tully. In March 1914, for example, when members of the league scheduled a meeting for Boyle, Tully cancelled it unilaterally. The organizers read about the cancellation in the *Herald*. Efforts to reschedule were successful, but opposition to their message was strong.[61] Further south there was league activity in Drum, but the only organized suffragette group in the Roscommon region was a small resident society in Athlone.[62] The *Irish Citizen* accused the county, along with Longford and Leitrim, of being 'a dark disfiguring blot on our suffrage map'.[63]

Various groups courted the support of Roscommon people by invoking the legacy of nineteenth-century movements such as Ribbonmen and Fenians. The IRB, with J.J. O'Kelly to the fore, were active in the county during the three decades prior to 1901 when the CI asserted it still had a significant membership.[64] By 1912 its position was less impressive. A decade of diminishing activity – largely consisting of unsuccessful efforts to infiltrate the UIL and GAA – had a predictable result. By 1909 the CI was describing the body as 'inactive'. Statements to the Bureau of Military History (BMH) and other sources support this. By 1912 the IRB in Roscommon was moribund.[65]

The late nineteenth and early twentieth century witnessed a renewed interest in cultural nationalism. This was typified by the Gaelic League, co-founded by Castlerea-born Douglas Hyde in 1893. First establishing a branch in 1901, Roscommon boasted ten the following year. All were 'under clerical control', which was encouraged by Bishop Clancy.[66] The aim of the Gaelic League was to arrest the decline in numbers speaking the Irish language. In Roscommon, 15.1 per cent of the population could speak Irish in 1901. By 1911 this had dropped to 10.8 per cent.[67] The CI believed the organization fostered 'a spirit of Irish Nationality opposed to the Union', and he may have been heartened by its poor growth, which saw just one additional branch by 1906.[68] The Roscommon Gaelic League declined from 1909 when a controversy raged regarding the opposition of the Roman Catholic hierarchy to Irish being a compulsory matriculation requirement for the National University. Insubordinate clergy were moved by Bishop Clancy and many distanced themselves from the Gaelic League to avoid his ire.[69] Their absence was a blow given that imbuing interest in Irish was considered a largely thankless task. By the summer of 1911, the number of branches had halved and were concentrated solely in towns like Castlerea and Boyle where politicians such as John Fitzgibbon and T.J. Devine provided support.

Cultural nationalists interested in sport looked to the Roscommon GAA. The first county board was formed in January 1889 with Jasper Tully as chairman. The majority of the affiliated twenty clubs were concentrated in north Roscommon. However, as happened in many counties, poor organization dogged progress. In April 1902 a reorganization meeting at Elphin saw eleven clubs convene. By late 1903, RIC reports indicated that the Roscommon GAA was making progress.[70] By the end of 1905, the year the county won its first senior provincial title, the Roscommon GAA boasted twenty-one clubs. Though deemed disloyal, the police did not believe that the county's GAA had much political influence. Connections were made between its likely politicization and the involvement of IRB men in 1906 and SF supporters in 1907. However, these facile observations did not prove that the GAA was controlled by advanced nationalists.[71] Land agitation during 1907–8 caused participation to decline and it was not until 1910 that signs of recovery were evident. By 1912, when a second Connacht title was secured, an IPP supporter, John Hession, chaired a county board that the RIC believed controlled seventeen official clubs.[72]

Whatever the organization or political personality, the RIC were studiously making their observations. Ostensibly an underpaid and overworked civil force, in 1912 the RIC in Roscommon operated in one of only three proclaimed counties in the country. The county had thirty-nine RIC stations, most of which remained in use until the War of Independence (see map 4).

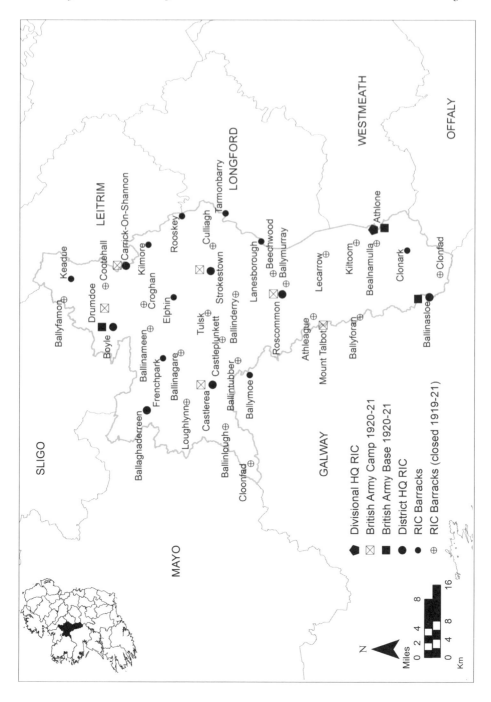

4 Distribution of the Crown forces

They accommodated one county inspector, five district inspectors, five head constables and 276 sergeants and constables. The ratio of police to population was higher than in most neighbouring counties, with the exceptions of Galway and Westmeath.[73] The largest police presence (twenty men) was in Roscommon town where CI Rutledge was located, one of four CIs stationed in Roscommon during the period under study. Outside of agrarian agitation, the county was not considered exceptional for crime between 1908 and 1912. The frequency of indictable offences (murder, larceny, sacrilege, arson and similar offences), although second highest in Connacht running at 100 per 100,000, was well behind Longford (155.2), Galway (169.9) or Westmeath (186.7) and largely matched Sligo (97.4).[74] In the case of less serious, non-indictable offences such as assault, road offences, drunkenness and labour unrest, Roscommon occupied a broadly similar position.[75]

In 1912 there were four local newspapers to which most in Roscommon turned for their news. All were nationalist and did little to cater for Roscommon unionists who looked to Dublin and Sligo for newspapers in tune with their politics. The *Roscommon Herald* was largely unchallenged in the north of the county. Produced in Boyle by Jasper Tully and his brother George, the newspaper evinced much of the contrariness for which Jasper became known.[76] After being expelled from the IPP in 1903, Tully ensured that the paper was an omnipresent thorn in the party's side. Editorials frequently denigrated the IPP and its members, especially Fitzgibbon, Hayden and John Dillon.[77] It carried some of the most detailed editorial commentary of national and international events of any provincial publication and was the only newspaper in the region to feature political caricatures on its front page. The county town boasted two rival titles, the *Roscommon Journal* (*Journal*), owned and edited by William Tully, Jasper's uncle, and the *Messenger*, another and less popular newspaper of J.P. Hayden, who took control of the title after the death of his brother, Joseph, in 1909.[78] An independent paper concerned with land issues, the *Journal* was by 1912 supporting the IPP in its pursuit of home rule. The necessary critiques were still present to disabuse any who had notions about local press homogeneity. The *Messenger* was the county's IPP paper, slavishly supporting the party in editorials that were often supplied by Hayden. Quite capable of taking on both the local and northern Tullys, the newspaper provided much-needed editorial balance. The largest newspaper in the region by page count and circulation was Athlone's *Westmeath Independent*. It was an independent title owned by Dublin Protestant Thomas Chapman and edited by Limerick man Michael McDermott-Hayes. Like the *Journal*, it saw the benefit of supporting the IPP efforts for home rule. Two other four-page titles operated at Boyle and Strokestown. The *Western Nationalist* (*Nationalist*) had the unenviable task of combating the *Herald* in Boyle. A dedicated IPP supporter, the newspaper incorporated the Irish parliament buildings at College Green, Dublin in its masthead. The *Strokestown Democrat* (*Democrat*) was little more than an advertiser that, by 1912, had not yet found its voice.

Looking forward from 1912, the people of Roscommon appeared to have a clear political future. A third home rule act was to be pursued by an IPP that occupied a prime position at Westminster. That legislation would provide for an Irish parliament that would quickly address the ongoing issues of land inequity. The bodies that supported the IPP were strong and largely unchallenged in Roscommon, with little to indicate that advanced nationalist elements had any weaknesses to exploit, or any great desire to do so – home rule could assist nearly all parties in achieving their ultimate aims. However, it was not to be that simple. A concatenation of events, both predictable and otherwise, would see home rule abandoned by most nationalists in favour of an Irish republic, which would then be abandoned by a majority who preferred a more readily gained Irish Free State. The forces that acted on politics in Roscommon and promoted change were varied. Unionist opposition to home rule, the First World War and the events of Easter 1916 demonstrated national and international influences. The desire for a republic and demands for more equitable land distribution indicated ideological and local concerns. Despite reflecting much of what was evident elsewhere, especially in the west of Ireland, Roscommon's experience was unique. From those who supported home rule to those who sought a republic, their earnest endeavours make for captivating history.

2 'Declare our unswerving faith': towards the home rule act, 1912–14

During the two years to 1914, the progress of the home rule bill at Westminster saw IPP supporters in Roscommon become confident that Irish self-government was imminent. Agrarian issues lost potency and complacency set in as the bill's positive progress convinced the land hungry to accept their MPs' advice of *mair, a chapaill, agus gheobhaidh tú féar* (live horse and you will get grass). Growing unionist opposition to home rule during 1913 caused that complacency to lift and Roscommon became one of the first regions in Ireland to organize to meet unionist threats of violence head on in the autumn of 1913. The Irish Volunteers, the great hope of home rule Ireland, were embraced in Roscommon from the spring of 1914, when British tolerance of unionist agitation and talk of concessions led thousands to flock to corps across the county. The swelling ranks forced the IPP to assume control of the Irish Volunteers in May 1914, as party leaders sought to manage the threat of civil war in Ireland. As the summer of 1914 progressed, a collision seemed probable and Roscommon's Volunteers sought arms. Their eyes were, however, diverted from unionist Ireland to the continent as a far greater conflict took hold, one that ensured home rule would no longer be centre stage.

During the months either side of the introduction of the third home rule bill in April 1912, Roscommon's constitutional nationalists made special efforts to show their support and promote enthusiasm. The *Messenger* provided blow-by-blow accounts of the bill's progress in Westminster and warnings to avoid the negativity of 'factionists'.[1] Supportive gatherings were numerous, with a North Roscommon UIL executive meeting at Kilmore in January 1912 hearing what became default resolutions for UIL branches: confidence in Redmond and the IPP, support for home rule and a call for funds.[2] The number of affiliated UIL branches increased, almost doubling to thirty-four by February 1912.[3] Optimism permeated the discourse. The Rooskey UIL looked forward to 'the home rule parliament in College Green', the league at Oran, Donamon and Cloverhill predicted that the Irish question would be 'once and forever … settled', while the Ballymore UIL believed the bill was so good that it would be enacted before the predicted time frame of mid-1914.[4]

As the months went by, UIL branches were reminded of the need to remain active. Some, such as that at Scramogue, near Strokestown, followed John Fitzgibbon's logic that the league would be superfluous when home rule was enacted and had already begun to disengage.[5] Branches were called on to remain focused, mainly so that they could coordinate fundraising to promote home rule. Thousands of pounds were collected, while the enthusiasm for the

predicted party atmosphere after the bill passed led the Tulsk UIL to pay
£28 for a celebratory banner.[6] Consolidation was another focus, with the unification of Athlone's two UIL branches in 1912 deemed a sign of unity and
strength in the national ranks.[7] By 1913, the CI reported that the UIL and
AOH had stepped up their efforts to act as 'a strong combination throughout
the county'; as a consequence both were 'in flourishing condition'.[8] Canon
Cummins and the RAEC did not facilitate further consolidation, however; the
canon instead opted for a 'hand-in-hand' relationship with the UIL that
ensured RAEC autonomy.[9] Hayden and Fitzgibbon, reassured by
Roscommon's support, focused on the British electorate, the target of much
unionist lobbying. Both joined speaking tours across Britain to ensure that
'the democracy of England is united with the National forces of Ireland'.[10]

Although the support of nationalist organizations was apparent, not many
others eagerly welcomed the bill. In his March report, the CI identified local
priorities. The people cared 'a great deal more about getting the land than
about government'. The following month he reaffirmed this view, noting that
the 'Irish government is not much discussed by people who seem to care little
where Parliament is, if only they could get the land'.[11] A *Freeman's Journal*
correspondent in Boyle wrote that locals saw the home rule proposal as a
'substantial advance' on similar bills from 1886 and 1893. Yet, outside of the
positivity of T.J. Devine, the reporter could find only a London visitor and
a local solicitor to provide evidence of satisfaction rather than delight.[12] The
Herald repeatedly highlighted the bill's weaknesses, especially when compared
to similar Canadian and South African legislation. It claimed that proposals
for Ireland's control over customs and excise was a route to more taxes on
farmers. The bill would not 'develop ... the greatness ... of the Irish
nation'.[13] The *Herald*'s pessimism was counterbalanced by the *Westmeath
Independent* and *Journal*. Both downplayed their earlier criticism of the home
rule bill, the financial aspects excepted. The *Journal* suggested that home rule
would 'win Ireland for a ... united British empire'.[14]

The celebrations in Roscommon after the first reading of the bill in the
House of Commons in January 1913 reflected that most were interested in the
headline of home rule rather than in the details. The *Messenger* cheered, but
omitted mention of growing unionist opposition, which was by then taking on
a military aspect.[15] However, shortly afterwards, it did report the emergence
of a dissenting group in Tulsk, the Ratepayers' Association. They struck a
discordant note by asserting that Irish politicians had proven themselves inca-
pable of prudent fiscal management. John Fitzgibbon rounded on the group
for 'supplying food to the Tory press and anti-home rulers in the north'.[16]
During a heated exchange in the county council chamber, a delegation from
Tulsk, 'currabucks' according to Fitzgibbon, were forcibly ejected.[17] District
Councillor John Healy, a member of the association, mused that the bill must

have been weak if a debate could not be entertained. Some of his neighbours in the Tulsk AOH disagreed and called Healy and his associates 'a pack of yahoos'.[18] By April the association had 250 members who continued to harry the council, which it termed a 'budding oligarchy'.[19]

Roscommon's unionist population also articulated its antipathy to the bill. At a meeting in Boyle in August 1912, Carrowroe landlord Captain Terence C.E. Goff offered reasons for opposing home rule, chiefly, destruction of the empire, less capital for investment and poor financial support from nationalists. The meeting did not overtly emphasize the issue of religion, though the Church of Ireland bishop for their diocese would do so soon after. It did, however, express their great anger, with calls for all home rule supporters to be drowned.[20] Ulster Unionist leader Edward Carson sent a letter of support, assuring Roscommon unionists that the 'tyrannical bodies' of the UIL and AOH would endanger their interests.[21] The *Messenger* lambasted Boyle's 'little unionist coterie', while Hayden rebuffed Goff's presumption of inadequate nationalist funds. The MP averred that nationalists too poor to donate had the unionist hierarchy to thank for their penury.[22] Ironically, north Roscommon unionists submitted a paltry sum to the anti-home rule fund; just £50 by June 1913, less than one per cent of the national total.[23] Hayden and Goff exchanged views through the *Irish Times* with Hayden suggesting that Goff, who had sold 1,200 acres to the CDB after his lands were driven in 1911, insulted his Carrowroe neighbours with his claims.[24] Goff gained support from unionist newspapers such as the *Belfast Weekly News*.[25] With the signing of the Solemn League and Covenant in September 1912, the unionist promise to resist home rule by every means, Boyle unionists again mobilized under Goff and established a branch of the Irish Unionist Alliance. The *Messenger* targeted Goff personally. Goff's father was a 'Tory' and his family were known for antipathy to Irish causes. Goff believed the allegations hit 'below the belt'.[26]

The unionists of south Roscommon were circumspect. In Athlone, where the region's largest unionist community lived, the introduction of the bill saw little overt opposition apart from that of Robert Baile, a covenant signatory and headmaster, who dismissed the bill entirely.[27] The covenant also elicited limited reaction from unionists in Roscommon town. The *Journal* reported that just five men had signed the pledge. It counselled them to be mindful of from where they extracted 'their living'.[28]

The most controversial incident involving south Roscommon unionists occurred in Dublin in December 1913 upon the delivery of an address to Conservative Party leader, Bonar Law. A memorandum signed by Lord Crofton of Mote Park near Knockcroghery in south Roscommon, stated that the actions of the UIL and the 'character of the AOH ... left us [unionists] no choice but to oppose home rule'.[29] Crofton was also said to have proclaimed that Roscommon nationalists were 'lessening in their ardour' for the act. The Kilbride AOH and Carniska UIL attacked him. They demanded that he indicate one instance of religious intolerance in the county. The AOH county board president, George O'Reilly, claimed that the assertions 'savoured of the deep-rooted intolerance of which they [unionists] are permeated'.[30] The incident was widely reported outside Ireland. The *Manchester Courier and Lancashire General Advertiser*, a newspaper that put itself at odds with the pro-IPP *Manchester Guardian*, carried the details under a headline 'angry at the truth' and offered examples of the Roscommon UIL intimidating landowners.[31] The unionist *Belfast Telegraph* reported that the peer was directed to issue an apology to mitigate the threat of being disallowed engage in hunts.[32] It was confirmed that Crofton, without knowing its details, had permitted others to append his name to an address from north Roscommon unionists.[33] John Keaveny accepted the clarification and sardonically acknowledged Crofton's need to clear 'with all haste ... the charge of libelling his neighbours'. The negative address actually originated with J.F. Murphy, Roscommon high sheriff, and Mr Merrick-Lloyd. Keaveny demanded that they instead be censured for their 'malicious lies and deliberate libels'.[34] Unapologetic about the inaccuracies, the *Messenger* queried why Crofton would stand on the anti-home rule platform in any capacity and published a letter from John Redmond that indicated increasing rather than lessening ardour in Castlerea. The town had doubled its donations to the home rule cause.[35]

Unionist opposition to home rule dictated much of both Roscommon press commentary and the discourse at nationalist meetings. When assessing the unionist threat, the *Messenger* used dismissive terminology common at the time: 'dying kick', 'bluster', 'bogey', 'hypocrisy', 'bluff'.[36] The newspaper counselled unionists to look to their bishop in Tuam, Dr Benjamin Plunkett, who saw home rule as nothing to fear, rather than the aged Dr Alfred Elliott, the Church of Ireland bishop of Kilmore, Elphin & Ardagh, who referred to 'fearful home rule'.[37] The *Herald* ridiculed Carson's 'dummy troops', and dismissed the wider unionist threat as too weak to derail home rule.[38] The only real threat, the Tullys averred, was that posed by the potential treachery of the Liberal Party.[39] Throughout the summer of 1913, the *Journal* and *Westmeath Independent* iterated much of what the *Herald* printed.

The largest meeting in Roscommon during 1913 was at Strokestown in mid-September. The muster of AOH divisions impressed CI Rutledge; they comprised 'the strongest body in the county'.[40] Thousands assembled to hear Hayden, George O'Reilly and others denigrate unionist military pretensions. The terms 'mimic army' and 'wooden gun brigade' were used to describe the Ulster Volunteer Force (UVF).[41] Hayden broached the subject of Liberal wavering, which, while not yet equating to treachery, had introduced the idea of offering compromises to unionists. Although Hayden dismissed the notion that home rule could be casually undone, he appeared to believe that union-ist agitation was influencing the debate in London in their favour.[42]

The most prominent compromise was that of partitioning Ireland. The IPP was opposed but did not reject it with the vehemence that many supporters wished. Redmond saw the Irish nation as indivisible. He was, however, willing to work with unionists to protect their interests, while safeguarding home rule for the entire island. He naively deemed partition more of a unionist ploy than a unionist policy. Roscommon's newspapers all issued warnings. The *Herald* described the talk as 'a stab in the back', and predicted the death of home rule.[43] In the *Westmeath Independent*, Michael McDermott-Hayes not only lamented the Liberal position, but assisted in establishing a nationalist coun-terweight to the UVF: the Midland Volunteer Force (MVF).[44]

The creation of the force in Athlone ensured that nationalists in south Roscommon were among the first in Ireland to begin military drills in defence of home rule. The *Journal* also promoted the MVF by summarizing the infor-mation presented in the *Westmeath Independent*'s exaggerated accounts of the force's activity.[45] Both publications and the *Herald* also carried news on the for-mation in November 1913 of the Irish Volunteers, the nationalist counterweight to the UVF that was in part inspired by Athlone's example.[46] Initial enthusi-asm for the Irish Volunteers was confined to the south of Roscommon, with the county town the first area in which the UIL and AOH were courted, albeit unsuccessfully.[47] The *Westmeath Independent* counselled that forming corps was essential to safeguard home rule.[48] By the turn of the year, the Ratepayers' Association, then boasting a county executive, offered to help north Roscommon 'join hands with south Roscommon', and promote the movement.[49]

Success was limited, however. With the exception of Athlone, which merged its MVF with the Irish Volunteers in January 1914, no new, official corps was formed in Roscommon until mid-March. Boyle was the first town to organize. Its corps emerged around the same time as the first Sligo corps.[50] M.J. Judge from Ballaghaderreen, a member of the Volunteer provisional committee, assisted in enrolling 800 men at the Boyle meeting, according to the *Irish Volunteer*. This figure was largely corroborated by the RIC, which gave a figure of 700.[51] The *Irish Volunteer* reported on the anti-unionist speeches of Volunteer inspector-general Colonel Maurice Moore and Judge, and noted the support of the clergy from outlying districts, such as Fr Thomas Flanagan of Cootehall. The Gaelic League was among the bodies represented; it was freer to operate after the death of Bishop Clancy in October 1912.[52]

In early 1914 an increasing tolerance of partition was in evidence. IPP newspapers, such as the *Messenger*, promoted the view that any separation was 'a reservation for a limited period, rather than an exclusion'. This reframing of partition was also promoted by the South Roscommon UIL executive; partition was a stopgap on the road to all-island home rule.[53] However, such equanimity was shaken in late March when unionists were perceived to have gained an advantage after an incident at the Curragh army in County Kildare. Widely believed to have been precipitated by the refusal of British army officers to comply with orders to deploy in northern counties, the incident was portrayed as a mutiny by the Roscommon press. The *Journal* demanded an end to talk of concessions for unionists, given that Carson and the British army had proven that they held 'the government in the hollow of their hand'.[54] Growth in the Irish Volunteers was essential. The British had, as the *Herald* put it, thrown 'dust in the eyes of the Irish people', by indirectly confirming that the army would not suppress unionist militancy.[55]

Given the gravity of developments, the ridicule hitherto heaped on the UVF gave way to moves to assess the threat from the north. A tour of Ulster to review the UVF led Jasper Tully to publish complimentary reports in the *Herald*. The fact that he was impressed was not lost on some British newspapers.[56] However, Tully believed that the 'fighting fury' of the 'Celtic' Ireland would win out if the Irish Volunteers were as well equipped. He also made the qualifying observation: 'they are not'.[57] In Knockcroghery in April, the company heralded its establishment with a fiery statement. They were 'prepared to a man to fight' for home rule, 'show unto Carson and his numerous blockheads ... that Irish Ireland requires full autonomy'.[58] The landing of thousands of guns at Larne a week after the article did not brighten the mood of Roscommon nationalists. They were assured the incident involved official collusion. The CI noted the disgruntlement, while the *Journal* published the common opinion that nationalists would be 'lodged in prison' if they attempted a landing similar to that at Larne.[59]

Volunteer companies across Roscommon mobilized to face the unionist threat. At Boyle in late April, the RIC reported that 300 men had taken up drill instruction during the month and joined 300 others in marching through the town on 3 May.[60] Charles H. Devine, T.J.'s brother, was the main organizer and the corps was backed by Frs Patrick Clyne and Francis Murray from St Joseph's and 'all sections of nationalists'.[61] Boyle's example spread to Keadue, Geevagh, Highwood, Corrigeenroe and Ballyfarnon later that month. C.H. Devine asked eager crowds in those areas if they were willing to show patriotism beyond simply the hanging of a picture of Robert Emmet in their houses.[62] Cootehall, Crossna and Cloonloo were reportedly eager to start companies as soon as spring farming duties abated; all that they needed were instructors, a role invariably filled by ex-British army soldiers.[63] Less populous areas combined to form corps. The rural district of Portaghard was the meeting point for volunteers from Callow, Rathkeary, Cloonmagnaune, Highbog, Ratra, Slieveroe and Raheen.[64]

The AOH were instrumental in organization efforts across the county as the third reading of the home rule bill approached. The national secretary J.D. Nugent MP made their duties clear. Even before Nugent's communications, the Roscommon CI noted that many Hibernians had joined the Volunteers in Boyle, while at Ballaghaderreen, the AOH participated in a muster of 300 men on 17 May 1914.[65] Support was also shown in Ballaghaderreen by diocesan administrator Fr J. Gallagher and his young subordinates, Frs Denis Gildea and J. O'Dowd. The clerics understood that, as the CI later expressed it, 'there is no use in their opposition, as they would only be left behind'.[66] The *Herald* saw the Volunteers as the most influential players in the home rule issue.[67]

The third reading of the home rule bill on 25 May 1914 provided another inducement to organize Irish Volunteer corps. Ballaghaderreen celebrated with an 800-man march, while the county town moved towards organizing a company. On 31 May J.P. Hayden, George Geraghty, Canon Cummins and Roscommon town's youthful curates Frs P. Flynn, J. Finan and O'Flanagan put their rivalries aside to promote the force. Fr O'Flanagan, who would become a prominent figure in SF during 1916, advocated meeting the UVF 'in a friendly spirit', but advised that if violence was needed, 'there will be nothing for it but blow for blow'.[69] At Kilteevan in the same week, a friendly statement invited 'Ulstermen' to assist in securing a free nation.[70] The AOH were to the fore at Strokestown alongside the clergy and UIL, who assisted in expansion at Scramogue, Mountpleasant and Cloonfree.[71] Shop owners in Strokestown were asked to 'show their zeal' by allowing their assistants the time to drill, while Úna and Eileen Sharkey's American Novelty Shop began to stock copies of the *Irish Volunteer* newspaper and sell 'volunteer shirts'.[72] Castlerea saw the AOH and GAA join forces to form its corps, with Canon Harte exhorting the men to assist in building the Irish Volunteers to be 250,000 strong and 'defend Ireland against all comers'.[73] Calls for a defence fund were greeted with enthusiasm and the women of Carniska were singled out by the *Democrat* for their generosity.[74] Hayden resorted to stating that the home rule bill was now 'in effect' an act, and therefore even more deserving of protection.[75] By the end of June, the CI reported that there were 2,300 men in twenty Roscommon corps. Sligo and Longford, which had similarly sized populations, had fifteen corps each, with Westmeath boasting twenty and Leitrim twenty-six. CI Rutledge observed that the companies 'are beginning to feel their strength ... when they get arms, their existence looks like being a serious menace to the peace of the county and to ... the minority who hold different political views'.[76]

Volunteer membership grew further after John Redmond's takeover of the provisional committee in Dublin. Hayden correctly believed that the movement would be welcomed more widely, given that it 'takes its direction from the Irish Party'.[77] The company at Crossna believed that the 'so-called Dublin Provisional Committee ... would mismanage ... the Volunteer movement only for Mr Redmond's ... intervention'.[78]

However, there was some dissent. Volunteers in Roscommon town and Cootehall deemed Redmond's action unnecessary. The Roscommon town resolution was controversial as only four of a five-member meeting issued it. George Geraghty and Michael Finlay were the most prominent of the four, whom Fr O'Flanagan criticized for their 'untimely' statement.[79] A follow-up meeting rescinded the resolution. The corps made clear its support for Redmond, alongside those at Ballaghaderreen, Boyle, Rooskey, Strokestown, Killina, Ballinlough and Ballyfarnon.[80] In late July, a review at Strokestown of the 'Roscommon (Central) Regiment' saw over 2,000 men parade in support of Redmond and home rule. The impressive muster involved less than half the county roster of 5,100 men.[81]

Activity in all other political organizations in Roscommon declined as people concentrated on the Irish Volunteers. Numerous publications reported on Roscommon's likely adoption of a boycott of Belfast traders given the anti-unionist rhetoric heard at many of the musters, which the *Ballymena Weekly Telegraph* suggested would show false all the nationalist professions of tolerance and fraternity.[82] Provocatively, the 4 July edition of the *Herald*, a newspaper now assisting the local corps, despite Tully's dislike of the Devines, ran with the front-page headline: 'Civil War in Ireland'.[83]

Roscommon Volunteers who looked fearfully at the headline had good cause. They were still largely unarmed. Calls to rescind the arms proclamation were made; J.P. Hayden stated that allowing the Irish Volunteers to arm would create mutual deterrence.[84] The CI, with fewer men than in previous years when Roscommon ceased to be 'in a disturbed state' from March 1914, referenced efforts to fundraise for weaponry, but reported few arms by August.[85] His subordinates appeared paranoid and, on one occasion, investigated straw bales that were delivered to John Beades, a Roscommon publican. Hayden raised the issue in the House of Common, querying whether the search for non-existent guns was legal.[86] The forensic police efforts in Roscommon and an absence of anything similar in the north of Ireland were highlighted. Additional proof of unequal treatment was seen with the shootings at Bachelor's Walk in Dublin on 26 July. The incident involved British soldiers firing into a crowd that had gathered to celebrate the landing of arms by the Irish Volunteers at Howth. A meeting in Roscommon town in the aftermath heard George Geraghty assert that 'the dirty hacks of the British Government' had confirmed the moral right of the Roscommon man to 'shoulder his rifle and take his place when the proper time comes'.[87]

However, the noise created around an impending civil war was drowned out when Britain declared war on Germany on 4 August. The *Herald* warned that home rule was to be relegated in importance. Tully counselled, however, that the European conflict could present an opportunity: 'Ireland may yet rise triumphant out of the ashes of her own past.'[88]

The changing political landscape in Roscommon from 1912 to the start of the First World War indicated a strong commitment to home rule. The measure was believed to have the potential to solve the county's land issues and, perhaps less importantly in Roscommon, give Ireland self-government. Apart from the organization, promotion and fundraising, reaction in Roscommon to the unionist threat illustrated that the measure was deemed worthy of exceptional sacrifice. Controversies surrounding local unionist opposition showed that Roscommon nationalists were outraged when the political minority sought to remould home rule. Although initially sluggish, support for the Irish Volunteers was driven by the increasing likelihood that unionist agitation and British politicking would lead to partition. John Redmond's adoption of the Irish Volunteers in May 1914 saw many more flock to the county corps, the men willing, it appeared, to protect home rule by force. Both constitutional and advanced nationalists in Roscommon sought arms to meet the unionist threat and, with the support of Catholic clergymen, readied themselves for civil war. Overnight, the start of the First World War halted that preparation. The continental conflict presented numerous challenges from the day war was declared, challenges that changed everything.

3 'People who trust Liberals have a slippery crowd to deal with': First World War to the Easter Rising, 1914–16

The early months of the First World War saw great change in Roscommon. Politics diminished in importance as people turned their attention to defending Ireland, supporting army enlistment and increasing food production. Believing that the war would be short, it was assumed that such support would copper-fasten home rule. However, as the war dragged on, an aversion to fighting for the British at the front ensured not only that willing recruits were limited, but that Irish nationalist unity was under threat. The expanding advanced nationalist section assumed a more vocal and active role in opposing enlistment. Roscommon grew increasingly unsettled as war price inflation impacted people's ability to feed their families and heat their homes. The prosperity that the demands of war afforded larger farmers stoked further resentment as graziers held on to lands that ought to have been subdivided. IPP inactivity on these issues ensured that people directed increasing criticism at their MPs. They were accused of focusing on the empire rather than Ireland. Unsuccessful recruitment drives conducted by army officers, gentry and MPs led to fears of conscription being imposed on the young farmers they targeted. This led to the emigration of hundreds of men until prohibited from doing so. Those forced to remain in Roscommon looked to advanced nationalists to protect their interests and moved away from the UIL and AOH, which did little to force the IPP to address their constituents' concerns. Speeches delivered by an increasingly prominent Fr Michael O'Flanagan ensured that anti-recruitment sentiment was well articulated as 1916 approached, his parishioners were among the thousands across Roscommon who demanded better conditions. Moves to wrest control of Ireland from the British in the rebellion of Easter 1916 had far-reaching consequences in Roscommon. The outbreak's suppression by the British government ensured that pre-existing antipathy to government policy increased exponentially as Roscommon reacted in horror to the executions, internments and widespread repression. The IPP's response to the Rising further underlined its disconnection from the people of Roscommon. Local MPs defended their efforts to reinvigorate home rule by conceding on the policy of partition. Large numbers of disillusioned constituents looked to SF for leadership as 1916 moved towards winter and released internees provided a focus for advanced nationalism. This began to take on the appearance of something the IPP had not yet faced: an existential threat to its political existence.

As preparations for war accelerated, the IPP recognized that their home rule strategy required overt support for Britain. On 3 August 1914 John Redmond committed the services of the Irish Volunteers to defend Ireland. He consulted beforehand only with J.P. Hayden and T.P. O'Connor, the Athlone-born MP for Liverpool, suggesting that he sought affirmation rather than challenge.[1] His pledge was widely welcomed. The *Messenger* predicted that 'lasting brotherhood' would result from the UVF and Irish Volunteers defending the nation, and congratulated Redmond for outmanoeuvring Carson.[2] The Gaelic Notes section of the *Herald*, as opposed to its editorial, saw such support as fair payback for home rule, while the *Journal* believed that Redmond 'properly pledged himself on behalf of the volunteers of Ireland'.[3] Irish Volunteer corps across Roscommon supported Redmond's position. The *Irish Volunteer* related that such was the county's enthusiasm, the Irish Volunteer county committee intended to raise a cavalry corps.[4]

Redmond's action was not only supported by nationalists. It promoted a rapprochement with unionists that appeared unlikely just days before. Captain T.C.E. Goff requested admission to the Roscommon Volunteer corps before his army redeployment. In common with other unionists, Goff saw little conflict between his antipathy to home rule and membership after Redmond's pledge.[5] The welcome he received from Canon Cummins was, however, judged too effusive by some existing members who were doubly annoyed at the gifting of the chairmanship of the county committee by incumbent Plunkett Taaffe to the Catholic Lord de Freyne.[6] Calls that such men should 'come in the same as every other body' were addressed by George Geraghty, who assured his audience that 'peer and peasant stand side-by-side'.[7] The Gaelic Notes section of the *Herald* reported that the changing profile led to efforts on behalf of a minority to limit 'unionist' enlistees, but that the 'sound common sense' of the main body prevailed.[8] Optimism surrounded the perceived elevation of the Volunteers to the status of, as the Ballyfarnon corps put it, being the 'recognised soldiers of Ireland'.[9] Moves by 30-year-old IRB and GAA member Micheál Ó Braonáin to foment anti-war sentiment with the circular 'Ireland and the War' were unsuccessful and the CI agreed with colleagues in adjoining counties that August saw cooperation and loyalty: 'Germany is hated and France loved'.[10] Discounting the unionist position, Roscommon nationalists believed that Ireland was fulfilling the home rule *quid pro quo*. As Plunkett Taaffe put it, the people needed to 'rally around [the] county flag', wait for the short war to end and the Dublin parliament to open.[11]

As ever, a jaundiced view appeared in *Herald* editorials. In early September Jasper Tully counselled that: 'People who trust Liberals have a slippery crowd to deal with'.[12] Others were also wary, with one attendee at a muster in Strokestown the same week bellowing: 'Why not put the home rule bill on the statute book before anything else is expected of the National

Volunteers'.[13] This did happen on 18 September but the measure was suspended for the duration of the war. The *Journal* was annoyed that the Irish were being treated to 'flapdoodle and humbug … in twelve months or longer, [we will] be as we are'.[14] The *Westmeath Independent* believed the likelihood of a short war made the suspension tolerable, while in a letter to the *Freeman's Journal*, John Keaveny, purporting to represent 'Roscommon nationalists', thanked Redmond for 'placing Ireland … among the nations of the world'.[15] The fact that the *Messenger* omitted news of the suspension in its editorials might have influenced the Irish Volunteers in Rooskey to celebrate as if the final hurdle had been crossed.[16] J.J. O'Kelly asked John Fitzgibbon to 'tell my people what they have got … explain to them the bill', a request that implied that even the disengaged O'Kelly understood that the majority in Roscommon knew little about the Home Rule Act.[17]

The most important consequence of home rule being placed on the statute book occurred on 20 September at Woodenbridge, County Wicklow, when Redmond called on Irishmen to fight at the war front; as home rule had been gained, full participation was now justified. The *Herald* protested and Tully put it succinctly that Volunteers had to decide if they were 'England's men or Ireland's men'.[18] Advanced nationalists on the Irish Volunteer provisional committee agreed and a schism resulted. Redmond supporters greatly outnumbered detractors and they broke away to form the Irish National Volunteers (INV). Consequently, the Irish Volunteers under Eoin MacNeill, whose article 'The North Began' influenced the formation of the Volunteers in November 1913, had a roster of perhaps 11,000 men, less than ten per cent of the pre-schism total. Resolutions of support for Redmond came from influential bodies and figures across Roscommon. T.A.P. Mapother, chairman of the Roscommon guardians and an ageing Kilteevan landlord, directed that resolutions of thanks be offered to Asquith for having 'fulfilled his promises' and to Redmond for ensuring that the Irish could assist the 'great Empire to which we belong in heart as well as in fact'.[19]

The split at the top of the Irish Volunteers filtered down to Roscommon. It was quickly apparent which side had more support. A vituperative editorial lambasting MacNeill's 'small body of malcontents' appeared in the *Messenger* on 3 October. The newspaper decried the 'impudence' of those supporting the man who had 'called for cheers for Carson'.[20] In Roscommon town, a minority of the local corps wrote to the *Irish Independent* denouncing Redmond. In response, M.J. Heverin, a county councillor and ally of Mapother, convened a Volunteer meeting that issued a statement condemning MacNeill's 'Sinn Féin' tactics and disowning the letter to the *Irish Independent*.[21] When Heverin organized a poll to ascertain loyalties, the result was a resounding win for Redmondites; it was replicated in Castlerea, Athlone, Boyle, Croghan, Ballyfarnon and Kilglass. Only the company at

Upper Arigna wavered before committing to the IPP. Roscommon, unlike some adjoining counties, comprehensively backed Redmond.[22] The CI reported that the number of advanced nationalist dissenters subsequently diminished.[23]

The support did not, however, translate into significant enlistment in Roscommon. Certainly, army reservists re-enlisted (reducing corps strengths and undermining drill instruction in the process); however, new enlistees were less common, a trend replicated across Connacht. The CI claimed that most were uninterested, especially 'the farming class of the Volunteers [who] are selfish and … have no idea of fighting for anyone'.[24] Large INV rallies at Lanesboro in early October 1914 promised much but delivered little, while meetings at nearby Ballyleague and, later, at Castlerea confirmed a general aversion to enlistment.[25] At Castlerea, Hayden couched his plea for recruits in an imperial context. The Irish had to defend their neighbour for political reasons, as had the Boers in South Africa: 'the place to defend England was on the battlefields of France'.[26] The meeting had a poor turnout, which the *Messenger* and *Weekly Freeman's Journal* could do little to conceal.[27] Fitzgibbon addressed the small numbers using what was to become familiar rhetoric. Those 200 present (fifty being INV), were the best men who, like his son, Michael, knew their duty.[28] The *Messenger* propagandized as best it could to support enlistment, even dedicating almost a full page to a small INV meeting in Knockcroghery in early November.[29] Most of the local press titles featured articles and reports that stressed the need for the INV to support enlistment but to little avail.[30] In a widely reproduced November letter intended to combat unionist criticism of nationalist enlistment, J.P. Hayden claimed that 180 men from Roscommon town had gone to war. He asserted that 'practically all of them were members of the local corps of the National Volunteers, which has been reduced almost to vanishing point'.[31] The claim was not supported by his own newspaper, which reported that sixty INV had enlisted to mid-November 1914. Another source suggested that only another thirty-five enlisted in the first six months of 1915.[32] Hayden's sole accurate assertion was that the INV had nearly vanished.

Fear that INV membership was a step towards the front drove organizers to promote its defensive aspect. The 'Roscommon battalion', which comprised south Roscommon INV companies, was promised guns for defence training, all financed by Hayden.[33] The arrival of fifty rifles was celebrated by the *Messenger*, which did not mention that the substandard weapons were returned to the vendor.[34] INV reorganization meetings were held across the county in early 1915. Yet, even Canon Cummins, also busily reorganizing the Gaelic League, could not arrest the decline, as news of corps training with Indian clubs and parallel bars brought ridicule.[35] The limited cache of weapons in the county, perhaps sixteen rifles in total, included many borrowed for the Roscommon town St Patrick's Day parade at which Cummins criticized men who left the INV on a 'whim'.[36] The low uptake for seats on trains bound for the national INV rally in Dublin in April 1915 confirmed the decline. There were fourteen Roscommon contingents. Most were depleted according to the *Herald* and *Journal*. The latter confirmed that just thirty men from Roscommon town took the train.[37]

The UIL also declined. By late 1914, the *Messenger* carried fewer meeting reports and in an editorial on 16 January 1915 criticized the 'premature' closure of branches.[38] Meetings to address the decline in the first three months of 1915 at places such as Drum and Clonown, near Athlone, heard Hayden and Fitzgibbon make empathetic statements. Hayden believed that UIL inactivity was not 'deliberate' and that Roscommon understood the need to support the 'movement that had gained so much for the Irish people'.[39] The meetings addressed topics that had driven IPP policy prior to the war. The MPs assured them that the IPP understood people's views on partition, the proposed home rule amendment bill and, more importantly in Roscommon, the need to address inequity in land distribution. Growing interest in SF was also noted. Hayden described the party as pro-German with a 'scissors and paste' approach to politics.[40] Rhetoric promoting the invulnerability of home rule in the context of solid Irish support for the war was commonplace.[41] Early mutterings against conscription at Rahara in the south of the county led Hayden to assure his audience that the measure would never 'pass the criticism' of the IPP.[42] Overall, however, the UIL remained quiet in Roscommon and adjoining counties.[43] Hayden and Fitzgibbon were in the unfamiliar position of speaking to unreceptive Roscommon audiences.

Outside of the Volunteer ranks, the first ten weeks of the war saw good enlistment in towns in Roscommon. The 4th battalion of the Connaught Rangers in Boyle received dozens of reservists, 'mostly old, seasoned soldiers bearing many decorations'. Major J.F. Murphy, the Boyle recruiting officer and an anti-home ruler, was reportedly inundated with men from Roscommon, Mayo, Leitrim, Sligo and Galway.[44] Even the *Daily Express* and *Weekly Irish Times* provided positive reports, the former using Roscommon's recruitment record to counterbalance news of strong unionist enlistment.[45] The constitutional nationalist press followed suit. The *Freeman's Journal* editorialized that the county had 'sprung to the aid of civilisation and national freedom'.[46] By November 520 men had enlisted in Boyle. Lady de Freyne claimed the figure accounted for one-sixth of eligible Roscommon men, a problematic assertion given the influx of recruits from other counties.[47] The *Messenger* claimed that the efforts of RIC Sergeant Doherty saw Roscommon town give more men per head of population than any other, an accolade also accorded to Athlone and Boyle.[48] Castlerea, the county's second recruitment office for the Connaught Rangers, was lauded for its contribution by Captain

Nicolas Balfe, the recruiting officer for Roscommon, Mayo and portions of Galway and Sligo.[49]

However, as early as mid-October 1914, opinions diverged. Writing proudly that 120 from Roscommon town had enlisted, the *Freeman's Journal* contrasted with the *Irish Times*, which regarded the 120 as a tiny proportion of the town's 1,800-strong population.[50] By early 1915 recruiters were certainly being portrayed inaccurately as 'busier than ever'. Only twenty men per week presented at Boyle military barracks, with the town's own contribution then qualified abstrusely as better than 'any other similarly circumstanced district in the United Kingdom'.[51] By February 1915 the CI reported there was little or no enlistment.[52] Efforts to enliven recruitment meetings using bands and Irish Brigade slogans proved ineffective, with letters from the front such as that from Royal Engineer Bernard Smith undoubtedly being dissuasive. He wrote of the 'rough time ... record marches ... heavy artillery fire ... we expect a most desperate battle at any moment'.[53] Similar accounts were common and, while exciting, few would have been enticed by the near misses or the increasing toll of Roscommon dead.

As recruitment numbers fell, rumours of conscription increased, prompting an uptick in the numbers seeking to leave Roscommon. In its 24 October edition, the *Journal* suggested that the Militia Ballot Act was a first step towards forced war service.[54] The following week, M.J. Judge, the only Roscommon attendee, joined committee members of the Irish Volunteers at a national convention to oppose conscription.[55] The Volunteers equated emigration with desertion and would not have been pleased that emigration agents' offices in Roscommon were 'thronged' in late October. Between Roscommon town and Strokestown alone, almost seventy young men booked passage, while an exodus from Frenchpark and Arigna was reported by the *Herald*.[56] The *Londonderry Sentinel* mocked the 'war shy west' and, in a widely-circulated article, claimed that some émigrés in Strokestown had abandoned farms.[57] The CI believed that around 200 men, mostly farmers' sons, left in October.[58] Interviews in Boyle confirmed that conscription was the cause. The *Messenger* was angered given that conscription rumours had received the 'flattest contradiction' from Redmond. What the paper did not recognize was that young men were disinclined to trust the IPP when it came to the war.[59] The outflow abated as government denials complemented Redmond's position. Nevertheless, emigration was never far from the minds of Roscommon's eligible young men.

Other push factors played a role. When the war commenced the cost of living rose sharply. As early as 8 August 1914, the Roscommon guardians sought regulations to prevent extortionate price increases.[60] Food hoarding became a feature of markets as the better-off purchased in bulk, with prices in Athlone reaching 'ridiculous' levels by September.[61] The cost of turf and coal rose so much that many were unable to heat their homes and feed their families adequately.[62] Graziers reduced tillage, increasing the more lucrative cattle stock by roughly twenty per cent, and received increased prices at fairs from Boyle to Athlone during the first year of the war. Bad weather in the spring and summer of both 1915 and 1916 had an adverse impact on the potato crop and fodder reserves, prompting graziers to hoard grasslands even more jealously.[63] The *Journal* and *Westmeath Independent* condemned their selfishness.[64] Outside of war time, the conditions were ripe for a reinvigoration of cattle driving. However, there were only two large-scale drives during late 1914 and early 1915, and one of those resulted from a family issue.[65] Aggression towards farmers at markets and fairs led many of them to use cooperatives to sell in bulk to the military, further undermining people's buying power. By November 1915, the CI believed that 'farmers were never so well off in their history'.[66]

Plans by Roscommon milk producers to petition the CDB to retain grazing lands and increase prices led George Geraghty to organize a protest meeting.[67] Recognizing growing anger at IPP inaction, J.P. Hayden complained about the export of crops in late 1915. By late 1916 when the government set food prices, locals in Roscommon town combined to force prices down at markets.[68] The *Journal*, which was reduced in size as paper costs increased, claimed it was an 'utter impossibility for the poorer classes ... to live with any semblance of decency', a point that was especially true in the towns of Roscommon where many were wholly reliant on markets and shops.[69]

The RAEC highlighted the consequences of unequal access to land, notably increased emigration and prices as well as numerous bullocks that 'were not suitable recruits'.[70] At Boyle in March 1915, the region's larger graziers were warned by disgruntled locals that they had to increase tillage or they would be boycotted. The *Daily Express* sneered that tillage complaints in Boyle were simply a 'pretext for adding fresh bitterness to the agrarian campaign'.[71] The CDB's straitened position saw it retain rather than redistribute lands, with the consequence that land purchases by smaller farmers slowed considerably.[72] The continued growth in cattle numbers – a forty-eight per cent increase nationally since 1914 – prompted angry scenes on the Roscommon leg of a tillage promotion tour undertaken by the vice president of the Department of Agriculture, T.W. Russell.[73] The meeting in the Harrison hall at the end of September saw Hayden and Fitzgibbon question Russell's assertions on increases already gained for tillage in Roscommon. However, Canon Cummins best represented the audience as he, in a 'stormy' presentation, highlighted how government inaction had actually made the situation more acute.[74] Cummins's intervention affected Russell, who a week later admitted that the actions of Roscommon's graziers had led to 'agricultural slums'.[75]

Inequity in land distribution did little to assist recruiters when they were appealing to young farmers. One approach was to propagandize that such men were enlisting in numbers. Increasingly fictional press accounts from February 1915 emphasized cases of farmers enlisting immediately after recruitment meetings.[76] Although a frequent speaker at meetings in early 1915, it took The O'Conor Don time to realize that Roscommon farmers were not motivated by the argument he deployed at Castlerea in March: 'you can't expect England to give us self-government if we don't join the fight'.[77] By April he understood the power of land and declared 'unofficially' that farmers whose sons enlisted would get preferable treatment from the CDB.[78] Captain Balfe petitioned the CDB in July to consider the proposal. The RAEC offered its support, with Cummins noting his 'pride' at the common sense being shown.[79] The *Journal* was not sanguine. It foresaw the continuation of the inequality between gentry recruits who left their families behind in comfort and 'the relatives of Catholic soldiers [who] are struggling on the worn bogtails and barren hillsides'.[80] The CDB agreed to append enlistment to their criteria but not until April 1916. This delay did not assist The O'Conor Don who, like many IPP MPs, was asking men to fight for a benefit that was not guaranteed.[81]

Frustrated recruiters resorted first to dealing with overt opposition and second to issuing threats. Athleague's Michael Purcell was arrested for breaching the Defence of the Realm Act (DORA) by 'interfering with recruitment' when he voiced his opposition to enlistment at a recruitment meeting. He was pilloried in the unionist press as an exemplar of nationalist opposition to the war effort.[82] Purcell fared little better in the *Messenger*, which stated hysterically that the ultimate sanction for his crime was death.[83] In the event he received two months' hard labour. Fears that conscription would imperil home rule saw the local press, local authorities and political organizations engage in heated arguments, many adverting to the effect of the newly formed British war cabinet in which Edward Carson was attorney general. The *Herald* believed Carson's appointment was 'the death and burial' of home rule.[84] The result of the recruitment aspect of these debates in the Strokestown and Roscommon RDCs was a decision to act as recruitment committees. Some members were convinced that conscription was more likely after Redmond declined a cabinet post.[85]

The most controversial criticism of recruitment in Roscommon came in July from Judge Walter Boyd at a Grand Jury session. While congratulating Roscommon on an absence of crime, the judge bemoaned the county's recruitment total of 438 men, a figure confirmed by the CI.[86] Excoriating 'slackers', Boyd declared that 'the respectable portion ... the gentry, are engaged in the war'.[87] His views fuelled anti-nationalist articles in the unionist press, while the constitutional nationalist press attacked his logic. The *Messenger* described his partisanship as a lesson in how 'not to do it'.[88] The *Evening Telegraph* accentuated Boyd's contrast between 'respectable' and '"ordinary" people' and claimed the slackers were mainly the ranchers that promoted emigration and the unnecessary extra RIC.[89] Boyd's views were soon repeated at recruitment meetings at Ballintubber, Castlerea, Roscommon and Strokestown. Myopic recruiters addressed 'themselves forcibly to the farming community', lauded the gentry and threatened conscription.[90] The *Journal* lamented the lack of introspection: 'A salutary hint is never made to the crimes that have banished the people of Roscommon from its fertile plains … whips and scorpions for the "populace" and "honour and glory" for the gentry'.[91]

Reluctance to enlist was not just an Irish problem. In August the British government moved towards introducing compulsory army service in Britain by passing the National Registration Act 1915. The measure was intended to quantify the manpower in Britain but had the unintended consequence of prompting the early return home of Roscommon seasonal labourers. Those who remained in Britain after January 1916, when compulsory service was introduced there, reportedly experienced 'some trouble' as a result of their reluctance to enlist.[92] Those who returned were subjected to a comprehensive voluntary recruitment scheme under the Central Recruiting Council for Ireland. The Roscommon committee was headed by The O'Conor Don, T.A.P. Mapother, T.C.E. Goff and other wealthy men with gentry connections.[93] The scheme led to 'a complete system of recruiting organisation' in Roscommon by late September when failed attempts were made to reform the INV at both Roscommon town and Castlerea.[94] The local newspapers ran one-page advertisements for the body, which sent letters to all men believed eligible for service.[95] Coinciding with efforts to revitalize north Roscommon UIL branches, continued voluntary recruitment in Ireland was heralded by Hayden as proof that 'factionists' were scaremongering. Faith in the IPP was being rewarded according to T.J. Devine, who deemed a muster of 2,000 Hibernians in Strokestown in September adequate proof that many shared his view.[96]

The new call to arms elicited a familiar result. The *Herald, Journal* (soon to be under the ownership of John McDonnell after the death of William Tully) and *Democrat* again noted increased emigration. The *Democrat* described the 'blue funk' of some men in Tulsk who 'made for the sea shore with all haste' before new regulations limited their ability to leave the country.[97] The Strokestown newspaper denigrated the 'women men' stuck to their mothers' petticoats, while the *Messenger* and *Journal* showed their support for recruiting by sending representatives to the meeting where Lord Wimborne, the Irish lord lieutenant, set out his vision for the scheme.[98] The obligatory recruitment tour had the same promoters and familiar propaganda. Major Murphy read old scripts. The reissuing of letters to unresponsive individuals was deemed intimidatory, while the receipt of letters by ineligible citizens provoked controversy, not least in the case of Fr O'Flanagan. The curate described his letter as an 'insult'. He reacted by further maligning recruiters and enlistees, each one of the latter being 'a traitor … and a fool'.[99]

By January 1916 the voluntary scheme had failed. The AOH county board was unsurprised. Men were needed on farms and Irish recruits were undervalued. The O'Conor Don agreed with the latter point. CI Rutledge maintained that most were more interested in farming than fighting but also blamed the influence of the 'pro-German' GAA for limiting enlistment in Roscommon.[100] Later recruitment plans remained uninspiring as Roscommon's upper classes did nothing to address the issues they caused by their own involvement. When a ladies' recruitment committee was formed in March 1916, its chairman, T.A.P. Mapother, admitted only one woman to the board.[101]

Even with the conscription threat, advanced nationalist growth, evident in south-western counties during the summer of 1915, was not replicated in Roscommon until the late autumn. There were small pockets of Irish Volunteers in the county; the CI estimated a combined figure of 259 SF and Irish Volunteers in July.[102] Like neighbouring Sligo, some corps still existed in Roscommon but had been reduced to a handful of largely inactive individuals.[103] At Athlone, a small Irish Volunteer cohort received drill instruction, while at Ballaghaderreen, the influence of M.J. Judge and John and Frank Shouldice, members of the most prominent advanced nationalist family in the town, assisted in drawing together aspiring Volunteers there during the summer.[104] In September a training camp near Athlone welcomed Roscommon men. Soon after that, the county's first branch of Cumann na mBan, the representative body for advanced nationalist women, was established in the town.[105] The more direct methods of the recruitment scheme of late 1915 increased advanced nationalist activity. At Ballaghaderreen, the corps mustered a reported (and likely overstated) 300 men for a parade in opposition to a recruitment meeting in November.[106] Reports of hostility towards speaker and Victoria Cross recipient Lieutenant Michael O'Leary were seized upon by Conservative Party leader Bonar Law as further evidence of nationalist antipathy to the empire.[107] Laurence Ginnell MP rounded on the town's magistrates after they withdrew permission for the corps to march, although they did reverse the decision when it became clear they acted without reliable evidence.[108] The Roscommon CI was worried and hoped that the inspector general (IG) would agree that Ballaghaderreen was, in reality, 'geographically in Mayo'.[109] RIC special branch reported that the corps trained throughout the winter, with thirty engaging in rifle practice. The CI suggested in spring 1916 that the corps had a 'good cache' of weapons and that it promoted advanced nationalist publications.[110]

There was controversy in Crossna when younger UIL members sought to follow Ballaghaderreen and promote the Irish Volunteers. John Regan, IPP stalwart and UIL branch chairman, proposed that 'any attempt to disrupt our national unity by trying to establish ... a foul and misleading movement known as Sinn Féin in the guise of Volunteers ... will be opposed'. Edward Doyle and P.J. Golden left the branch after being in the minority third that opposed Regan. The Crossna Irish Volunteers were quickly reorganized, with honorary secretaries J.J. Doyle and Thomas Moran goading Regan by stating that the IPP did not invent Irish nationalism in 1879 when they started the Land War. The discord spread to the Crossna AOH, of which both Golden and Regan were members. Brethren in nearby Cootehall supported Golden, asserting that Redmond had an 'imperialist attitude'.[111]

The discord was fuelled by Fr O'Flanagan who was posted to Crossna after being removed from Cliffoney, County Sligo, by Bishop Bernard Coyne. When he arrived in his new parish in October 1915, O'Flanagan continued the criticism of the IPP that precipitated his removal. Consequently, in the interests of 'ecclesiastical discipline', the bishop denied O'Flanagan permission to harangue 'the congregation ... inside, or in the vicinity of, the church'. The curate complied in his own way by reminding parishioners that 'I can think and so can you'.[112]

Visible support for the Irish Volunteers increased. In the south, John Brennan formed a company between Athleague and Roscommon town in December 1915. The *Irish Volunteer* claimed he had sourced guns.[113] Efforts were made to reorganize Irish Volunteer corps in Roscommon town and in Kilglass, where it was declared that partition was 'political heresy'.[114] Arguments that advanced nationalism was the force keeping conscription at bay were dismissed by John Keaveny. He told a Breedogue audience that SF were 'malcontents, harpers, with penny-pistol ideas of emancipating Ireland'.[115] The meeting was, however, one of an increasing number held by constitutional nationalists who feared that the Irish Volunteers and SF were making gains in Roscommon.[116]

The advanced nationalist resurgence gathered momentum from February 1916. CI Rutledge reported the mobilization of 110 men at Ballaghaderreen and Crossna who had access to forty-six shotguns and fifteen revolvers. Curiously, he did not comment on the Athleague corps, which, by March, according to the *Daily Express*, was displaying an 'aggressive demeanour'.[117] February also saw a Cumann na mBan branch established in Lisacul, while RIC reports from Ballaghaderreen indicated that anti-British protests were made after GAA matches.[118] The North Roscommon UIL executive decried the 'soreheads' who protested and were likely unnerved when similar rhetoric was heard at local authority meetings.[119] At a meeting of the RTC, Alfred McCrann excoriated the IPP for its £400 annual MP parliamentary salaries, supplementary incomes from recruitment efforts and doing little to stop food exports.[120] The *Irish Independent* relayed the *Herald* view on the 'colossal impudence' that advanced nationalists were promoting: 'We fear Mr Redmond is in for a run of this "colossal impudence"'.[121]

The war and conscription were relegated in importance after Easter week 1916. In a special 27 April edition, the *Herald* evinced the common reaction to the Irish Volunteer-led Easter Rising: condemnation. While acknowledging that the *Belfast Daily Telegraph* was its main source and that judgment was premature, the Boyle newspaper described the rebellion as a 'crime against our people's highest interests', yet another 'tragic bloodsplash'.[122] In their 29 April editions, other Roscommon newspapers rounded on Carson, trade unionist Jim Larkin and the Liberal government for creating the conditions that fostered the 'mad' rebellion.[123]

A week later, when details were clearer, there was little moderation. The *Herald* presented the Rising inaccurately as a SF-led event. Tully's review of the 'bombastic' Proclamation of the Irish Republic described it as 'windy nonsense', full of 'crank notions' such as equal voting rights for men and women.[124] The *Journal* and *Messenger* agreed, and while the latter acknowledged that those involved had patriotic motives, the British response ensured the 'so-called Irish Republic is no more'.[125] The *Westmeath Independent* struck a charitable note by calling for the British to cease executing the leaders.[126] Following the lead of the local press, UIL branches across Roscommon condemned the Rising. Carson was to blame, as were SF. Patrick Regan of the Crossna UIL believed that SF obstructed home rule simply to 'serve the German demand'.[127] Fr O'Flanagan, somewhat incongruously given his previous rhetoric, described the Irish Volunteers who fought in Dublin as 'murderers'.[128] The CI reported that the Ballaghaderreen Volunteers ceased drilling to show their opposition to the rebellion.[129]

The release of testimonials from people caught up in the Rising and the continued execution of the ringleaders led to reappraisals. At the Castlerea guardians, John Fitzgibbon qualified their initial condemnation by acknowledging the 'greatest esteem for the manner in which the insurgents conducted the insurrection'.[130] In a letter to the guardians, J.P. Hayden assured them that the IPP had done all it could to save the executed leaders and acknowledged the change in sentiment. He counselled that the loyalty of the majority of Irish people in the aftermath of the Rising would invigorate the weakened claim for home rule.[131]

The influence of Jasper Tully on the county council ensured that its resolutions reflected the evolving mood. Tully, Mapother and Devine argued about the formulation of a resolution that eventually, among other issues, blamed Carson, condemned the actions in Dublin of the 'dupes' of German agents and indicated that the British repression was having a disastrous effect on opinions in both Ireland and the United States.[132] Unexpectedly, Tully congratulated John Dillon MP on his condemnation of the British response in the House of Commons.[133] Calling for the immediate imposition of home rule, Fitzgibbon noted the irony that, if it was instated: 'England had taught

Irishmen … that nothing but armed rebellion would ever gain the full independence of the country.'[134] Mapother's stronger position in the Roscommon
RDC saw a resolution pass condemning the 'Rising of the Sinn Féin party'
and calling for the executions to halt. He did, however, draw criticism when
he claimed that the 'entire Irish nation is … opposed to … Sinn Féin'.
Patrick McDermott said that he would have supported the Rising had it any
chance of success, while John Farrell damned the government for shooting
Irish Catholics but not Carson, a man who deserved a bullet.[135]

Public bodies complained bitterly about the imposition of sanctions in areas
where there was no activity connected with the Rising. The only pro-Rising
displays in Roscommon were the erection of a SF flag on Roscommon Castle
in Roscommon town, two 'republic' notices posted on Easter Sunday and the
removal of some Union Jacks in Boyle by boys from the previously quiet local
Na Fianna Éireann branch. The new CI, St Laurence Tyrell, allowed the flag
to be burned in two instalments, first on Abbey Street and then in the Market
Square.[136] Few from Roscommon participated in the Dublin Rising. M.J.
Judge, Micheál Ó Braonáin, John and Frank Shouldice and Joe O'Kelly were
all in Dublin during Easter week, O'Kelly having sourced gelignite for the
Dublin Volunteers.[137] Understandably, people in Roscommon town were,
therefore, dismayed by the arrival of 600–700 members of the Sherwood
Foresters, King Edward Horse and Royal Field Artillery during late April.
Press reports stated that 'Notices of Martial Law were immediately posted', a
curfew was imposed from 9 p.m. to 5 a.m. and pickets were set up on all
approach roads.[138] Twenty-six men were arrested. After courts martial in
Athleague, nineteen were released. The remaining seven – Geraghty, Ó
Braonáin, John Brennan, Edward and J.J. Doorly, Alfred McCrann and Pat
Smith – were sent to Dublin.[139] The Roscommon GAA county board supported Ó Braonáin, its chairman, by informing the Rebellion Commission that
the GAA was non-political, 'its programme contains nothing that can be con-
strued, except by slanderers, into opposition to the British'.[140]

There were eleven arrests in Ballaghaderreen (John and Frank Shouldice
were arrested in Dublin), a town in which Crown forces were active even
before the Rising.[141] There were no arrests in Castlerea ostensibly due to the
local DI, while the King Edward's Horse regiment at Strokestown seized only
Michael Cassidy, a national school teacher.[142] The visit of the Sherwood
Foresters to Tulsk was proclaimed a wasted journey by locals, 'there being no
Sinn Féiners about the place', while the army's activity in Boyle led to the
arrest of commercial traveller Peter O'Rorke.[143] In total, the sweep by the
army led to sixty-five arrests. Of this number, nineteen were sent to prisons
such as Wandsworth, Wakefield and Barlinnie in Britain.[144] Roscommon was
placed fifth nationally for arrests, an incongruous position for a county that
was considered the least disturbed during Easter 1916.[145] J.P. Hayden assured

readers of the *Messenger* that he was working energetically on the prisoners' behalf.[146] A bitter CI reported that the sympathy for those arrested and executed did not extend to dead RIC or soldiers. This was possibly a reference to Killina-born RIC Sergeant John Shanagher who was killed at Ashbourne, County Meath on 28 April.[147]

By June the initial version of the Easter Rising was being revised. An account submitted to the *Journal* by Dermot McDermott, a Roscommon solicitor held prisoner by the Volunteers during the fighting, presented a picture of intelligent and courteous men under the command of Countess Markievicz.[148] The *Herald* published 'Tales of the Rebellion', accounts that provided new context to the efforts and actions of 'The Crazy Poets that made the Crazy Rebellion'.[149] The *Westmeath Independent* told its readers that 'the poets, dreamers, Irishmen all' had been grossly mistreated, an editorial line that led the authorities to request that McDermott-Hayes publish a more loyal assessment.[150]

This increasing admiration for the Irish Volunteers was in stark contrast to the growing anger at the IPP. The *Irish Independent* reproduced Jasper Tully's editorial rant that was printed when Redmond looked to facilitate partition to save home rule.[151] Demanding that the IPP recognize 'a three-quarters nation … would expire of ridicule', the Boyle newspaper was joined by the *Westmeath Independent* in condemning the move. The Athlone publication began its gravitation away from the IPP by writing about 'bastard home rule'.[152] The IPP position so shocked Patrick Morahan, editor of the *Democrat*, that he departed from his staid editorials to excoriate the party. Redmond wanted to 'mutilate the country to please … Carson', while his followers continued with 'the tommy rot of passing resolutions of confidence' in the IPP leader.[153]

In a highly charged county council meeting on 23 June that received three columns in the *Weekly Freeman's Journal*, numerous county councillors decried the partition of the country. Calls for faith in Redmond's calm and wise leadership heard from Fitzgibbon, Hayden, Mapother and John Galvin did not quell the unrest. Long-time IPP follower and Land League activist D.J. Kelly was horrified. He stated that ninety-five per cent of constituents were against partition, while the UIL's John Drury queried whether 'the Irish Party has delegated their power to Mr Carson'. Jasper Tully dominated the meeting. He spoke of British duplicity, the imminence of conscription and the likely tax-heavy subjugation of the twenty-six counties after partition. Moves to resolve confidence in the IPP saw Galvin and Tully argue when Galvin blocked the latter's amendment on a united Ireland.[154] The *Westmeath Independent* wrote angrily of Hayden's rhetoric and the position adopted by the IPP in backing temporary partition. McDermott-Hayes editorialized that 'it is the duty of the representatives to obey the expressed wish of their constituents', a point commended in the *Democrat*.[155] By contrast, the *Messenger* applauded Hayden's 'masterly exposition' that framed partition as a unionist bluff and clarified that strict time parameters would anchor separation.[156] The position adopted by Redmond led several AOH divisions and UIL branches to condemn their leader. The Kilteevan UIL described partition as the 'mutilation of our country'.[157]

However, support for Redmond was also demonstrated. Resolutions with unquestioning faith were passed by the UIL at Ballynaheglish, Crossna, Kiltrustan and Corrigeenroe.[158] Led by Fr Kelly, the Knockcroghery UIL declared that rejecting partition outright was 'playing the game to suit Carson', a point with which Fr O'Flanagan agreed. Total opposition to partition would, O'Flanagan believed, see the Irish dismissed as an 'impossible race'.[159] The *Messenger* inaccurately asserted that the northern counties were to be temporarily excluded by their 'own wish' and published a Roscommon town UIL resolution that thanked northern nationalists for their 'self-sacrifice'.[160] The Strokestown guardians, although angered at a letter sent by Joseph McCrann, a guardian, to the *Irish Independent* directing the IPP away from partition, appeared unconcerned; Redmond should be left to work.[161]

The negativity was not something to which the IPP was accustomed. The CI noted that partition was the only aspect of home rule that had aroused local emotion.[162] The Killina UIL wanted to stem the flow away from the IPP and asked the party to seek 'a general amnesty' for Irish internees. Its members were certain, however, that only the dismissal of partition would quell the growing antipathy. At Ballaghaderreen, councillors and JPs told John Dillon that the release of detainees was 'necessary in order to allay the feeling of irritation and discontent which is now very widespread'.[163] J.P. Hayden's echoing of the government position that the 'advisory committee' would decide the prisoners' fate heightened the impression of a passive IPP and led angry Roscommon activists to look to Laurence Ginnell MP for assistance. Propaganda derived from the experiences of internees like Ballaghaderreen's Tom McCormack also damaged the IPP. It was reported how his internment conditions deteriorated with his move to Frongoch, a prisoner camp in Wales.[164] A county-wide fund to support the release of all Roscommon's internees was started by the AOH. Issuing a statement that must have alarmed the IPP, AOH chairman George O'Reilly declared: 'The rebellion demonstrated the spirit of courage and freedom which yet animates the hearts of Irishmen.' He called for a fund 'worthy of the insurgents ... and worthy of Roscommon'.[165] By August the *Westmeath Independent* was lauding SF for 'awakening' the Irish to the risk of trusting the British. A month later it was agreeing with Bishop O'Dwyer of Limerick that the 'principle of Sinn Féin' embodied the 'true spirit of the country'.[166]

Predictably, increasing anger in Roscommon found expression in land agitation. At Falty, between Athlone and Ballinasloe, a conflict on the 8,000-acre holdings of Presbyterian farmer James Mather in late June and early July saw the deployment of 120 RIC men and an army battalion. Hundreds from the parish of Moore targeted his 1,000 strong livestock herd and dozens were prosecuted for unlawful assembly. Almost by itself, the unrest led the county to be proclaimed under the Crimes Act.[167] Along with the RTC, the county council condemned the coincident imposition of castle rule, a more resolute form of government. The former termed it a 'breach of faith', especially given that nationalists had accepted the 'reasonable temporary solution' of partition.[168] The *Journal* indicated that castle rule was proof that Ireland was regressing under the IPP.[169] A newly radicalized *Democrat* excoriated home rule and the resolution obsessed UIL and AOH. The two bodies had fostered an inertness in Irish politics that had made people forget the need to criticize their MPs.[170]

Mounting unrest focused the minds of the authorities, who released some Roscommon internees. When George Geraghty, John Brennan and others returned to Roscommon town in late July, they were welcomed by a massive crowd.[171] The return of Michael Cassidy to Strokestown and the release of five Ballaghaderreen men heralded similar celebrations, as did the liberation of Patrick Moran of Crossna.[172] Their homecomings contrasted sharply with the glee-filled English mobs who, the *Herald* asserted, greeted news of the hanging of Roger Casement at Pentonville on 3 August.[173] Geraghty reassumed his role as RTC chairman. Pushing back against the IPP members, he condemned Casement's execution and called for the Irish to assert their rights.[174] The increasing distaste for home rule, now qualified by the *Herald* as 'a sham of the worst type', drove more people towards SF, while resolutions at UIL branches were ever more focused on the advanced nationalist threat.[175] Enmities increased, not only in already volatile places like Crossna, where Patrick Regan raged against those criticizing the 'most successful leader Ireland ever had', but also Kiltrustan, where established local disunity found new expression in advanced and constitutional nationalism.[176]

Advanced nationalists in Roscommon recognized that better organization was required if they were to pull people away from the IPP. To begin that process, the county's first unofficial SF club was set up in Roscommon town in November. Run by George Geraghty, 'The O'Rahilly Club', was officially named the 'Roscommon Social Club' and established under the 1904 Social Club Act.[177] In December the Roscommon UIL disparaged the 'starting of any organisation tending to create dissension', echoing J.P. Hayden's earlier denunciation of the 'insidious attempts to undermine' the IPP.[178]

The late 1916 conscription threat saw the local press continue to support voluntary enlistment but direct people away from the IPP. The *Herald* claimed that Redmond offered only 'mock opposition' to conscription – it was certain he would undermine the Irish just to get home rule.[179] The *Messenger* disagreed, of course, as did many UIL branches. The still loyal AOH county board also backed Redmond but issued a resolution to J.P. Hayden, which notably lacked a declaration of confidence.[180] T.J. Devine tried to counterbalance Tully's anti-conscription rhetoric in the county council. Like the Roscommon UIL, Devine directed people to stop reading the lie-laden *Irish Independent* and to consult instead the *Freeman's Journal* and *Evening Telegraph*.[181]

The death of J.J. O'Kelly, MP for Roscommon North, in December 1916 offered an opportunity for confidence in the IPP to be tested in a by-election in Roscommon. At O'Kelly's funeral in Glasnevin Cemetery, Hayden, Fitzgibbon, John Galvin and T.J. Devine took turns in helping to support his coffin.[182] Both the IPP and the new prime minister, Lloyd George, understood that the general release of the internees in December 1916 might not quieten the political atmosphere as intended. Pre-election discourse both in Ireland and Britain made it clear that an advanced nationalist candidate would have significant support in north Roscommon. The *Yorkshire Post and Leeds Intelligencer* set the scene: 'Sinn Féin [are] ... fairly strong in the constituency ... the United Irish League will have some difficulty in securing the seat for its own nominee, and the election is almost certain to prove interesting.'[183]

During the two years prior to O'Kelly's death, much had changed in Roscommon. The early months of the First World War seemed to confirm Redmond's strong position. However, as the conflict continued, the IPP's pro-war position became a liability. MPs did little to address the deprivations that the war economy created. Higher prices for scarce provisions placed pressure on those with the least capacity to bear it, while, in contrast, larger farmers prospered. Despite the assertions of J.P. Hayden, INV members were as averse to enlistment as Roscommon's young farmers. The criticism and threats that issued from recruitment platforms manned by IPP MPs, unionists and gentry speakers did not endear the MPs to their young, male constituents, many of whom emigrated. The Irish Volunteers became a natural harbour for those who were forced to remain and who sought to oppose voluntary recruitment schemes. While the increases in Volunteer corps in Roscommon up to early 1916 were modest, the reawakening of the UIL indicated that they recognized the threat. Although initial reaction to the 1916 Rising appeared favourable to IPP interests, the draconian British suppression ensured that Roscommon redirected its antipathy towards the government. Raids and arrests across the county during May indicated that Roscommon's quiescence during the rebellion was of little benefit. The imposition of the Crimes Act in Roscommon alongside Castle rule further fuelled the sense of persecution and gave additional credence to many of the arguments being promoted by advanced nationalists. J.P. Hayden's assertions that the IPP would protect the interests of nationalist Ireland jarred with his party's decision to accept partition to save home rule. With the exception of a minority of IPP stalwarts, partition was denounced across the county. The by-election occasioned by O'Kelly's death gave advanced nationalists in Roscommon their first opportunity to challenge the IPP in the electoral arena.

4 'Their decisions might not represent the real views of the electors': the Roscommon North by-election, 1917

The Roscommon North by-election in February 1917 changed the approach of advanced nationalists to the fight for Irish freedom. Previously convinced that politics could only taint the fight, the Roscommon North contest assured separatist doubters that the electorate could be persuaded to abandon Westminster. This profound shift in advanced nationalist policy led to electoral victories from Longford South to Clare East in the months that followed. The small number of advanced nationalists who came to Roscommon to test their political strength were a disparate collection of groups and individuals who defeated an IPP that had not faced a challenge in the constituency in over two decades. The contest was held during some of the worst weather conditions Roscommon had experienced in the twentieth century. Driving snow and severe cold limited the number of meetings that heard all sides discuss the merits and demerits of home rule, partition, army recruitment, access to land and parliamentary involvement. The support of Roman Catholic clergymen was essential to electoral success for political parties in Ireland. The exceptional energy of the loquacious Fr O'Flanagan ensured that the advanced nationalist side attracted many young clerics who secured key votes. The headline policies and presentation of the IPP and advanced nationalists were starkly different. Uninspiring IPP speakers continued the rhetoric that had typified their public engagements since the start of the war. By contrast, their opponents emphasized the stagnation of Irish politics during the war, the empty promises of the IPP and the sacrifices made at Easter 1916 by those who sought an Irish republic. The fact that their candidate – George Noble Plunkett – drew on the legacy of that rebellion was essential to his eventual success. The repercussions of the Roscommon North by-election were momentous. For the first time, a majority of voters decided that the IPP was no longer best suited to represent Ireland's interests.

As soon as O'Kelly died, ten potential IPP successors were touted. The most prominent were T.J. Devine; George O'Reilly; John Keaveny; UIL organizer, W.G. Fallon (reportedly John Dillon's preference); Professor John Conway, a Belfast-based Roscommon academic (reportedly in Joe Devlin's favour); and John Doherty, a London barrister, formerly of Roscommon.[1] Keaveny and O'Reilly ruled themselves out. Fallon's soundings convinced him that 'no stranger was wanted', with John Dillon confirming that the *Irish Independent* had spread a mistruth regarding his support.[2] Conway was san-

43

guine, despite Joe Devlin distancing himself, as was Doherty who organized meetings to explore his chances. Devine was the frontrunner. The IPP hoped that its nominee would be elected unopposed; there had been no challengers in the constituency since 1895.

When a small group of advanced nationalists saw merit in offering a candidate who could draw on the legacy of 1916, so did some voters in Roscommon. After Dr Michael Davitt, son of the famous land agitator, declined, an approach was made to George Noble Plunkett. A papal count, the 65-year-old former director of the National Museum in Dublin was largely selected because he was father to Joseph, one of the Rising's executed leaders, and George and John, two imprisoned 1916 veterans. Kevin O'Shiel, a SF member from Omagh, recalled that 'no one had ever regarded the Count as anything other than a conservative Catholic gentleman with harmless literary and cultural tastes'.[3] Plunkett, then living in Oxford, given a government order excluding him from Ireland, agreed to stand. He promised to shun the 'vile party systems' that compromised Irish representatives.[4]

When Plunkett's candidacy was confirmed, various press organs sought to denigrate and malign him. The *Messenger* dismissed him as 'the father of some of those' in the Rising, and asserted that he had no discernible policies or allegiances.[5] The *Freeman's Journal* focused on the count's January 1917 expulsion from the Royal Dublin Society, relating that such was his malignancy that a margin of 236:58 voted him out.[6] Northern unionist titles disdained his papal title, while British conservative titles emphasized his 'rebel' son, his own deportation and the threat the 'Sinn Feiner' posed to the empire.[7] The *Daily Express* was more accurate in suggesting that Plunkett had not declared himself a Sinn Féiner; indeed, he had 'not described himself at all'.[8]

Recognizing the value of a good start, Plunkett's promoters descended on Roscommon in mid-January. The county's IRB circles became active, as did additional Irish Volunteer corps, both groups using the by-election to reorganize. Michael Dockery and Micheál Ó Braonáin were to the fore for the IRB and worked alongside a then little-known Michael Collins. George Geraghty and Lanesboro man, P.J. McCrann, a former Frongoch internee, drove the Volunteers' efforts.[9] Other backers included the Irish Nation League (INL), a splinter group of mainly northern former IPP supporters; William O'Brien of the Dublin Trades Council and, most prominently, Laurence Ginnell MP and Fr O'Flanagan.[10] Plunkett's canvass was started with a circular that promoted his 'patriotism, intellectual ability and command of several languages'. The last point was important, as advanced nationalists sought Irish representation at the peace conference that was predicted after the end of the First World War.[11] Setting the tone for an arduous campaign influenced by the heaviest snowfall in fifty years, Ginnell demonstrated his dedication during the first week of electioneering by trudging ten miles to a meeting in Frenchpark.[12] The positive response there led him to assure Plunkett that 'all the young, male and female' were behind his candidacy.[13] Boyle's Michael Ward, a former UIL man, informed Plunkett that a virtue had been made of his enforced absence. Patrick Morahan of the *Democrat* printed a poster entitled: 'The West's Awake', which called for voters to end Plunkett's exile.[14]

The IPP faced its first fight in the constituency in twenty-two years. Unlike the 1895 contest, they were not facing a candidate who represented a different strand of constitutional nationalism, but one whose support came from people ready to reject much of what that stood for. To combat this existential threat, the IPP needed to be unified. As the constituency convention drew near, it was confirmed that Devine was unopposed. Devine's coronation was not without incident, however. With men from Crossna and Cootehall, Fr O'Flanagan staged an incursion and requested that Plunkett be nominated unopposed. Efforts from the floor to facilitate O'Flanagan were opposed by chairman J.P. Hayden given that Plunkett was not affiliated with the IPP. Devine was duly selected, with the *Freeman's Journal* claiming that the convention was the 'most representative ever held in the constituency', one that was 'free, untrammelled … unfettered'.[15] The same newspaper pointed out that the selection of Devine, a friend of Bishop Coyne, was apposite given 'his grasp of the land problem and public affairs generally'. Indicating the need for 'national discipline' to realize 'Parnell's plan', voters had one question to answer: 'Whether … the Irish Parliamentary Party can be trusted to speak and act for Ireland in the … critical times that are ahead … ?'[16]

Jasper Tully, a man well able to afford the £295 election deposit, joined the fray in opposition to both Plunkett and Devine. He claimed that if a 'real Sinn Feiner' such as Eoin MacNeill stepped forward to replace the count, he would withdraw.[17] Tully presented a confusing set of policies. On conscription and partition he would act as he saw fit, but on 'all other issues he would support the National Party'.[18] The *Messenger* believed that Tully's 'own estimate of his merits' led him to enter and weaken Plunkett's chances.[19] The *Nationalist*, which despised Tully, suggested that a loss to him would be as deplorable as defeat to the count, while the *Freeman's Journal* rebuked Tully's offer of partial IPP support.[20] The ballot paper for the Roscommon North presented T.J. Devine, 'Irish Parliamentary Party'; Count Plunkett, 'Independent Nationalist' and Jasper Tully, 'Independent'.[21]

The cold weather played a prominent part in the campaign. It was so severe that it led to several deaths, the loss of livestock, the cancellation of church services, the postponement of funerals and delayed markets.[22] When IPP rallies did convene two weeks after Plunkett's canvassers had started, Devine and Hayden were the main figures. Devine, though speaking to large, enthusiastic crowds at places like Ballyfarnon, was an uninspiring candidate. His recourse to staid pro-IPP rhetoric led *The Leader* to portray him as an 'I say ditto automaton'.[23] His inexperience showed when, instead of downplaying Plunkett's nationalist credentials, he stated that no-one with 'nationalist blood in him would say a word against' the count.[24] Notably, the IPP 'big guns' of Redmond, Dillon and Devlin were absent.[25] They were undoubtedly complacent and appear not to have understood that the election drew sufficient numbers of IPP enemies together to pose a serious threat to the party. Additional efforts by Fitzgibbon, John Keaveny and George O'Reilly were supplemented by Richard Hazelton, Francis Meehan, William Doris and Daniel O'Leary MPs.[26] Clerical backing came from Boyle's Fr Sharkey, Loughglynn's Canon Whyte, Kilmaryl's Fr M.J. Connellan, and Ballaghaderreen's Fr Gallagher, the last town a rallying venue outside the constituency.[27]

IPP speeches referenced the legacy of O'Kelly and Parnell; the Land Acts; old age pensions; dividing ranches; the uselessness of 'one-man parties' as exemplified by Ginnell; the failure of force and SF policy; the IPP defeating conscription and successfully agitating for the release of Irish prisoners. The ultimate argument centred on home rule, with disingenuous assertions made that the 'temporary exclusion' of the six northern counties – partition – was now off the negotiating table.[28] When attacking Plunkett, IPP speakers focused on his unproven republican credentials, his uncertain affiliations, support network and policies and his unconfirmed views on parliamentary attendance.[29] Hayden claimed to possess a copy of a letter Plunkett sent to Dublin Castle disavowing all knowledge of and support for Easter 1916.[30] The *Freeman's Journal* attacked some of the count's supporters by re-publishing *Herald* pieces that depicted Ginnell as a venal materialist who grovelled to access the £400 MPs annual salary, and Fr O'Flanagan as an 'erratic' partition advocate.[31]

The IPP spent considerable time attacking Tully, whereas the Plunkett side dealt with him summarily. Darryl Figgis indicated that Tully 'did not count in the election'.[32] Tully engaged in fewer meetings than the other candidates. He instead relied on the 'Roscommon Election News' pamphlet that he produced almost daily. Promoting himself as an experienced, politically attuned local man fighting conscription, partition, high rates, taxes and land issues, his approach to his opponents was anything but subtle. Characterized quite fairly in the *Freeman's Journal* and *Nationalist* as a 'mudslinger', Tully concentrated on personal abuse.[33] Plunkett was a former 'amiable Whig', 'a feeble old man' who was unfairly deriving sympathy from his sons' travails. Tully's most ill-advised attacks were on O'Flanagan, who he described as disingenuous, someone 'who danced to every tune'.[34] This elicited a furious response from the curate's superior, Fr Thomas Flanagan, who felt compelled to rebuke the 'blackguard attack on his curate' and publicly support Plunkett.[35] Flanagan's opposition exemplified Tully's inability to attract priests to his campaign. Apart from Tulsk's Fr Michael Monahan, Tully had no overt clerical support. He did not attack his long-time enemy Devine with the same energy. Tully saw the IPP man as a non-entity who followed Redmond slavishly. His censure of the IPP concentrated on home rule, partition and conscription.[36]

Plunkett's campaign was driven by the exceptional energy of Ginnell and O'Flanagan. Labour and the GAA also assisted, with O'Flanagan's influence in Roscommon GAA circles securing support from that quarter. Clerical support was widespread. The curates of Keadue and Arigna, Frs Kelly and Goodwin, were just two of the curates that assisted on 28 January when twenty-five Plunkett meetings were hosted in the constituency's church-yards.[37] The varied backgrounds of those supporting Plunkett ensured that little in the way of policy was heard on the hustings. Some 'borderline disloyal' speeches and seditious songs caused the RIC to contemplate prosecutions. However, a realistic CI agreed that, in the case of O'Flanagan, it was better to petition the ecclesiastical authorities to rein in the curate. Prosecutions against Ginnell and others did not proceed.[38] The *Irish Times* singled out O'Flanagan for his effort as he toured the constituency 'like a whirlwind … talking in impassioned language'. Kevin O'Shiel believed that the curate's 'extraordinarily melodious and emotional' voice mesmerized audiences.[39] Ginnell's sharp-edged rhetoric was also persuasive. He ably dismantled the 'sham' home rule act at Elphin, where O'Flanagan claimed that the Act already had its legs cut off and that the amending (partition) bill would 'cut its arms off'.[40] Keen not to unsettle voters or promote antipathetic official action, the curate made repeated reference to SF being a party of 'passive resistance'. Recognizing the value in claiming links to Parnell, Ginnell emphasized Plunkett's unbroken support for the legendary leader at an election meeting in the Corrigeenroe AOH hall. At Strokestown, Ginnell maintained that Roscommon ranches were evidence of IPP failure and scorned the party for the Irish death toll at the war front. O'Flanagan's reference to the freedom of small nations at the same meeting was mocked by the *Daily Express*, which claimed that the Count had as much chance of representing Ireland at the Paris Peace Conference as 'the Man in the Moon'.[41]

When Plunkett returned to Ireland on 31 January, O'Flanagan hoped that the count would refute the IPP 'deceit' whereby they told the 'young men that he was not Sinn Féin enough, and the old men that he was too much Sinn Féin'.[42] Upon his arrival, the *Irish Independent* printed the IPP prediction of a 500–800 favourable majority, alongside Plunkett's supporters' compatible claim that he had 2,000 votes.[43] A UIL circular issued after Plunkett's arrival warned deliberately against hoisting 'the red flag of rebellion in Roscommon', a certain threat to old-age pensions and the work of the CDB.[44] Plunkett added little of value to his campaign. O'Shiel believed him an 'old man, bowed down and rendered feeble … almost in a daze' during his first meetings. William O'Brien believed that few paid attention to Plunkett anyway, 'he being … supported because he was the father of Joseph Plunkett'.[45] An address delivered to

Plunkett on 2 February at Elphin by Fr M. Clyne outlined the essential considerations: Plunkett's education; papal title; the efforts and sacrifice of his sons;
and for Plunkett to 'be not a mere member of the British Parliament, but
Ireland's representative at the Peace Conference'.[46]

The most significant meetings on the day before polling were at
Ballaghaderreen. Both Devine and Plunkett were present, Plunkett's supporters deliberately setting up opposite the house of John Dillon. P.J. Ryan
presided over the meeting that heard Ginnell restate a well-publicized canard
that IPP MPs cheered when news of the 1916 executions was heard at
Westminster.[47] Standing alongside a papal cross and a Parnell portrait,
Plunkett continued his unimpressive rhetoric.[48] O'Flanagan was present but
permission to speak in public had been withheld by Bishop Morrisroe of
Achonry, even though the bishop was himself questioning his IPP support.[49]
At Devine's meeting, Fr Gallagher directed voters not to allow 'sympathy …
to warp their judgement'. They had to abide by the convention vote because
'if Mr Devine were not returned it would be said in England that the Party
… had no longer any right to represent Ireland'.[50] The *Freeman's Journal*
underestimated the 'voteless young men' who attended the Plunkett meeting.
Their inability to emigrate and widespread underemployment allowed them
to invest much energy into the campaign.[51] O'Shiel asserted that Devine's
platform was, in contrast, orientated towards 'hundreds of elderly men'.[52]
This generational difference was reflected in families according to the
Freeman's Journal; the sons backed Plunkett, their fathers supported Devine.[53]

According to the electoral register of September 1914, 8,418 men were
entitled to vote in Roscommon North. The 'couple of hundred unionist
voters' identified by the *Journal* were generally discounted.[54] The *Freeman's
Journal* commented on the arrival of Arthur Griffith the night before polling
and claimed that roughly 6,000 were present to cast their ballot. The *Belfast
News Letter* predicted that the weather would see a poll restricted to towns,
something O'Flanagan attempted to address by coordinating herculean efforts
to clear roads across the constituency.[55] The *Freeman's Journal* dismissed
Tully, but admitted that Plunkett was a threat to Devine who should,
nonetheless, be elected 'by a substantial majority'.[56] The *Democrat* asserted
otherwise and supported Fr O'Flanagan's exhortation that 'young men …
carry the old people on their backs through the snowfalls', presumably only
if they would cast a vote for the count.[57]

Polls opened on 3 February. By midday, fewer than 100 had cast a ballot
due to the weather.[58] Transport was provided by the Devine and Plunkett
sides, with some electors misrepresenting themselves to avail of a lift to a
polling station. There was little friction. O'Shiel noted some bellicose 'inebriated Hibernians' later in the evening being ignored by inattentive policemen whose indiscipline was counterbalanced by Irish Volunteers.[59] Early

tallies indicated that Devine and Tully split Boyle, the former also dominating Rooskey, while Plunkett had majorities in Cootehall, Croghan, Frenchpark and Elphin. When the polls closed, Devine's supporters reined in their optimism and expected to win by a 'small majority'.[60]

At 2 p.m. on Monday 5 February the results showed that Plunkett gained 3,022 votes to Devine's 1,708 and Tully's 687. The election fought on 'a wave of national emotionalism, and on no particular policy' proved to advanced nationalists that politics could play a more prominent role in their stratagem.[61] Speaking outside Boyle courthouse after the result, Devine unselfconsciously blamed the weather for limiting his canvass. Tully rejoiced in his townsman's loss and claimed that the constituency had raised 'the flag of revolt'.[62] He proclaimed that his votes should be added to Plunkett's. In his victory speech Plunkett referred to his abstention from Westminster. He gained the loudest cheer when he referenced O'Flanagan as the 'best priest in Ireland'. The curate, gagged by his bishop, later remarked that his silence was 'eloquent' given 'so glorious, so great and so magnificent' a win.[63] Plunkett declared that Roscommon had let the IPP know that it was with Wolfe Tone and Robert Emmet. The *Herald* carried a front cover illustration depicting the IPP being given the boot.[64] Plunkett's victory was celebrated locally and nationally.

The *Irish Independent* editorialized gleefully on the 'disagreeable eye-opener for "the leaders"', who were punished for 'belauding the Liberals'. It also reprinted extracts from the *Westmeath Independent*, which predicted the demise of the IPP as a result of the 'Roscommon revolt'.[65] Both the *Irish Independent* and *Democrat* believed the emphatic outcome was derived from an almost exhaustive poll, which led to queries regarding personation.[66] The *Leader* warned that the IPP should 'recognize ... that what North Roscommon did today, the rest of nationalist Ireland will do tomorrow'.[67] Blaming the government policy since 1916, the *Freeman's Journal* bemoaned the 'heavy blow to the Irish Party and ... home rule'.[68] The 'wholly unexpected' win for the 'old man' was a sympathy vote that delighted unionists and made a 'blood collision' more likely.[69] In a disbelieving editorial, the *Messenger* queried whether the convention system was broken. Blaming British 'bloodthirstiness', the *Messenger* did, however, suggest that SF comprised 'men ... whose views are nationalist and patriotic'. The paper maintained that Plunkett's political ambiguity was key. The 'temporary defection of North Roscommon' would not have occurred if his platform were better defined, a point with which Joe Devlin and the *Nationalist* agreed.[70] Numerous provincial IPP papers underestimated the election's significance by asserting that 'one swallow does not a summer make'.[71] The *Irish Times* incisively drew attention to the influence of the numerous curates who supported Plunkett.[72] Of the thirty priests in the constituency, O'Flanagan later believed that nineteen were for Plunkett; eight or nine for Devine and two or three for Tully, with perhaps two neutral.[73]

The unionist and British press organs struggled to analyze the result. The *Irish Times* stated that Roscommon had voted against the IPP, rather than for SF, while the *Daily Express* and *Belfast News Letter* deemed the result proof that resolute government was essential.[74] British press reaction varied from the *Daily Herald*'s lauding of Plunkett's cultural background, to the *Liverpool Echo* predicting Plunkett's firm support for Redmond to the *Derby Daily Telegraph* depicting him as an extremist.[75] A correspondent to *The Scotsman* thought it was simply continuity: 'Roscommon has always been, with … Galway, the stronghold of disaffection in Ireland, and … Mr. Parnell, even at the height of his power, was unable to secure the election of his nominee there.'[76] At Westminster, the MP for Enfield, England, Major Pretyman Newman, ruffled feathers. Described by John Redmond as 'a type … of the English members … so inveterate in their hatred of home rule that they wish "God-speed" to the revolution and … the destruction of the constitutional movement', Newman claimed that if he were a Roscommon North voter, he would have voted for Plunkett.[77] His assertion that Roscommon unionists had done just that led the *Freeman's Journal* to damn their 'purblind morality'.[78]

The North Roscommon by-election was a decisive moment in the emergence of the post-Rising Sinn Féin and, indeed, the Irish Revolution. The long dominance of the IPP in Roscommon was broken and many saw it as a harbinger of the party's demise. On his own merits, Plunkett was an unimpressive candidate. However, the sacrifice of his sons, the exceptional work carried through by his support network and the weakness of the IPP campaign helped to ensure his victory. The indifference of the IPP's leadership is difficult to understand given ample evidence that their interests in Roscommon were under threat since 1915. The party's loss of so much backing by Roman Catholic clergy was an ominous portent, as was the exceptional support given to their opponent by youthful citizens. The inference was that any increase in the franchise on the basis of age, something expected at the end of the war, would cripple the IPP. The by-election experience gained by Plunkett's supporters led to better organization that was put to effective use in later contests. Furthermore, the by-election helped advanced nationalists understand how best to frame policies to attract voters who undoubtedly sought change but not, at least in 1917, revolution. There is little doubt that the contributions of Fr O'Flanagan and Laurence Ginnell were hugely influential. O'Flanagan's work was exceptional. The press reaction to the result encapsulated much of what John Dillon himself worried about – if the IPP could not 'carry an ordinary rural constituency in the Province of Connaught, where can [it] be sure of its position?'[79] It was yet to be seen whether the result was an indication that the Irish electorate wanted to adopt a more advanced form of nationalism and discard the IPP and home rule.

5 'Sick of the childish mentality which parliamentarians for years ascribed to them': Sinn Féin growth and the 1918 general election

Count Plunkett's victory provided a boost for advanced nationalism. Although he did little in the short term to assist SF, from May 1917 further by-elections affirmed SF's ascendancy. In Roscommon, dozens of branches that embraced both new republicanism and older nationalist legacies were formed. The efforts of J.P. Hayden to maintain the IPP's relevance led him to become the target of SF attentions in Roscommon. For support, he had to rely on ever-diminishing numbers in the largely defunct UIL and the imploding AOH. RIC actions against SF supporters in 1917 saw the ostracization of the police commence, while police activity during land agitation in Roscommon in 1918 crystallized their enemy status. IPP inactivity on land gave SF the opportunity to supplant the parliamentarians and it led the agitation on food production and ownership issues. The 1918 agitation once again underlined the centrality of the land issue in Roscommon and convinced SF to manage it as part of their political strategy. The threat of conscription during the spring of 1918 again saw SF at the vanguard of the opposition when thousands mobilized across Ireland. Roscommon reflected the nationwide increase in Irish Volunteer numbers, as young men organized to face the threat with the support of advanced nationalist women in Cumann na mBan. A pervasive move away from the IPP was occurring. British attempts to subvert SF by arresting its leaders proved counter-productive, as men like Fr O'Flanagan continued to propagandize ably on their behalf. As the general election of December 1918 approached, it was apparent that the expanded electoral register posed an existential threat to the IPP. The contest in Roscommon South confirmed that the IPP had lost vital clerical support. The majority of those who braved the Spanish Flu to vote ensured that the search for Irish independence took a new turn.

During the weeks after his win, Plunkett adopted the mantel of political hero. He spoke to audience after audience and accepted the freedom of both Sligo and Kilkenny. According to O'Shiel, he was a figure transformed who 'no longer supplicated, he commanded', much to the annoyance of his allies.[1] In an address delivered at Strokestown one week after the election, Plunkett confirmed that he would not attend Westminster and attracted much notice when he challenged the Speaker of the House of Commons to have him arrested.[2] The *Messenger* was disgusted; his arrogance made 'extreme unionists jubilant', as their influence in Westminster increased.[3] General Bryan Mahon, British army commander-in-chief in Ireland, found the count's tour, with 'his avowed object of rendering British government in Ireland impossible', so injurious that he sought to deport him.[4]

The election result was interpreted by the IPP as a directive to pursue a more aggressive policy at Westminster. T.P. O'Connor tabled a motion to instate Irish home rule, and, while the *Freeman's Journal* was impressed by his alacrity, the London correspondent to the *Yorkshire Post and Leeds Intelligencer* viewed the move as a sign of panic: 'unless they can persuade the Government to offer them a settlement before the election … the Irish Nationalist party will almost disappear'.[5] In the event, the move failed. The *Herald* scorned the action as a 'trick [that] imposes on nobody'.[6] In Roscommon, the pro-IPP press sought to show that the party was not as inactive as its opponents alleged with Hayden indicating that he would assume the duties of MP for Roscommon North. Jasper Tully mused that, given how little O'Kelly had done, the workload would be a small burden.[7]

Growing into his self-conferred position as Irish nationalism's leading light, Plunkett set about defining policies. At a meeting in the Mansion House in Dublin in early March, he revealed his desire for 'perfect and complete independence'. Plunkett set about creating the Liberty League and issued an invitation to local authorities to discuss his programme.[8] Delighted that most bodies marked the invite 'read', the *Freeman's Journal* tallied an 18:115 rejection by April; the unpopularity of Plunkett's plan was undeniable.[9] Plunkett's invitation occasioned heated discussions in Roscommon. At a meeting of the Roscommon guardians, T.A.P. Mapother described the invite as 'unadulterated impudence'. John McGreevy's censure of Mapother did little to avert a nineteen votes to seven decision to ignore it.[10] Both the Castlerea and the Strokestown guardians marked the invite 'read'. Strokestown chairman, J.J. Carlos, believed Plunkett a 'humbug' and sought to exclude him from communications. He was undermined by the vice chairman Joseph McCrann, who continued to send memoranda to the count.[11] Equally uncharitable talk was heard during the six-six tie at the Boyle RDC No. 1 vote, where a concerned John Keaveny broke the deadlock with his chairman's ballot.[12] The Tulsk UIL believed the local and national rejections 'sealed the doom of factionism', while J.P. Hayden wrote that they disabused all those who thought that 'the verdict of North Roscommon was the verdict of Ireland'.[13]

At Plunkett's convention on 19 April, the large Roscommon contingent heard shouts of 'Up Roscommon'.[14] According to the *Daily Express*, only a quarter of the bodies invited attended.[15] Plunkett, who had excluded the INL, issued a 'Declaration of Liberty' as part of an agenda which featured land issues and the establishment of a country-wide network of Liberty clubs. The count and Arthur Griffith clashed. The SF founder was aggrieved by what he regarded as Plunkett's overreach in attempting to remould political policies that were years in the making.[16] Fr O'Flanagan mediated to find a consensus between the two men. The *Nationalist* suggested that Plunkett's 'unworkable policy' would see only 'fools' having faith in it.[17] The Liberty clubs elicited some support in County Roscommon and the count received requests for information from several others. However, Plunkett's move also caused confusion, as it appeared to present the Liberty clubs as an alternative to SF. Some correspondents assumed overlap, others that Plunkett was endorsing SF when promoting Liberty clubs, and others that the two bodies were incompatible.[18]

The disunity buoyed IPP supporters organizing for the Longford South by-election in May. Roscommon promoters canvassed for both candidates: SF's interned Tarmonbarry man, Joe McGuinness, and the IPP's Patrick McKenna. Both the *Westmeath Independent* and *Herald* supported SF, whose canvassers showed the value of the experience gained in north Roscommon.[19] Despite having lost business as a result of its support for Plunkett, the *Democrat* also rowed in behind McGuinness.[20] SF badges and flags were conspicuous; the RIC were kept occupied both removing the flags and tracing their owners in Athleague, Strokestown, Ballaghaderreen and Roscommon town.[21] Fr O'Flanagan was restricted to letter writing for the campaign; his bishop's interdiction kept him from the hustings. The curate's influence was still apparent, however. He rounded on Hayden for the MP's accurate observation that the Longford contest was at least devoid of Plunkett's 'false pretences'; O'Flanagan disingenuously asserted that Roscommon North voters knew that parliamentary abstention was certain if Plunkett won.[22] George Geraghty spoke for McGuinness, thereby making himself a target for the police, who hassled him repeatedly and ransacked The O'Rahilly Club.[23] IPP supporters in Ballymahon assaulted Geraghty, who, though reported as 'all but murdered' in the *Journal*, recovered to celebrate McGuinness's narrow but significant win.[24]

Victory celebrations took place across Roscommon. Large gatherings were held in Castlerea, Rooskey and Ballaghaderreen; in the latter, an RIC man sustained a gunshot wound from an inebriated Joe O'Kelly who shouted that he was a 'soldier of the Irish Republic'.[25] Slieve Bán glowed with bonfires and over 1,000 people marched through Strokestown when John Brennan and Úna Sharkey confirmed the final result.[26] SF flags flew over the town's courthouse, as well as at Scramogue cross, Athlone Castle, Clashaganny Protestant church, Tulsk, Cloonfree and on the Caslin hills.[27] When George Geraghty was praised by a crowd that gathered outside his house, he declared that 'Irish people shall be slaves no longer'.[28] Some houses mocked the IPP by closing their shutters and placing IPP 'in memoriam' cards in the windows.[29] By a vote of six to three, the Boyle guardians moved a resolution for McGuinness, the man 'doing penal servitude in an English dungeon for the love of his country'.[30] The result left the *Messenger* bereft: 'Ireland is thinking of disbanding her army ... before the battle is won'.[31] Like many in the IPP, the paper found solace in the thirty-seven vote margin.[32] J.P. Hayden believed that SF finances, enough to 'fight several constituencies', were key, as was a letter from Archbishop Walsh of Dublin that criticized the IPP.[33]

Soon after the by-election, reports of British efforts to temporize on the Irish question emerged. To reduce American unease, Prime Minister Lloyd George created the Irish Convention, a forum in which Irish politicians, nationalist and unionist, could negotiate a home rule proposal. Welcomed by the *Messenger*, *Nationalist*, *Westmeath Independent* and *Democrat*, T.A.P. Mapother, one of Roscommon's two delegates, deemed it 'the greatest opportunity which ever came before the Irish people', while John Fitzgibbon, the other delegate, thought it capable of 'framing a constitution for ... self-government ... satisfactory for all Ireland'.[34] Crucially, it was disdained by SF, a point emphasized by Fr O'Flanagan at the foundation meeting for the county's first official SF branch in Crossna on 27 May 1917. Describing the Convention as a 'sham', the priest, ignoring his bishop's interdiction in this context, directed the 100 members of the Tom Clarke branch to focus on the Peace Conference.[35]

SF's growing confidence was evident in the formation of a branch in Roscommon town just days later. Harrison hall was 'filled to the limits of comfort' when George Geraghty told the ninety-five members to ignore the 'packed' Irish Convention, in favour of a petition for representation at the Peace Conference. To generate goodwill ahead of the Irish Convention, the government had released SF prisoners, among them Boyle man Séamus Redican, Count Plunkett and the remaining 1916 prisoners, including Thomas Ashe and Éamon de Valera.[36] Fr O'Flanagan addressed the releases with the members of the 'Sean MacDairmuide Sinn Féin Club' and claimed that they were designed 'to take the wind out of our sails'; focus needed to be maintained. He exhorted that 'if two elections can free 125 people, ten or twelve ought to go a long way towards freeing the four millions'. Describing the RIC as 'an army of occupation', he asserted that the Peace Conference petition was hugely popular. In Crossna, 878 signed out of the available 950; those who did not sign were, according to O'Flanagan, 'Redmond's out-and-out pot wallopers'. After committee positions had been confirmed to include Gaelic League activists, Mrs McCrann and Margaret Doorly, as well as Geraghty and Michael Finlay, the meeting concluded with 'The Soldiers' Song'. Membership doubled the following week. The local deanery assisted in forming clubs in nearby parishes.[37]

Cloontuskert, Tarmonbarry and Strokestown soon followed, with priests leading the way. George Geraghty and P.J. McCrann assisted in all three cases, presenting SF policy as 'constructive ... and ... constitutional', mindful as they probably were of the uncertain support for anything more revolutionary.[38] In Cloontuskert, James Oates did what he could to promote a similar situation when he stood down as SF branch president in favour of Fr James Kearney. Oates hoped that the priest's presence would remove any 'erroneous ideas' about SF being a party of revolution.[39] The branch soon boasted 'nearly all the self-reliant, self-respecting young men in the parish ... women [also] ... well to the fore'. Similar intentions may have been at play in both Scramogue and Kiltrustan, where curates Frs Mannion and McGowan drove branch formation; 'several hundred' joined up.[40] Thanks to the efforts of the Shouldice family and the newly released Harry Boland, branches were formed with the assistance of the GAA in Ballaghaderreen and Edmondstown. Ballaghaderreen, like Fairymount, honoured local man William Partridge, a labour internee who died on 16 July 1917.[41] While many like Cootehall's 'P.H. Pearse', Killina's 'Joseph Plunkett' and Kilgefin's 'John MacBride' clubs honoured 1916 patriots, others looked to older legacies. Ballyfarnon's 'Robert Emmet', Rooskey's 'Michael Davitt' and the Dysart and Ballyforan 'C.S. Parnell' clubs all joined the growing network. In July the CI noted twenty-two SF clubs, one of the highest totals for any county. This was in part accounted for by Plunkett's direction that Liberty clubs amalgamate with SF clubs. CI St Laurence Tyrell enumerated a total membership of 1,100 in Roscommon, roughly ten percent of the national roster.[42]

There was a concomitant decline in grassroots support for the IPP that followed an almost nationwide trend. UIL branches at Kiltrustan, Kilgefin, Kilbride, Cloontuskert and Rooskey continued to meet, yet their membership was shrinking. The branch at Cloontuskert damned the *Herald* and 'foolish' young men for promoting the change.[43] By December even reports in the *Messenger* referenced single figure attendances.[44] The Tulsk AOH joined the local UIL in issuing hyperbolic statements, declaring that SF had only 'a half-dozen voices' in the area.[45] When the South Roscommon UIL executive met to strategize, John Fitzgibbon made the awkwardly phrased request that people 'judge our movement, not us, by the past'.[46] *Journal* editor John McDonnell observed that while some still called SF 'factionists ... none soon will be left to be orthodox', and predicted that the general election would end the IPP and their 'honour and jobs' supporters.[47]

Roscommon's local authorities began to show signs of IPP vulnerability. The election for chairman of the Boyle No. 1 RDC in June saw John Keaveny re-elected by fourteen votes to thirteen.[48] Even when handling supposedly 'safe' co-options, IPP loyal bodies could be surprised by the opportunism of the co-optee. Stephen Hannon, president of the Roscommon UIL branch, accepted an invitation to join the RTC in July but then defected to SF the next month.[49] The unrepresentative nature of local authorities was tackled by Jasper Tully in the county council. He denounced some councillors' support for the Irish Convention and indicated that they were 'repre-

senting worn-out constituencies'.[50] Conceding that he too was not popular
with the electorate, Tully reacted furiously to Mapother's accusation that he
lacked respect for William Redmond, brother of the IPP leader, who died at
the front on 7 June. Tully demanded that the council remember its condem-
nations of 1916 and accused IPP supporters of throwing stones at the mothers of dead Easter men in Longford. After the exchange with Mapother,
when members were asked to stand in silence for William Redmond, Tully
remained seated alongside four others. He was certain that the council was
out of touch with the new political reality.[51]

J.P. Hayden did all he could to stem the SF tide in Roscommon. In mid-
July at Kilroosky, north-east of Roscommon town, he declared that Ireland
had a choice: 'constitutionalism against revolution'.[52] A week later, near
Fourmilehouse, he claimed that SF was inexperienced, had incoherent aims
and sought to take up arms against the British. He predicted that the outcome
would not be independence, but conscription and land seizures.[53] Lauded in
the constitutional nationalist press for his 'exposé' of SF and its plans for a
'paste board Parliament', Hayden counselled in a letter to the *Evening
Telegraph* that once people moved past 'hysterics', they would discover how
counter-productive SF's 'abstention folly' was.[54] The *Freeman's Journal*
thought Hayden's efforts reinvigorated the UIL in Roscommon, Hayden himself noting its 'remarkable revival' during September.[55] Evidence of that reinvigoration included the controversial burning in August of a SF flag near
Cremully church by Fuerty IPP followers, an incident that saw additional
priests make public their support for advanced nationalism.[56]

Hayden became the main target for SF in the region. One opinion that
carried great weight was that of councillor D.J. Kelly. The week after
Hayden's Kilroosky speech, at a SF rally in Athlone Kelly declared that the
IPP had 'deserted him and Ireland'. He called for Hayden's resignation.[57] The
Journal undertook a month-long offensive against the IPP and its 'place-
hunter' supporters, describing Hayden's meetings as reminiscent of the Land
War, the MP protected by RIC with their 'rifle, bayonet and baton'.[58] The
newspaper threw its support behind a September *aeraíocht* (festival) for the
county town, which was organized by the newly formed branches of Cumann
na mBan and Na Fianna Éireann. The 3,000 in attendance heard another call
for Hayden to resign.[59] Of the many newspapers that covered the meeting,
only the *Daily Express* indicated that the resignation demand 'met with a considerable amount of dissent from those present'.[60]

The most important event in driving people to SF in September 1917 was
the death in Mountjoy prison of Thomas Ashe, a republican hunger-striker.
Given that John Redmond's son-in-law, Max Green, was the prison governor, the *Herald*, *Journal* and SF branches at Rooskey, Castlerea, Kilgefin and
elsewhere agreed that the IPP was to blame.[61] The *Nationalist* instead blamed

the government for their 'official callousness', as did the Roscommon guardians and RTC, while a large Roscommon contingent, including 180 Cumann na mBan, attended Ashe's funeral.[62] In Strokestown, a banner spanning the main thoroughfare read: 'We mourn Thomas Ashe'.[63] The CI recorded that Ashe's death 'caused excitement', with well-attended requiem masses. New SF clubs at Rahara, St John's, Ballynaheglish and Cam all took Ashe's name and Irish Volunteer corps welcomed additional members as the nationwide reorganization that began in August benefitted from the increased anti-British feeling.[64] The film periodical, *The Bioscope*, related details of a screening of Ashe's funeral in Roscommon town. Renditions of the 'Soldier's Song' and shouts of 'Easter Week' came from the general audience, while British soldiers present replied with 'God Save the King'. The expected clash did not materialize. *The Bioscope* observed that Roscommon town still had many IPP supporters: 'it is interesting to note, a shout of "Up Redmond!" met with a good response'.[65]

Given the groundswell for SF, the party needed defined structures to manage its burgeoning membership. Both North and South Roscommon divisional executives were formed in September, the latter tentatively and informally. Fr B. Keane ably assisted Joseph McCrann and B.J. Goff in the north.[66] Both executives sent delegates to the SF national convention in the Mansion House in Dublin on 25 and 26 October, where the party's national executive confirmed Éamon de Valera as president. Fr O'Flanagan was elected a vice president alongside Arthur Griffith. Plunkett's desire for the vice presidency did not attract much support.[67] De Valera was also appointed president of the Irish Volunteers, confirming the synergy between SF and the militant wing that was reflected in Roscommon by men like George Geraghty and Seán O'Hurley.[68]

SF in Roscommon grew more active. Clubs in Boyle, Curlieu Pass and Arigna joined the two separate branches at Croghan, the 'Dr O'Dwyer' and 'Sean Heuston' clubs, in staging organizational drives.[69] By the end of November, the county boasted fifty-five branches, thirty-five being in the north.[70] Cumann na mBan branches also emerged. The women of Athleague, Castlerea, Kilteevan and Strokestown mobilized alongside those in Cootehall.[71] Antipathy to Hayden also increased. D.J. Kelly accused the MP of being a turncoat: 'No one has been a greater friend of the present member … than I have, but … Mr Hayden … has become a Liberal.' Reframing his own political conversion, Kelly asserted that he was 'a Sinn Feiner at heart before the Sinn Fein party was brought into prominence', and dismissed accusations that the party was funded by German money.[72]

Kelly put special effort into assisting with the organization of a meeting on 25 November at Ballygar, where de Valera spoke. An 'enormous contingent' greeted the SF president in Roscommon town as he passed through on his way to the east Galway town. The Boyle guardians' welcome signalled John Keaveny's declining influence.[73] Although the Ballygar meeting was deemed disappointing given the smaller than expected turn out, John Brennan attended in full Volunteer uniform, which, though banned under DORA, showed commitment to the idea of the Irish Volunteers acting as the army of the republic.[74] The follow-up meeting in the Harrison hall was lauded, however. With an 'overflowing' attendance, the meeting saw Ballygar parish priest, Dr Kielty, preside with Fr O'Flanagan, who was soon suspended by Bishop Coyne 'for refusing to remain in his parish and attend to his religious duties'.[75] The meeting heard criticism of the *Freeman's Journal*, whose local representative was the only pressman charged for entry.[76] Many newspapers noted de Valera's reluctance to address the antipathy of Cardinal Michael Logue, the primate of the Irish Roman Catholic Church. The SF president instead quoted the *ex cathedra* assertion of Pope Leo XIII that, once the Catholic faith was maintained, it was not wrong to prefer a particular form of democratic government.[77] The *Journal* reported on the number of mature clerics present. The discourse led the CI to believe that 'Sinn Fein are adopting a more moderate tone'.[78]

The meeting inspired Geraghty, D.J. Kelly and others to inaugurate the South Roscommon executive. Geraghty was elected president; Kelly assumed the joint vice presidency alongside Micheál Ó Braonáin. Michael Finlay was a joint honorary treasurer.[79] Many of those involved joined Seán O'Hurley at Lecarrow that week to promote Irish Volunteer participation. While satisfied with SF growth, O'Hurley counselled that political statements needed 'something to back them up'.[80] Both he and fellow speaker Geraghty were targeted by the authorities for the Lecarrow speech: Geraghty's declaration that it 'would be better for the young men to die in Ireland than to be buried in nameless graves in France' was taken as an incitement to violence.[81]

By the end of 1917, the AOH provided the starkest measure of the decline in grassroots support for constitutional nationalism in Roscommon. After the Roscommon North by-election, Hibernian leaders were reported to be 'very sore at the defection of some … divisions and their officers' in the constituency. This was, in part, a reference to P.J. Neary, the county secretary, who voted for Plunkett. The by-election crystallized differences already apparent in Crossna and Cootehall, with divisions also emerging publicly in Drumlion and Ballyfarnon, the latter seeing brethren join an Irish Volunteer corps formed during the election.[82] Certainly divisions loyal to the Board of Erin such as Tulsk, Ballynaheglish and Fuerty continued to back Redmond but the Longford South by-election marginalized them further.[83] Support for McGuinness from AOH men in Roscommon, including Neary, caused a 'Hibernian sensation', with 'open antagonism' between county board members. This forced AOH president, J.D. Nugent MP, to step in, suspend

Neary (giving him time to explore establishing a Liberty club) and soon thereafter accept the county board's dissolution.[84] Nugent's letter of censure was printed in the *Whig* and *Londonderry Sentinel*; both reported how adjoining counties followed Roscommon's example.[85] Divisions in Cootehall and Drumlion called for Nugent and Joseph Devlin to be expelled; Drumlion referred to Nugent as a 'temporary MP'. Both divisions, as well as those in Tarmonbarry and Croghan, congratulated SF in Longford for beating 'the corrupt and discreditable so-called Irish Party'. The Hibernian's national committee condemned them for publishing 'resolutions ... calculated to injure the Order'.[86] At Ballinameen, Ballynaheglish and Ballyfarnon, schisms developed – the latter's resolution on the 'jobbery and intrigue' of the IPP caused local consternation.[87] Some divisions, such as those in Roscommon town and Tarmonbarry, abandoned the AOH and re-emerged as Catholic Young Men's Associations.[88] In May, the CI noted the move of many brethren to SF, clear evidence of the latter's ascendency.[89] The late summer saw the Drumlion and Elphin AOH inaugurate SF branches, both, like divisions across the country, making no effort to mask the defection.[90]

By late November 1917, Roscommon had the fourth highest ratio of SF clubs to population in Ireland.[91] By contrast, a county board reorganization meeting saw the previously dominant AOH muster only fourteen divisions, one-third of its peak total: Boyle, Slatta, Ballyfarnon, Strokestown, Tulsk, Crossna, Creeve, Ballinameen, Fuerty, Kilbride, Fourmilehouse, Cloontuskert, Ballynaheglish and Kiltrustan. The latter division was the only one to record new members and an active ladies' auxiliary.[92] By January 1918, just nine of those divisions were still active; the previously supportive *Herald* believed the Roscommon AOH to be 'dead for all intents and purposes'.[93] The Roscommon CI confirmed the decline. Many of the former divisions transferred their funds when they switched allegiance to the dominant SF party.[94]

Coinciding with the growth in SF during 1917 was ongoing agitation for increased tillage farming, land redistribution and reductions in the cost of provisions. The tillage issue was the first that saw some amelioration, as north Roscommon farmers increased their crop acres during the spring. The *Daily Express* reported that many 'who had never previously owned a farm implement' attended instruction courses held by the Roscommon Agricultural and Technical Committee chaired by Canon Cummins.[95] South Roscommon farmers were less enthused. J.P. Hayden did what he could to address resistance around Fuerty, Athleague and Roscommon town.[96] Various UIL branches criticized the CDB for doing little. Its moratorium on purchasing lands during the war continued alongside its unpopular practice of renting some of the lands it held to graziers. The UIL itself was not considered of much use either. John Healy DC assisted in establishing a 'Landless Men's League' in

February at Tulsk to push for local land reform.[97] Count Plunkett lectured
the land hungry on the need to await the republic before seeking land, a
directive that was redolent of IPP rhetoric on land and home rule during the
war. This showed poor understanding of his constituents' concerns and
encouraged them to look towards locally directed agitation.[98] Moves by some
owners to let lands on conacre – the piecemeal letting of small tracts or strips
of land – were accepted in some areas but resisted in others.[99] The RAEC
continued its work, Canon Cummins on different occasions noting how the
'English point of view' dominated attitudes towards land in Ireland. He criticized the 'unproductive' nature of T.W. Russell's promises on tillage and
framed the government's focus on using Irish land to supply the war as part
of a decades-old reluctance to act in the best interests of the majority of Irish
farmers.[100] One government measure did make a difference, however, and
gained a compliment from Cummins when it targeted intransigent graziers.
Compulsory Tillage Orders (CTO) saw Roscommon achieve the second highest percentage increase in tillage after Meath in 1917–18.[101]

Price controls on foodstuffs were enforced by the RIC from February
1917. Annoyed farmers at the Roscommon town market reacted by following their Athlone counterparts in withdrawing produce.[102] At a prosecution of
one farmer in April 1917 who defied a price order, DI Hetreed testified that
'Roscommon market was practically devoid of potatoes … the farmers were
behaving scandalously'.[103] Reports from a year later showed little improvement
in farmers' attitudes as they chased a price control official out of the town
because his monitoring of pig sales was unwelcome.[104] Some shopkeepers also
resisted. The police seized two tonnes of butter from Roscommon merchant,
P.J. Doorly, after he refused to reduce prices.[105] Farmers left potatoes to rot,
contributing to a food scarcity that occasioned desperate scenes at markets.
Roscommon workhouse staff resigned when the shortages left them unable to
feed their charges adequately.[106] Part of the problem across Ireland was that
beef cattle continued to be 'most remunerative to the farmer'; this had consequences not only for tillage but also for dairy cattle.[107] Canon Cummins testified that, by the winter of 1917, milk shortages forced mothers to give
mulled porter to their children.[108] This impacted those seeking porter for
recreational consumption. The tipple had already become both scarce and
expensive from that summer.[109]

By late 1917, some SF members in Roscommon moved to act. In October
Plunkett, presumably after gaining a better understanding of his constituents'
concerns, counselled men to combine and break up the lands. However, he
directed that as a first step, they had to commit to the republic by joining
both SF and the Irish Volunteers.[110] SF in Roscommon attempted to conduct
a food census and implement its own food orders. Having failed to conduct
the census, George Geraghty advised Roscommon town SF branch members:

'Guard the food you have to tide your own people over till the harvest comes again, and by that time, please God, the Irish Republic will have been built up.'[111] Other SF branch meetings heard rhetoric redolent of UIL meetings a decade previously when the ranch war raged. The branch at Ballaghaderreen adopted a hands-on approach by seizing supplies from local farms.[112]

SF branches at Mantua and Kilmaryl were the first to drag the party into land agitation in Roscommon during 1918. Branches in Clare, Galway and south Sligo also acted, the western counties reminding SF that land was key to retaining their support.[113] The presence of many young men forced to remain in Roscommon owing to restrictions on emigration was a significant boon to SF efforts. In January 1918 members seized lands being let under the eleven months system, a short lease arrangement designed to avoid leasee benefits that started from the twelfth month. SF and Irish Volunteers in Frenchpark followed suit with cattle drives, which freed up land that was then let to small farmers at what was deemed a reasonable rent.[114] Around Boyle, some of the five dozen Irish Volunteers, who drilled regularly under James Feely, seized land for the 'Irish Republic'.[115] The billeting of Crown forces had made food supply a serious issue in the region, with Major Pretyman Newman telling the House of Commons of one incident near Boyle that involved over 1,000 men from Roscommon and Sligo.[116] The *Herald* supported the land agitation and presented a picture of a confident, quasi-military Irish Volunteer-led operation: 'Headed by bands, young men carrying loys and spades with the iron portions upwards, representing fixed bayonets, and followed by ploughs on carts, representative of artillery ... crowds ... lustily cheered them.'[117] Similar acts at Ballinameen led CI St Laurence Tyrell to initiate a baton charge and introduce the Roscommon Volunteers to their first large-scale violent engagement with a police force that was increasingly depicted as the enemy.[118]

The last two weeks in February 1918 saw a series of incidents that indicated SF would have difficulty in controlling the land issue in Roscommon. The gates of the Packenham Mahon estate at Strokestown were pulled down and a grave dug nearby to intimidate the landowner. The local SF branch repudiated the act and Fr Roddy, the branch president, condemned it outright.[119] Unrest at Mockmoyne on the lands of John Cox led Fr Clyne of the North Roscommon SF executive to step in to negotiate a settlement. His arbitration had limited success and indicated the reluctance of the land hungry to submit to SF authority.[120] The most violence was seen on lands held by John Keaveny at Arigna/Keadue. About 150 SF and Irish Volunteers, including George Plunkett, son of Count Plunkett, clashed with sixty RIC. Described by one policeman as the 'fiercest riot' he ever took part in, the intervention of the local clergy was required to stop the violence.[121] Arrests led to a court case that saw the *Gloucester Echo* sneer at claims that Roscommon farms were being seized for tillage; they were 'seized … because their owners do not happen to be rebels'.[122] A letter from Irish chief secretary, H.E. Duke, to Mrs M.J. Ffolliott of Boyle did not reassure unionists. Duke claimed it was not possible for the RIC 'to anticipate … every act of lawlessness … no exertions of the Department of Agriculture … will prevent … the creation of disorder'. Many unionists agreed that the letter proved that Duke was out of his depth.[123]

On 23 February, as violence increased and the political support of a growing section of farmers was threatened, the SF comhairle ceanntair directed local executives to 'restrain all who may be incited … into foolish or indiscreet action'.[124] The North Roscommon executive wanted the agitators to seek the consent of landowners in all cases, a naive request that was largely ignored. The South Roscommon executive was more nuanced in its appreciation that 'elementary justice' had to be the cornerstone of all efforts for the republic.[125] Unlike Sligo, where there was a high level of compliance, Roscommon branches that acted with restraint did so only when an owner submitted to SF arbitration, the forerunner of the republican court system. Where arbitration failed or was rejected, conflict continued. Some disturbed areas did see the Department of Agriculture and Technical Instruction take over lands seized by SF and convert them to tillage. It was claimed that this had an 'excellent effect' and reduced agitation.[126]

The worst conflicts were around Boyle. Lord Justice Ronan, adjudicator of the Roscommon assizes, described the lawlessness there as 'horrid'.[127] Court sessions involved dozens from Crossna, Corrigeenroe, Drumlion and Curlieu's Pass and saw defence solicitor B.J. Goff frequently come up against DI Kearney of Boyle, the policeman who had become a focus of enmity for the land hungry.[128] P.J. Neary, then using his secretarial skills on behalf of SF, was jailed for a month in Belfast for commandeering lands. When he, like so many others, was denied political prisoner status, which was not accorded for agrarian crimes, he undertook an unsuccessful hunger strike.[129] The defiance demonstrated at court proceedings provided SF with good propaganda but also hardened judicial attitudes. For example, at the Athlone assizes, Judge Wakely railed against the 'so-called Republic' and described six Frenchpark men as 'common thieves'. The *Herald* rounded on Wakely, who continued to mock the republic and hand down harsh sentences to those who transgressed in its name.[130]

As tensions mounted during the spring, additional RIC from Donegal, Tyrone and Derry were drafted into north Roscommon. The unionist press reported that an attempt to derail a train carrying some of the supplementary force was made at Kilfree junction, north of Ballaghaderreen, a town where 130 Irish Volunteers regularly drilled under Frank Shouldice, Joe O'Kelly and Joe Flannery.[131] The newly deployed RIC were active in seeking out smuggled weapons. They closely monitored republicans, such as Séamus Redican, whose frequent trips to Dublin were, the RIC believed, a cover for arms importation. The 'mere labourer and ... dangerous Sinn Féiner' was difficult to track, however; the RIC resorted to reviewing his bank records for evidence of illicit payments.[132] Purloining weapons already present in the county was deemed more productive by republicans who raided Rockingham House, home of Sir Thomas Stafford.[133] News reports stated that thirty quality guns and 1,000 rounds of ammunition were taken, an exaggerated estimate according to testimony from James Feely. He confirmed, much to his own chagrin, that Sligo's Alec McCabe took the guns away and 'we never saw them again'.[134]

The raid prompted Bishop Coyne to write to Fr Thomas Flanagan of Cootehall, the parish priest nearest to Rockingham. Coyne denounced those involved as 'the dupes of criminal cowards' whose 'reckless display of patriotism' was only 'a mask for selfishness or treachery'.[135] Five arrests were made. They included Feely (the only Roscommon man involved) and George Plunkett, who had been staying with Arigna's Fr Joe Goodwin while organizing an Irish Volunteer corps in the area.[136] Doing little to ingratiate himself with his bishop, Fr Michael O'Flanagan juxtaposed the Rockingham raid with that at Fr Goodwin's where Plunkett was arrested with strong-arm RIC tactics. He directed people to ask themselves which act was cowardly.[137] Crowds gathered in Boyle to support the hunger-striking prisoners when they returned for trial. Providing the best propaganda of any Roscommon trial yet held, the men refused to recognize the court and sang 'anti-English choruses' throughout proceedings. Three of the five were released due to lack of evidence. One of the three, Plunkett, was immediately rearrested for the Arigna land grab. Feely was one of two that went to trial.[138]

Constitutional nationalists were dealt a further blow by the death of John Redmond in March 1918. The *Herald* noted brusquely that Redmond had 'outlived his ... usefulness to Ireland by at least four years'.[139] By contrast, the *Westmeath Independent* and *Journal* were measured and remembered Redmond's early victories as well as his later missteps. The latter made it clear, however, that 'Roscommon en masse is behind Sinn Fein', and that people were, 'sick of the childish mentality which parliamentarians for years ascribed to them'.[140] The *Messenger*'s editorials evinced the paroxysms of Redmond supporters; the man, 'like his great predecessors O'Connell and Parnell ... has died of a broken heart'.[141] At a meeting of the Roscommon guardians, T.A.P. Mapother regretted that Redmond's 'last days should be embittered by unsympathetic references by some of his fellow countrymen'.[142] A number of UIL branches and AOH divisions met to pass resolutions of sympathy and, secondly, to celebrate the IPP retention of Redmond's seat in the Waterford by-election.[143] During IPP celebrations in Ballaghaderreen,

Thomas Doherty from Mayo, a SF target in the land campaign, died follow-ing an assault. Having allegedly shouted 'Up Dillon' to the annoyance of Bertie Shouldice (brother of Frank and John) and Thomas Maguire, Doherty was killed in an 'attack by Sinn Féiners', according to the *Messenger*. The coroner attributed his demise to 'pleurisy and pneumonia ... accelerated by violence'.[144]

Any improvement in IPP fortunes after their by-election success was reversed by government moves to impose conscription. During the spring of 1918, the need for troops increased to such an extent that the government passed a new Military Service bill that included Ireland. John Dillon, the new leader of the IPP, withdrew the party from Westminster in protest. A meet-ing in Dublin's Mansion House led to an alliance against conscription that the *Journal* described as: 'priests and people, bishops and leaders, Sinn Feiners and party men, unionists and northerns [sic] all ... in the one league to fight the latest mad ... policy'.[145] Government efforts to entice the Irish with another offer of attenuated home rule only angered people further and thou-sands mobilized in opposition. In Roscommon, conscription diverted the focus of local attention away from land, at least temporarily, as many sought to repulse the conscription threat.[146] The county town hosted a rally 'of dimen-sions seldom exceeded' during the first week in April. Canon Cummins, with the backing of Bishop Coyne, called for resistance to 'the vilest tactics that ever a tyrant nation performed against another'.[147] Signatories to the Roscommon covenant against conscription vowed to 'use every means in my power to render its operation null and void'.[148] Under the subtitle 'Roscommon's Threat', the *Aberdeen Press and Journal* reported that the people promised 'open rebellion against the government', while a number of other British titles feared that Roscommon's penchant for violent agitation would promote exceptional unrest.[149]

Dozens of rallies followed that in Roscommon town throughout the rest of April. At Boyle, Athlone, Strokestown, Elphin, Tulsk, Scramogue, Fourmilehouse and Fairymount, thousands turned out. They often did so under the direction of younger clergymen who assisted in inducting hundreds into SF branches.[150] Labour showed its strength when towns across the county observed the national general strike organized by the national labour movement on 23 April. Merchants closed their businesses and joined anti-conscription processions.[151] At Ballintubber, a large Irish Volunteer contingent undertook a protest march to Ballymoe, while at Creggs, on the spot of Parnell's final oration, 1,800 signed the anti-conscription pledge. A police baton charge against SF members in Castlerea a week before the pledge cir-culated convinced a reported 5,000 to sign there.[152] Protestants in Roscommon town circulated their own, separate and 'exhaustively signed' anti-conscrip-tion memorandum.[153] At Ballinlough, Hayden and Fitzgibbon pledged strong, passive resistance. Some attendees were aware of Hayden's apoplexy in the Commons when it was asserted that Ireland had not played its part in the war.[154] At Ballaghaderreen, 'Sinn Féiners and Dillonites united in common cause', for a meeting at which both de Valera and Dillon spoke. The *Herald* denounced Dillon for 'posing as a patriot'. Similar views across the county ensured that neither the UIL nor AOH benefitted from their association with the campaign.[155] SF had supplanted them in Roscommon; they were remnants lacking the capacity to reinvigorate. Cooperation in the Roscommon county council saw D.J. Kelly support Fitzgibbon's resolution against the 'blood tax', while John McGreevy in the Roscommon guardians indicated his continued antipathy to Hayden by recommending action more definite than sending messages to MPs; 'no good results follow from sending resolutions'.[156] In Boyle, a women's anti-conscription day saw 500 women assert their opposition and Women's Day marches across Roscommon were organized by Cumann na mBan.[157]

The conscription crisis also boosted the Irish Volunteers. Although their numbers had grown during 1917, this increase was neither geographically comprehensive nor sustained in Roscommon. Ballaghaderreen was the only overtly active area by early 1918.[158] The conscription threat saw the ranks across the county swell as many believed that a large Volunteer body would undermine conscription. In Kiltrustan, the IPP-loyal AOH brethren joined the Volunteer corps en masse, making the honest declaration that they joined 'purely for the purpose of defeating conscription'.[159] Volunteer numbers in Kilgefin and Knockcroghery quadrupled in a few short weeks.[160] Modest increases at Curraghroe were accounted for by the corps refusing to admit members whose commitment was conditional as in Kiltrustan.[161] The growth coincided with efforts by Volunteer organizer Ernie O'Malley to provide better training in Roscommon, define brigade areas, assess Crown forces strength and create a structured reporting process with General Headquarters (GHQ), the national body intended to coordinate Volunteer efforts.[162] In this, he was supported by Tarmon national school teacher Daniel O'Rorke, who experienced first-hand the common exodus of men from the Volunteers after the crisis passed: 'I visited a company there [south Roscommon] where 103 members [were] present. I told them that any man not willing to fight for a Republic was not wanted ... eighty-nine ... left'.[163]

In general, the Volunteers were not targeted by the police, who were themselves unenthusiastic about Irish conscription. However, the spike in Volunteer numbers did see the RIC act on a DORA arms proclamation in early May that focused on Roscommon and eleven other counties.[164] In Castlerea, they seized all guns and ammunition on sale in local hardware shops. In Roscommon town, married RIC men were ordered to sleep in the barracks as the night guard was doubled, owing to fears of a raid.[165]

Roscommon's Cumann na mBan also increased its presence. While never accurately capturing either branch or membership numbers, the CI recorded new Cumann na mBan branches at Boyle, Deerpark, Cloontuskert and Kilgefin. They followed those at Cootehall, Keadue, Athleague, Strokestown and Knockcroghery, where most provided first aid training.[166]

Thousands of pounds were pledged to the national defence fund to fight conscription. Dozens of areas subscribed with £400 donated in Roscommon town and £276 in Kilteevan.[167] By mid-May, almost £7,000 of the £136,000 national total had been collected in Roscommon. This was the highest total per head in any Connacht county. Galway, with twice its eastern neighbour's population, collected £10,000, while Mayo, with a population greater still, only equalled Roscommon's contribution.[168]

Conscription in Ireland was to be implemented by former British army commander Lord French, the new lord lieutenant. He had a house at Drumdoe near Boyle, a fact that ensured especial RIC scrutiny of SF activists in the region. People around Drumdoe regarded French as an 'unassuming, kindly man' before his appointment as lord lieutenant but his later actions against SF belied this view.[169] He set about trying to dismantle the party, believing it the main obstacle to army recruitment. In May 1918 the 'military dictator', as he was described in the *Westmeath Independent*, acted on a contrived plot that alleged SF collusion with Germany. He ordered the arrest and deportation of dozens of SF party members.[170] Dismissed across Ireland as a canard, the *Herald* called the plot a 'sham', while the *Messenger* editorialized on the 'cowardly' arrests that were transacted without due process.[171] Co-ordinated from Ballinasloe, RIC raids in south Roscommon resulted in the arrest of the newly married George Geraghty on 17 May. His seizure made the front page of many British titles, as editors presumed he was an important SF leader.[172] Frank Shouldice and Seán O'Hurley were also arrested at Ballaghaderreen and Athlone. All three were interned in jails in England. Reports of their poor conditions inspired anti-internment rallies in Athleague, Cam and Ballaghaderreen, as well as a resolution from the RTC, which was forcibly removed from the minute book by a RIC delegation.[173] Shouldice endeavoured to influence SF activities in Ballaghaderreen, sending numerous letters to associates. Prison officials concluded that in many cases his code was 'not intelligible', at least not to them.[174] Arrests across the country led to all SF lay leaders, including Count Plunkett, being interned. The task of leading SF then fell to Fr O'Flanagan.

Allied to the arrests were other acts of suppression. A marked increase in action against drilling and meetings reduced overt republican activity. At Athleague, both Canon Cummins and Revd Dr Kielty spoke of their surprise at the heavy-handedness of the RIC when engaging in their duties.[175] Swathes of Roscommon were trawled by both police and soldiers, who dodged bullets both near Strokestown after an Irish Volunteer drill, and at Ballymoe after attempts to arrest an instructor, possibly Ernie O'Malley.[176] The resource-heavy nature of the operations led the IG to direct CI St Laurence Tyrell to avoid mass arrests and, instead, request that the clergy use their influence to stop the drilling.[177] In individual cases, clerical intercession was not deemed appropriate. Frustrated Crown forces failed to capture Micheál Ó Braonáin who joined a number of other men 'on the run'. In a show of solidarity and defiance, his neighbours tended his farm with SF flags flying from their carts.[178] Whatever about such failures by the Crown forces, at the 1918 summer assizes Lord Justice Ronan deemed that their successes had alleviated the land-related 'Boyle temporary insanity'.[179] Even with Boyle's improvement, a decision was still made to impose the special jury provision of the 1887 Criminal Law and Procedure Act on Roscommon and most adjoining counties. It allowed for the relocation of court proceedings in cases of jury intimidation, which were reported in relation to the trial for the Rockingham raid.[180]

The actions against SF affected the usually perfunctory annual votes for the chairmanships of Roscommon's local authorities. The most controversial was in Strokestown, where J.J. Carlos, the IPP chairman, resisted the challenge of SF's Joseph McCrann. Controversially, Carlos won after he disallowed a co-opted member to vote and then used his own ballot to break a deadlock. The clerk's confirmation that correct procedures were applied did little to prevent a 'wild scene of disorder' during which Carlos was accused of malfeasance.[181] Surprisingly, Carniska SF supported Carlos. Its committee, some of whom had defected from the AOH, indicated that Carlos had shown his commitment to Ireland by acting as chairman of the local defence fund; opposing him was unnecessary.[182] The North Roscommon executive suspended Carniska, while SF branches at Rooskey, Strokestown and Frenchpark censured it for 'playing into the hands of Dublin Castle'.[183]

The IPP was also successful elsewhere, though again signs of greater opposition were apparent. In Roscommon County Council, John Fitzgibbon defeated D.J. Kelly by just twelve votes to seven. Jasper Tully declared that Fitzgibbon had voted for 'sham home rule ... [at] the [Irish] Convention appointed by Lloyd George' and should not be in charge. Tully claimed that the vote was a 'swan song' in any event; the new voter register would kill off the IPP.[184] At the Roscommon guardians and RDC T.A.P. Mapother was reinstated to both chairmanships without opposition.[185] John McGreevy refused to reassume the vice chairmanship. He was aggrieved at their unrepresentative makeup.[186]

SF fared better in Boyle. John Keaveny's sixteen-year chairmanship of the No. 1 RDC was ended by Crossna's newly released SF member, Edward Doyle. Decrying the twenty-six to thirteen vote margin, Keaveny resigned 'after a vile speech against the priests and his colleagues ... to whom he attributed acts of terrorism'.[187]

By the end of June, it was apparent that conscription could not be enforced in Ireland. Lord French did, however, continue to target SF and proclaimed the party suppressed along with the Gaelic League in July. The *Journal* wrote presciently that the move would strengthen SF, with even the *Messenger* somewhat aggrieved given the contrast between the approach to unionist and nationalist agitation.[188] Speaking at a 'patriot fête' at Rockingham, French noted that most Irish people were loyal, but some had minds 'filled with mischievous sentiments and poisonous lies'. The aim of the proclamation was to break the networks that promoted these.[189] While reports stated that it was 'business as usual' for Roscommon SF, the CI noted that there had been 'little open display since the recent proclamation'.[190] A humorous Roscommon SF badge read: 'Hush – we're suppressed.' With the exception of 15 August, when Roscommon participated in a countrywide reading of Éire Abú, a SF national executive statement on the proclamation, overt SF activity declined, as it did in neighbouring Westmeath, Longford and Sligo.[191]

French's tactics forced Fr O'Flanagan into a more prominent SF role, much to the annoyance of Bishop Coyne. Aggrieved by the priest's canvass for the imprisoned Arthur Griffith in his by-election victory in East Cavan in June, Coyne suspended the curate. Crossna parishioners were aghast and closed the local church in protest on the penultimate Sunday in July. The *Irish Independent* reported that O'Flanagan's replacement, Fr Clyne, a SF-supporting curate from Elphin, made his 'ingress through a sacristy window' for the second Mass of that day, attended by twelve parishioners.[192] Subsequently, all entry points were padlocked and a sign was placed at the churchyard entrance: 'The next Mass that will be read in this church will be by the Rev. M. O'Flanagan'.[193] SF branches at Ballinameen, Arigna and Ballyfarnon censured Coyne for furthering the British agenda. O'Flanagan tried to cool passions by requesting that the church reopen, something his followers allowed under protest.[194] RIC assertions that the issue then ended were proved incorrect when demonstrations for O'Flanagan at Strokestown and Tilly Hill, near Ballaghaderreen, were staged. The priest issued an emotive letter to the press: 'It is a dreadful thing to find myself torn from the altar, but I have this consolation at least, that I have not yet been torn from the hearts of the people.'[195] O'Flanagan's time away from the pulpit was put to good use. He focused his redoubtable energy on SF preparations for the 1918 general election.

The greatest influence on the election was the new voter register. The expanded franchise included 21-year-old men with six months' residency in a district, women older than thirty (subject to valuation), the wives of voters and soldiers older than nineteen.[196] Numerous challenges to eligibility were lodged in the courts, however. B.J. Goff represented dozens of potential SF voters, while M.J. Heverin protected the interests of the IPP.[197] Women were disproportionately represented in complaints to the council clerk, who asserted that incorrectly completed forms caused the most issues. A common problem was people's unwillingness to sign the necessary paperwork. Some presumed that the details would be used for a purpose other than the expansion of the franchise. In many areas, a priest's reassurance was needed to sooth the nerves of young men who still eyed the continent warily.[198]

The proclamation of SF made promoting the party difficult, while RIC raids for SF promotional materials and merchandise made it harder still. From late August, the CI had increased activity against both SF and the Irish Volunteers, both of which he reported were increasing their activity, albeit surreptitiously.[199] In September his men raided shops across the county. They targeted that of Mrs George Geraghty in Roscommon town, whose letters to the British authorities protesting with 'great indignation at Geraghty's continued detention … without a trial' earmarked her for special attention. Other targets included the Sharkey sisters in Strokestown. Both women were arrested and sent to Sligo gaol after Crown forces ransacked their premises, confiscated their stock and closed the shop.[200]

SF supporters took advantage of the latest round of recruitment meetings to promote their message. They hectored the new The O'Conor Don and Major Murphy at Ballaghaderreen, Strokestown and Elphin and probably gained supporters when Murphy warned his Elphin hecklers that 'obstruction to a friendly appeal was rendering conscription absolutely necessary'.[201] A meeting scheduled for Boyle was cancelled to avoid a repeat, while a baton charge was required to clear a meeting in Roscommon town, where Mapother and Murphy derided SF achievements.[202] Such was the hostility manifested at recruitment meetings that both of Boyle's recruitment offices also relocated. The regional recruitment office was moved to Sligo, while the local office was moved to the courthouse, presumably because the military no longer wanted unknown civilians accessing the barracks.[203]

The SF proscription provided organized Labour with an opportunity to become better established. Moves to form an ITGWU branch in Strokestown got underway in August, followed by Ballyfarnon in September. Athlone and Roscommon town followed in early October; the latter quickly claimed 220 members. Enrolling both men and women, the branches sought an eight-hour working day, 30s. per week, a half-day on Saturday and overtime payments, as well as better houses and three acres of land per labourer.[204] While organizers sent mixed messages regarding army enlistment, they were united in opposition to conscription. The CI suggested that the ITGWU in Roscommon was 'controlled by Sinn Feiners' and in January 1919 counted nine branches.[205] When the Labour party decided not to contest the general election, the Sinn Féin Notes section of the *Journal* stated that both parties would speak with 'one voice'.[206]

Early indications did not favour the IPP. John Fitzgibbon withdrew from the political arena after the death of a second son in the war, Revd John Fitzgibbon. The Mayo South MP cited 'circumstances of a private character'.[207] Hayden confirmed that he would enter his first general election contest in his twenty-one-year parliamentary career. He started the process of rousing the long-dormant party machinery in South Roscommon so that he could, as the *Herald* put it, 'win or lose on Redmond's policy'. In his first election speech in Ballynaheglish on 15 September he extolled the virtues of the IPP legacy, disparaging 'sham republicans' and their 'mongrel inventions' which would bring 'perpetual coercion'.[208] The *Herald* mocked the report of the meeting submitted to the press and claimed that some of the forty-seven attendees noted were actually dead. Castlerea's Tom Egan tried to break the link between the 1880s IPP that Hayden referenced and the IPP of 1918. In a letter to the same newspaper, he criticized Hayden for being 'bereft of that integrity which actuated his dear brother Luke'.[209]

Count Plunkett, Birmingham Prison's newest internee and one of many SF candidates in prison during the election, remained the SF candidate for Roscommon North. Despite indications of a contest, the North Roscommon UIL executive was unable to find someone willing to oppose Plunkett, even after an appeal to the UIL National Directory.[210] B.J. Goff sent the necessary documentation to Birmingham Prison to ensure Plunkett's unopposed return, one of many in the December 1918 election.[211]

Hayden supporters did become active. Some South Roscommon UIL branches convened for the first time since John Redmond's death to fundraise; those at Cloontuskert, Athleague, Fuerty and Kilgefin were prominent.[212] The Cloontuskert UIL issued warnings about the likelihood of 'another rebellion' in the event of an IPP loss.[213] The *Freeman's Journal* remarked on the success of the Roscommon South election fund (Hayden subscribed £50, the largest individual contribution), noting the contribution of Major Gerald Dease of Westmeath, a man whose logic proved attractive to the newspaper, despite his politics: 'I have no particular regard for the Irish Party; but I prefer it to Carsonism and national lunacy and suicide.'[214]

Harry Boland was confirmed as Hayden's opponent in September. A major IRB figure with links to Roscommon through his grandfather and the Shouldices of Ballaghaderreen, he had to appeal to more voters than in any previous electoral contest.[215] Both at national level and in Roscommon, the electorate tripled. The Roscommon South register for December 1918 numbered 14,819 men and 7,224 women.[216]

In anticipation of unrest, the British military commandeered Boyle workhouse to accommodate extra troops. Some of the men were deployed as disinfectant soldiers, recruits who targeted the Spanish Flu, a powerful strain of influenza that had spread across Europe during 1918.[217] The virus entered

Athlone in June 1918 and slowly spread across Roscommon. Reports indicated that it had reached Strokestown by October, when it was cited by the Sharkey sisters as an excuse for missing a court date.[218] The effects of the virus in Ballaghaderreen were so severe that the general election and the end of the First World War in November were deemed 'secondary considerations'.[219] Reports from Ballinlough, Arigna and Castlerea indicated similar severity and, while fatalities were in single figures early on, the death of younger citizens was concerning.[220] By mid-November, the flu was 'claiming new victims every other day', schools were closed and social activities curtailed.[221] While Roscommon town appeared to have 'practical immunity' during October, forty cases were reported by mid-November.[222] By December, the flu was pervasive. Athlone reported 300 diagnoses and fourteen deaths; hundreds more followed across Roscommon.[223]

For those capable of electioneering, the contest was stimulating. Boland launched his campaign in Athlone on 23 November, relying on the SF manifesto of October 1918 that both he and O'Flanagan (who canvassed in opposition to John Dillon) had a part in conceiving.[224] His meetings at Fourmilehouse, Cloontuskert and Kiltoom were described as 'triumphant' in the *Herald*, a 'procession of huge proportions' in Roscommon town, making his return seem assured.[225] The county town meeting was staged at Essex Lawns, on the outskirts, due to the 'epidemic on Main St'.[226] Speakers Michael Finlay and P.J. McCrann decried Hayden's £400 parliamentary wage and the IPP's support for the war. George Geraghty, on compassionate leave from Usk, related that his internment prevented him from seeing his sister before the Spanish Flu claimed her life.[227] The most significant contribution was a letter from Canon Cummins. Likening the IPP to a 'blunted ploughshare', he exhorted people to support SF and disdain the British – the *Journal* capitalized Cummins's contribution where it saw fit: 'The hour is gone to fawn or crouch like supplicants ... Now is the time. NOW OR NEVER.'[228]

Boland's speech indicated his recognition that the electorate could be unnerved by talk of revolution. He started by speaking in Irish and stressing that the contest was about the republic, not Hayden and the IPP. He was vague as to how the republic would be achieved, but stressed that the route of constitutional nationalism – 'repeal to home rule ... home rule to partition' – had to be abandoned.[229] He highlighted Labour's decision not to oppose the 'national party', SF, and concluded by asking supporters to shout not 'Up Boland' but rather 'Up the Republic'.[230] At subsequent meetings on Boland's first five-day 'flying tour' in Castlerea, Cloonfad, Ballydangan and fourteen other districts, there was similar rhetoric and chants of 'liberty, liberty, liberty'.[231] The *Messenger* disparaged Boland's supposedly disorganized meetings. It claimed that crowds were small and that at Kilbegnet locals trampled on Boland's election pamphlets.[232] The newspaper did not print Boland's name until the 7 December edition. Instead it referred to him as the 'young man' who 'darkly hinted' at the violence that would be needed to gain a republic.[233]

Reports of Hayden's meetings suggest that they were not as successful as Boland's. Certainly, the *Messenger* claimed that at Ballinlough, Cloonfad, Kilbride and Athleague enthusiastic crowds cheered the MP. However, even it had to admit, alongside the *Freeman's Journal*, that Hayden was repeatedly heckled in Athlone and that D.J. Kelly had undermined him in rural areas.[234] The *Herald* reported that the MP was booed in Moore, greeted with 'silent contempt' in Ballyforan and 'pelted with scraws and mud' at Taughma-connell. When departing Taughmaconnell, Hayden reportedly shouted: 'Go and cheer for the Kaiser and his pro-Germans.' Numerous titles agreed that Hayden was hit with a lump of clay at St John's.[235]

Hayden's rhetoric concentrated on the IPP's historic record, their affinity with the land hungry and, of course, home rule. At Castlerea and Castleplunkett he declared that SF internees were simply mimicking the IPP men who 'took the prison food, wore the prison garb, slept on the plank bed'.[236] SF claims to greater sacrifice were disingenuous. Like John Dillon in Ballaghaderreen, Hayden asserted that an IPP defeat would see the land issue regress. If a proposed bill passed, Crown forces would be gifted Roscommon acres in exchange for their war service – it required the IPP in Westminster to stop the legislation.[237] He disparaged Micheál Ó Braonáin for his alleged reluctance to fight when in Dublin during Easter 1916, implying that Roscommon's SF leaders were cowards. Boland handled the assertion smartly; Ó Braonáin had followed orders at the time while Hayden was 'applauding Mr Asquith's decision to show us no mercy'.[238]

After Canon Cummins made his support for Boland clear, some SF sup-porters moved to depict Hayden as an enemy of the church. Letters and arti-cles reminded people that Hayden, a Roman Catholic married to a Belfast Presbyterian, had spearheaded the effort to limit the influence of priests in the 1898 Local Government Act, or, as one letter put it, 'outdistanced the greatest No Popery bigots … to disqualify the priests from the … councils'.[239] Reintroducing this 20-year-old issue contributed to Hayden's difficulty in attracting clerical support in the constituency. Just six priests backed him.[240] The *Herald* claimed that Hayden became 'vicious against the priests' as a result, most prominently against Cummins.[241] The canon indicated his distress at Hayden's opposition but confirmed that twenty-two priests in south Roscommon opposed the IPP's partition plan.[242] The *Messenger* maligned Cummins and sourced pro-IPP articles from the bishop of Ossary and dean of Cashel in an attempt to counterbalance Cummins's claims.[243]

Polling day in Roscommon on 14 December was 'carried through qui-etly'.[244] The only newsworthy clash in the constituency occurred in Curraghboy, near Athlone, where those 'opposed to Sinn Féin were hustled

about'.[245] The RIC disarmed Irish Volunteers in some areas but did little
when Boland's car was attacked in Athleague, a town where free drinks were
offered to IPP supporters.[246] Cummins toured the constituency on the day to
promote SF and was criticized by Hayden after the polls closed for introducing 'personalities … and slander'.[247] Controversy arose when the high sheriff,
The O'Conor Don, disallowed the Irish Volunteers a custodial role for the
ballot boxes. It was agreed that the RIC could guard them but only after the
boxes had been covered in tape to prevent tampering.[248]

A win for SF was certain. The *Herald* reported a 'demoralized' Hayden
arriving at Roscommon courthouse. He sported a John Redmond badge, while
Boland had a 'tricolour riband with crossed rifles and camán'. The MP had
polled well only in Aughaderry, where promises made by John Fitzgibbon
carried weight, and Roscommon town. He was beaten decisively in Athlone,
Castlerea, Ballinlough, Cloonfad and Mount Welcome (near Athlone), the
final district showing a 487 to 6 vote in favour of SF.[249] The *Journal* reported
that Hayden's supporters – party men, unionists, separation women (the
wives of soldiers in receipt of a separation allowance) and RIC – were too few,
reports from areas such as Cams showing that people voted contrary to IPP
expectations.[250] Personation was not a major feature as there was little need
for it. Only the polling station at Taughmaconnell was deemed problematic
in this regard.[251] When the Roscommon South results were announced, the
Freeman's Journal remarked that Boland's victory 'took no-one by surprise'
but the margin of victory by 10,685 to 4,233 certainly did.[252] Jasper Tully was
so happy with the defeat of Hayden and John Dillon that he sent his delivery cars to spread the news before the *Herald* went to press.

Hayden had few complaints. The 'well conducted' contest was part of an
election that confirmed 'the passing away of a movement that has achieved
untold good for Ireland and the substitution for it of a new movement'. While
sceptical, he hoped that the SF party 'will be one for the advancement of the
county, for its development and … freedom'. Boland revelled in the victory.
He agreed that the election was 'very orderly', and distanced himself from the
Cummins/Hayden personality clash. Magnanimously, and confusingly, he
stated that: 'Mr Hayden and I are pursuing the same object by different
means.' Newspapers carried reports of celebrations across the constituency as
well as those in north Roscommon for Count Plunkett, who was released from
Birmingham Prison on 31 December.[253] Overall, SF won seventy-three seats.
Some candidates took two constituencies. The IPP was reduced to six MPs;
five in Ulster and one in Waterford. The party was dwarfed in Westminster
by twenty-six Irish Unionist MPs.

On the penultimate day in December, Boland addressed a crowd in
Athlone. While he reiterated much of what he had said on the campaign trail,
he indicated more clearly that SF was not solely reliant on the Peace

Conference: 'If the Conference fails us we will put forth such an organization in Ireland as will make it clear that there can be no peace in Western Europe so long as Ireland remains under the heel of the English oppressor.'[254] The nature and methods of that organization were not defined. Only time would tell what was required and whether the people of Roscommon would be willing to participate.

The rapid growth of advanced nationalism in Roscommon in the aftermath of the February 1917 by-election was impressive. Although initially undermined by Count Plunkett's vanities, it was apparent after the Longford South by-election that Roscommon was embracing SF. The IPP appeared naïve, as it placed its faith in the Irish Convention, while SF built up its grass roots organization. The new branches supplanted the moribund UIL and overwhelmed the AOH, which was much reduced in numbers and influence by 1918. The reaction to the death of Thomas Ashe showed that republican martyrs were a potent means of promoting advanced nationalist sentiment. The efforts of J.P. Hayden, though showing an honest commitment to the IPP and its policies, were both ineffective and counterproductive. His disparaging of SF policies made him appear myopic and he haemorrhaged support, even from long-time allies. The reinvigoration of land agitation in 1918 was the culmination of people's exhaustion at the static position that had pertained since the war began and the growing sense of IPP impotency. The actions of the RIC in suppressing the agitation ensured that the police began to be marginalized, while SF's limited success in controlling their supporters indicated that in Roscommon the pursuit of the land wielded more influence than the pursuit of a republic. The crisis of conscription saw Roscommon men and women unite to oppose government plans for forced enlistment. Although the IPP and its followers allied with advanced nationalists to repel the threat, only the latter increased their support base through SF, the Irish Volunteers and Cumann na mBan. The fact that the growth in the Irish Volunteers was temporary showed, however, that as of mid-1918, there were few in Roscommon who were willing to take up arms for the republic. As often typified British policy, the German plot arrests in May 1918 and associated repression had the opposite effect to that intended. SF gained traction in Roscommon's local authorities as additional criticism of the government's strategy was heard. By the time of the 1918 general election, there was no sense that the IPP would benefit from the expanded register that enfranchised younger electors. The Roscommon South contest proved the strength of SF, which drew clerical support away from the IPP and reflected the almost nationwide abandonment of home rule. The result signalled that Roscommon electors had joined the growing clamour for Ireland to seek her independence by another route.

6 'The rebel organisation is acting as if it alone has the right to govern': the republican counter-state, 1919–21

The 1918 general election gave SF a mandate to pursue an Irish Republic. From early 1919, the party set about the essential, if unglamorous, task of gaining control of local government and supplanting the Crown courts with a republican equivalent. The local authority strategy was initially limited to appointing republicans to county council posts and harrying IPP councillors. It was not until the local elections of 1920 that both SF and Labour won control of Roscommon's councils and disengaged from the British administration. However, managing local authorities in the absence of British revenue led them to the brink of collapse and caused some in Roscommon to question their commitment to the republican administration. The republican court system, although primarily dealing with criminal and civil cases, was embraced from the summer of 1920, as it dealt with the issue that most exercised the people of Roscommon: land. As the courts gained support, there was a concomitant abandonment of the Crown courts. This suggested a growing sense that the Irish Republic was no longer an aspiration but a reality.

Many of Roscommon's councillors had been elected on a wave of IPP enthusiasm in 1914. By 1919, the continued control of most councils by the same men was incongruous. Given that elections were not scheduled until 1920, SF supporters were limited to symbolic efforts to wrest control from the IPP. A high-profile example in Roscommon came in February 1919, when the interned B.J. Goff was proposed for the position of county council relieving officer. The 'old guard' won by fourteen votes to nine; Patrick Drury wondered sarcastically whether, if Goff had won, his receipt of 'an English salary … [would] suit the policy of Sinn Féin'. Roscommon SF branches, preoccupied about what to do with defence fund monies in the absence of the conscription threat, condemned the vote.[1] The result pleased the Tulsk UIL and the AOH county board. They believed that the margin of victory reflected IPP support in Roscommon.[2] J.P. Hayden interpreted such votes and the non-convening of Dáil Éireann for a second sitting during February or March as signs that republicans were not as well positioned as they claimed.[3]

Other votes signalled that IPP councillors were well aware of their position being under threat. Upon the death of T.A.P. Mapother in February 1919, a handful of Roscommon guardians assembled in the offices of the *Messenger* to install their first new chair in thirty-seven years: James Kilroe, 'a member of the old stock'.[4] SF was able to exert greater influence in the county council with the death of John Fitzgibbon in September 1919. D.J. Kelly was elected chairman, while Fitzgibbon's co-opted replacement was his Castlerea adversary, Pa Beirne of SF.[5] At Strokestown, no man from the still dominant IPP membership sought the position of chairman. After intervention from the Local Government Board (LGB), a chairman was found. Yet, even then, many of the meetings for the remainder of 1919 failed to attract a quorum, or, indeed, any members at all.[6]

The municipal elections in January 1920 confirmed that local authorities in Roscommon were as unrepresentative as SF claimed. The contest was the first to use the proportional representation (PR) system. The ITGWU branches in both Roscommon town and Boyle were primed to exert an influence through Labour candidates who, unlike the 1918 general election, were to compete directly with SF.[7] The *Westmeath Independent* and the *Journal* supported both Labour and SF and highlighted the parties' compatible manifestos. The *Journal* emphasized, however, that a win for SF would be the most suitable repost to the 'farcical' Government of Ireland bill, which sought to establish separate parliaments for northern and southern Ireland.[8] No contest was required for the RTC, as just nine candidates – five Labour and four SF – presented for the nine seats.[9] Along with Callan in County Kilkenny, the RTC was joint first in Ireland in declaring its composition.[10] As happened in many councils, the Labour majority, which included chairman George Geraghty, was re-framed as a republican-labour majority.[11]

In Boyle, an energetic contest was expected on 15 January. Labour sought all nine seats and competed as the largest party against SF, unionists, Redmondites and independents.[12] Among the Labour hopefuls was an unnamed 'lady shop assistant', who had to abandon her bid along with all the other candidates when their candidature was 'declared void through some informality'. Legal action was taken to address the issue and the incumbents were re-elected without a contest.[13] Roscommon was, therefore, one of few counties in which tallies offered by the PR system are unavailable. National results showed that SF had taken 30.8% of the vote, Labour 21.7% and constitutional nationalists 13.1%. The underwhelming win for SF convinced Harry Boland that SF needed to review its position.[14] Given the closeness of SF and Labour, the *Journal* saw the result as a victory for the republic.[15]

Increasing republican control and support by June 1920 influenced the local elections for unions, district councils and county councils. The newly formed Irish Farmers' Union (IFU), a natural harbour for larger farmers who had backed the IPP, supported independents. The IFU had spread across Roscommon during 1919 and formed a county executive that October.[16] The association of unionists like T.C.E. Goff and, of course, Redmondites ensured that it was not welcomed in all localities. In Ballynaheglish, SF blocked efforts to organize by instructing locals to allow only those bodies 'who are prepared to take their stand as true soldiers to Ireland on the platform of Sinn Féin'.[17] Even with such opposition, by May 1920 the IFU had twenty-five branches and 2,000 members 'of all political shades of thought'.[18]

Few electoral contests were held, as Labour's weaker rural organization benefitted SF. The number of candidates and seats were equal in Elphin, Rooskey and Tulsk, while in some areas coerced withdrawals ensured the same balance.[19] Boyle union initially had three independents but republican pressure led to their change of mind.[20] In Roscommon, Michael Petit of Cloontuskert, an IPP man, was warned of 'what he might expect' should he stand.[21] He withdrew. The *Messenger* lamented the loss of the 'good servants' in the union, which saw Athleague host an eight-candidate contest for five seats and Cam host a six-candidate contest for four seats.[22] Most incumbents had withdrawn in Castlerea and Strokestown too, with only one independent standing in each. Charles Gunn, the Strokestown independent, pitted himself against Úna Sharkey, who aspired to be the first woman elected to Roscommon County Council.[23]

A comprehensive republican victory led the *Journal* to cheer that the Irish were about to manage the local government of their 'own nation'.[24] Of the six Strokestown seats for the county council, five went to SF/Labour. IFU support enabled Gunn to take the final seat from Úna Sharkey.[25] SF dominated in all the other electoral contests with twenty-one councillors elected under the republican banner. This result reflected SF dominance across the west of Ireland, while the CI's opinion that the men were 'extremists of no standing' reflected British prejudices that led the Crown forces to underestimate republicans.[26] Jasper Tully's delight in the victory 'for a whole people' inspired him to denounce British policy in *Herald* articles, which in turn caused the British authorities to censure the newspaper.[27]

The 'republican' county council made an event of its first meeting. D.J. Kelly presided as national school teacher Andrew Lavin TD was elected chairman and Micheál Ó Braonáin vice chairman. Lavin first addressed the council in Irish, before he confirmed the repudiation of British institutions and pledged allegiance to Dáil Éireann. He thanked the Irish Republican Army (IRA) for its campaign against RIC barracks (see chapter 7), 'fortresses of oppression', and 'on the run' members such as the officer commanding (OC) the North Roscommon Brigade, James Ryan, and John Brennan, both of whom were present.[28] The *Belfast News Letter* reported attempted 'embezzlement' with the unsuccessful proposal to give the council's £1,000 bank credit to the IRA 'Paymaster General'.[29] Calls to burn LGB documents were heard, while written requests for additional RIC were also deemed good tinder. Malicious claims 'arising out of the state of war between the Republican forces and the army of occupation' were to be ignored.[30] A close vote of eleven to eight led the council to burn its predecessor's condemnation of the 1916 Rising.[31]

Other Roscommon local authority bodies also set about demonstrating their republicanism. The Strokestown guardians and RDC, though soon to mirror the dismal attendance record of their predecessors, had a strong start. They pledged their support to the republic and co-opted Úna Sharkey 'to make amends' for the election.[32] The Roscommon RDC declared its allegiance to Dáil Éireann on 14 June and co-opted Ó Braonáin and John Burke, a Kilteevan republican, to replace Mapother.[33] The *Journal* suggested that the RDC should also burn its condemnation of the 1916 Rising. The Castlerea union followed the suggestion in part by voting to delete the condemnation of the Rising from its minute book. Athlone union adopted a realistic approach when it made its pledge of fealty to the Dáil. Its chairman, Seán O'Hurley, expressed initial hopes to 'make use of the existing Castle institutions until ... Dáil Éireann [had] set up a substitute authority'. As it transpired, the Dáil had no appetite for such pragmatism and repudiated the LGB before the end of June.[34]

While the Dáil's position was clear, the need for funds ensured that some local authorities were slow to disassociate overtly from the LGB. On 29 July, a LGB memorandum declared that local authorities had to acknowledge its authority (and therefore Westminster's) by submitting to audits.[35] The RTC, Castlerea and Strokestown unions rejected the LGB demand and disassociated in response. However, the Boyle and Athlone unions were reluctant.[36] Seán O'Hurley asserted that LGB grants had to be accessed for the 'good of the people'.[37] The quandary was acknowledged in Roscommon union. Chairman George Geraghty wanted the union to be 'abolished altogether', a call that prefigured the Dáil's plan to do just that and influenced numerous staff to resign.[38]

The difficulty of running local authorities without British funds quickly became apparent. In September, when the LGB denied funds where audits were refused, the RTC dissolved, its already poor financial situation beyond hope.[39] The county council predictably declined to submit to audits, while its refusal to contest malicious injuries claims closed off access to Local Taxation (Ireland) Account funds; rates then remained its only income. Rate collection had been an emerging issue since early 1919 when some SF clubs in Roscommon and Leitrim promoted non-payment as a form of protest. Roscommon town was deemed a 'shopkeeper riddled bedlam', as many merchants there sought to evince their support for the republic, and, more attractively, their bottom line by avoiding payment.[40] The uncertainty that the escalating military conflict caused in 1920 led many ratepayers to withhold payment and, in turn, contractors rejected council work, fearing bad debts.[41] Some, especially smaller farmers, advanced valid economic reasons for retaining their funds, while others simply tried to take advantage of the uncertainty to avoid their obligations. In some cases, even IRA members refused to coop-erate with new Dáil-approved collectors. When long-standing rate collectors had money to deposit, they were often unwilling to hand it over to the trustees that Dáil Éireann nominated. Banks, which had usually taken the deposits, were deemed too likely to follow Crown court rulings directing pay-ments for malicious injury claims.[42] Some rate collectors, such as Joseph Jordan, instead lodged the money in their own accounts and sought LGB assistance.[43] Jordan was arrested by the IRA, and after four months in deten-tion, it was reported that a gun to his head persuaded him to sign two cheques.[44] A Roscommon rate collectors' meeting in mid-November con-firmed the 'awful state' of rates collection in the county, which forced the county council to suspend wage payments, dismiss the coroner, vets and court-keepers, default on bank repayments and deny revenues to the county's unions.[45] The absence of revenue led the Roscommon and Boyle guardians to reduce relief, cut staff pay and discharge 'healthy' inmates. Cheques issued by the Strokestown guardians bounced in December.[46] Invitations from banks for loan applications guaranteed by men with satisfactory 'means and reliabil-ity' gave hope. However, the seizure of account books by the Crown forces ensured that the applications were rejected.[47] As desperation set in, the Roscommon guardians sold their meeting room clock for £10.[48]

As in neighbouring Leitrim, Longford and Sligo, improvements were slow to register, even when Roscommon County Council re-instated the trustee status of the National Bank.[49] Deeming the situation impossible to solve otherwise, the guardians in Boyle and Athlone re-engaged with the LGB.[50] The fact that many republicans could not attend meetings due to the activities of the Crown forces ensured that arguments advanced at the rele-vant Boyle guardians meeting carried disproportionate weight: 'What harm would submitting the books do to the cause of Ireland?'[51] The permitted audit in Boyle saw £3,000 released in February. However, the capitulation 'soured' relations with the county council, which largely suspended its activ-ities in spring 1921. The Boyle union chairman later admitted that the cause had been injured.[52]

When the county council reconvened after the truce in 1921, rates were still the most contentious aspect of its work. Though Ó Braonáin reported that the council was £10,000 in credit in August 1921, he purposefully did not refer to the dearth of council work, much-reduced payroll, or, indeed, the books that had not been balanced and accounted for much of the nominal sur-plus.[53] The areas around Athlone, Castlerea and Ballaghaderreen had devel-oped into rates black spots. In an attempt to leverage payment, the council ceased work in non-compliant districts. Coercive measures were also rolled out against rate collectors, unfortunately for them, by both sides. The council set targets and imposed penalties for non-collection. Those who did not wish to pay issued beatings and produced guns. Even with low rates of 2*s*. in the pound for land and 3*s*. for houses, by June 1922 over £30,000 in rates were deemed uncollected or uncollectable. By March 1923, that figure stood at £55,000 and prompted the IFS to adopt a judicial solution.[54]

One of the main cost-saving schemes advanced by the Dáil Department for Local Government was the amalgamation of union workhouses and the creation of a national network of county infirmaries. The workhouses at Castlerea, Strokestown, Athlone and Boyle began to close in May 1920, although Athlone and Boyle unions again proved uncooperative.[55] The intransigence of Athlone union saw it deprived of all funds from April. The workhouse there closed in any event when amalgamations concluded in September.[56] The move was opposed by political figures in each town on grounds of lost business, employment and patronage. Every town was also left with a large empty building to repurpose.[57] In Boyle, part of the workhouse became a branch hospital, while the county infirmary was located in Roscommon town workhouse.[58] The 100-bed Sacred Heart County Home was promoted as a social revolution, given that its approach to managing destitution would be more humane. It would, press releases claimed, lead to the eradication of the 'stigma of pauperism'. Bishop Coyne donated £100 so that the authorities could 'do away with "the union garb"'.[59] Even allowing for expenditure on the amalgamations, it was reported in January 1922 that managing the new system had reduced costs by one-third.[60]

The republican judicial system gained more widespread support during the summer of 1920. In Roscommon, its most important use was in addressing the contentious land issue. Rolled out as part of a system of parish, district and, later, circuit courts (referred to variously as SF courts, republican courts and Dáil courts), the first land courts in Roscommon were held in the county town and Castlerea during the second week in May.[61] Early reports from the *Democrat* were positive; at last the 'poor man is coming in for a little of his just rights'.[62] The *Messenger* was compelled to agree. Both sides were happy in most cases, although Hayden's newspaper did indicate that cases from Tulsk, Creggs and Strokestown saw resolutions accepted by landowners only after they were forced to engage with the court.[63] Indeed, it was reported that landowners near Castlerea were 'terrorized' into cooperating.[64] J.L. Cotton was subjected to multiple cattle drives before agreeing to arbitration, while M.G. Sweeney's house at Cahir was burned to convince him to come to terms.[65] B.J. Goff, often the solicitor representing small farmers, admitted to using robust methods but was unapologetic. In the case of one Protestant grazier, Goff purposefully noted the man's opposition to the republic before telling the court that when his client put a gun to the man's head, it was simply to 'induce' cooperation, rather than cause duress![66] By June, Ian

MacPherson, the Irish chief secretary, reported that in seven Roscommon cases, 5,847 acres had been sold due to 'threats and acts of violence'. This report was counterbalanced by news that an unnamed Protestant farmer donated £20 to SF when a 'scandalous' request for land was dismissed. At times, such men were happier to deal with the republican process rather than the less effective British system.[67]

The work undertaken by land courts in Roscommon was vast. Between May and August, dozens of claims were lodged. The RIC, which observed proceedings in both Roscommon town and Castlerea, was chastised by the *Belfast News Letter* for its inaction, the newspaper perhaps unaware that arbitration systems were not illegal.[68] Kevin O'Shiel, a judicial commissioner appointed by Dáil Éireann, heard sixty-nine cases pertaining to Roscommon that concerned 11,575 acres. O'Shiel thought Roscommon worse than Galway or Mayo, which also came under his remit:

> I had harder work ... in that county than in any of all the thirteen counties I ... held my courts in. There was an aggressive, "bolshie" spirit about the Roscommon litigants that was ... not so obviously present in the other counties, even the worst of them.[69]

The prevailing view in Roscommon was reflected by Fr McDermott, parish priest of Ballinlough. He exhorted all to appreciate the 'services to the cause of justice rendered by the Arbitration Courts'.[70] The RIC, while admitting that its data was incomplete, noted a massive fall in agrarian offences as the courts spread. Although not admitting the courts' role (the RIC instead blamed the end of letting season), the CI reported a fall from forty-four cases in May to thirteen in June and three in July.[71] The republican judicial system proved the viability of the republican counter-state. Even Roscommon's 'loyal' resident magistrates admitted that people were so impressed 'it would be difficult to shake their belief in the reality of a Republic'.[72]

The parish and district courts gained similar support, as did their custodians, the 'republican police'. Usually IRA men (the police arrested lawbreakers) protected post offices (at least in areas where the post master or mistress was sympathetic) and enforced court rulings. They held transgressors in 'unknown destinations', often abandoned houses, and engaged in the work for free, fitting it around their jobs.[73] According to Thomas Lavin, their no-nonsense approach instilled caution in those who 'often gave a bit of trouble', while their impartiality was generally recognized not only in Roscommon but elsewhere in Ireland.[74]

Publicizing the competency, impartiality and effectiveness of the largely locally directed courts was essential. Excessive localism, with all of its longstanding enmities, had been an early issue but courts did become generally impartial quite quickly, with propaganda reports helping publicize their professionalism. A trial held at an abandoned house that concerned post office raids at Knockvicar and Cootehall saw a 'well-known Irish Professor' act as judge and an invited journalist record a detailed account. The blindfolded defendants claimed that they had been well-treated, given four meals a day, the option of a glass of whiskey and were permitted to write letters.[75] Similar articles on orderly courts that heard cases involving trespass, vandalism, breach of contract and bog access in Boyle, Roscommon town and Ballaghaderreen, helped legitimize the system.[76] By the end of May, solicitors were frequently engaged. The Croghan parish court saw several working under Andrew Lavin TD in July, while the Cootehall district court hosted solicitors from three counties and a guest arbitrator, Fr Appleby, from Lancashire.[77] The court system borrowed from Brehon law to reduce reliance on English common law. Inventive sentences resulted. One convict was made to parade outside a church wearing a sign stating he was a thief. Another was 'tonsured in a manner that would do credit to a friar'.[78] Fines, deportations and the equivalent of community service were also handed down.[79]

The success of the republican courts required the failure of the Crown courts. IRA man Patrick Brennan recalled that he convinced 'people about to take cases into the enemy courts ... to recognize IRA courts instead'.[80] JPs were also 'convinced', with reports from Ballaghaderreen, Rooskey, Athlone, Boyle and Castlerea indicating effective republican pressure.[81] Other JPs resigned in protest at the British war strategy. Between April and October, 1,000 (or one-fifth of the national total) did so. Many were replaced, but had little work, as a pervasive disinclination to use the British system developed.[82] In Strokestown in June, Judge Wakely had 'nothing to do' at a quarter session when only two RIC, four court officials and four solicitors turned up.[83] Similarly quiet sessions were reported in Castlerea, Elphin, Frenchpark, Athlone and Hillstreet. Tulsk set a county record in November when the sessions did not convene for the sixth month in a row.[84] In mid-July, when the summer assizes were held in Roscommon town, the presiding judge lamented developments. As in many neighbouring counties, cases referred to the assizes had increased greatly: six-fold in Roscommon when compared to 1919.[85] Nevertheless, no defendants and fewer than half of the jurors presented. Such civil disobedience was a strong measure of growing belief in the republican counter-state. British sanctions for being absent had lost their potency.[86] By the late summer, the republican courts were supreme. To underline this, the IRA burned Ballaghaderreen courthouse and also engaged in a calamitously unsuccessful attempt to burn the courthouse in Strokestown.[87] Soon after, Roscommon County Council decided to stop paying for court buildings not in its ownership; they were no longer needed.[88]

The domination of local electoral contests in Roscommon by SF and Labour was inevitable. The 1918 general election had confirmed that the elec-

1 *(above, left)*, J.P. Hayden, Irish Parliamentary Party MP for Roscommon South, 1897–1918.

2 John Fitzgibbon, Irish Parliamentary Party MP for Mayo South, 1910–18.

3 *(below, left)*, Jasper Tully, co-owner and editor of the *Roscommon Herald*.

4 Canon Thomas Cummins, parish priest of Roscommon town.

5 A Roscommon Gaelic League trip to Quaker Island in 1909. Michéal Ó Braonáin and his brother, John, are pictured holding fiddles in the centre of the group.
6 The Roscommon Gaels hurling team in 1904. George Geraghty, the team captain, is pictured in the centre of the group.

7 Castlerea Irish Volunteers, 1914.

8 & 9 Boyle Volunteers at Keash, County Sligo, 26 July 1914.

10 (*above, left*), Count Plunkett, winner of Roscommon North by-election, February 1917.
11 Badge worn by Plunkett supporters while canvassing in 1917.
12 (*below, left*), The West's Awake election poster printed by Patrick Morahan of the
Strokestown Democrat for the 1917 Roscommon North by-election.
13 Why you should support Count Plunkett by-election poster, 1917.

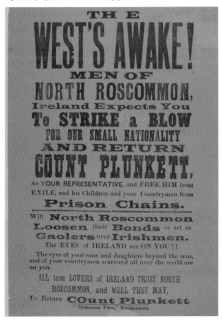

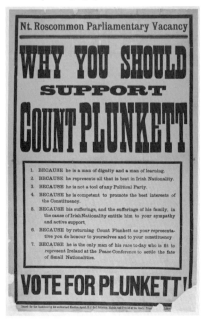

14 Father Michael O'Flanagan.
15 Laurence Ginnell, MP for
Westmeath North.

16 Anti-conscription rally, Ballaghaderreen, 5 May 1918.

17 John Dillon at an anti-conscription rally, Ballaghaderreen, 5 May 1918.

PROCLAMATION
NO CONSCRIPTION

▶■ WE ■◀

THE MEMBERS OF THE BALLAGHADERREEN CUMAN NA mBAN hereby PROCLAIM that we will NOT CONSCRIPT any person who does not wish to COME VOLUNTARY TO OUR MONSTER

AERIDEACHT

Consisting of Choral Recitals, Irish Songs, Dances and Recitations, to be Held in

Sports Field. Ballaghaderreen,
ON SUNDAY, JUNE 23RD INST.
AT WHICH
COUNTESS PLUNKETT.

And Other Prominent Speakers

• Who have kindly Consented to Attend, will Deliver Short Addresses.

The above Programme will be preceded by the following Athletic Events :
1. 220 Yds. Race, Boys under 16 Free entry
2. 100 Yds. Race, Open Handicap,
3. 220 Yds. Race, Open Handicap,
4. High Jump, Open.
5. Obstacle Race, Open.
6. Old Age Pensioners' Race.

Entrance Fee for Each of the above Events is 6d. General Entry 1s Valuable Prizes will be Given to Winners [First and Second] of above Events. To Conclude the Athletic Part of the Programme the Strength of our Manhood will be Tested by a **TUG OF WAR** (Open to any Team in the West). Teams to be Limited to 10 Men A Splendid Set of SILVER MEDALS, with Gold Cent e and Scroll, will be Presented to the Winning Team. Entrance Fee for Tug of War Teams is **5**s. N.B.---Entry for the Tug of War must be made through the Secretary of the Club. Intending Competitors should, if possible send in their entries to JOSEPH BEIRNE, or THOMAS F. O'HARA (Flannery's), Receivers of Entries, before Saturday, 22nd Inst. Entries will also be taken on the Field,

FIRST ITEM WILL BE "RAN OFF" AT 2.30 O'Clock, OLD TIME.

PRICE OF ADMISSION - 1s. (Centre of Field). 6d. Side Line.

:. :. PROCEEDS IN AID OF THE LOCAL CUMAM NA MBAN. :: :

Owen Mirahan, Brinter, Castlerea. # A Dhia Saor Eire.

19 Harry Boland, Sinn Féin TD for Roscommon South.
20 Úna and Eileen Sharkey, Strokestown.

21 Burial of John McGreevy, 4 May 1920. Fr Michael O'Flanagan is pictured in the middle-left section of the image.
22 Crown forces checkpoint, Athlone bridge, 1920–1.

23 Roscommon County Council, June 1920. *Front row (l–r)*: James Oates, J.J. Colgan, Denis Creaton, Andrew Lavin TD, Micheál Ó Braoináin, Patrick Duignan, Joseph McCormack. *Second row*: James Feely, P.J. Neary, James Kenny, James Ryan, Thomas Lavin, John Brennan, Michael Ward. *Back row*: William Donnelly, B.V. Lavin.

24 Paddy Moran of Crossna who was hanged at Mountjoy Gaol, Dublin on 14 March 1921.

25 Knockcroghery in ruins after attack by Crown forces, June 1921.
26 Seán Mac Eoin leading an IRA company to take over Victoria Barracks, Athlone, 28 February 1922.

27 Handover of Roscommon RIC barracks, 24 March 1922. This image was included in the 29 March 1922 edition of the *Freeman's Journal* in the section headed 'New army in old barracks'.

28 National Army Brigadier General Michael Dockery who was shot dead at Boyle workhouse by anti-Treaty IRA forces on 2 July 1922.

29 (*above, left*) Michael Cullen, Ballinlough, in National army uniform.
30 (*above, right*) Patrick Hestor, Tarmon, in National army uniform.
31 James Creighton, Feigh, Castlerea, in National army uniform.

32 Destroyed railway bridge at Kiltoom, April 1923.

torate repudiated the IPP. From early 1919, the party's councillors and guardians realized their political fate. Although in Roscommon, the municipal elections of January 1920 provided little detail, they indicated that Labour was a growing force, especially in Boyle. The SF dominance of the June elections proved that its rural support was largely unchallenged. The exceptional difficulties faced by local authorities indicated a clash between republican aspirations and the exigencies of service delivery. The loss of revenue caused much hardship but the positions adopted by the Athlone and Boyle unions undermined the Dáil's authority. In Roscommon, the success of the republican land courts bolstered both SF and Dáil Éireann. The generally fair arbitration was an important step in promoting compliance with verdicts and defused much of the tension surrounding land in the county during 1920. The speed with which Roscommon embraced the other strands of the republican court system and the abandonment of the Crown courts demonstrated the success of the republican counter-state.

7 The War of Independence in Roscommon, 1919–21

The formation of Dáil Éireann in January 1919 was a bold assertion of independence that needed pervasive grassroots support. As the Irish Volunteers (the IRA from 1919 on) became more active in Roscommon, attempts by the Crown forces to quell republican support by means of raids, arrests and internments intensified. These actions made the ostracization of the Crown forces easier, with IRA intimidation of prospective RIC recruits, destruction of RIC stations at Easter 1920 and a social and commercial boycott further marginalizing them. The re-emergence of violent land agitation in 1920 once again highlighted the centrality of land for people in Roscommon. The Dáil was forced to address the issue lest it threaten the pursuit of independence. With the use of arms in fatal IRA ambushes from July 1920, that pursuit entered a new phase in Roscommon. The British response of drafting in the Black and Tans and Auxiliary Division RIC forces heightened tensions and resulted in a tit-for-tat campaign of violence that saw republicans target suspected informers. Disruption to the railway lines as a result of strike action and damage to infrastructure made living conditions difficult for the people of Roscommon. The spring of 1921 was marked by exceptional violence after the execution of Crossna's Patrick Moran further motivated the IRA. The Roscommon press felt pressure from both sides while reporting on developments, especially during spring 1921, when violent encounters between the IRA and the Crown forces intensified around Castlerea. The destruction of Knockcroghery village in June 1921 proved the lengths to which the Crown forces would go to find their targets. When news of a truce broke in July, moves to engage in score settling saw the IRA show the risks they would take to execute one of their most hated enemies.

After the 1918 general election, SF supporters promoted the Irish Republic. Canon Cummins and Count Plunkett hosted the Roscommon instalment of nationwide anti-internment rallies on 5 January 1919. Plunkett suggested that Ireland needed to be ready to strike down England if required, while Cummins, seeking to influence the American delegation at the Peace Conference in Paris, called for cheers for the 'stars and stripes'.[1] In the event, the Peace Conference did not give the Irish demand for a republic a hearing. Plunkett, who was denied a passport by the British to attend, was calling it 'a soulless thing' by the third week in January.[2] Cummins also rallied support for those still interned, including George Geraghty, who escaped with Frank Shouldice during a prison transfer two weeks later. The two men benefitted from an amnesty given to German Plot prisoners in March after the death from Spanish Flu of Pierce McCann TD, a fellow internee.[3]

SF established the Irish parliament, Dáil Éireann, on 21 January 1919, with Fr O'Flanagan opening proceedings with a prayer. Welcomed by the *Westmeath Independent*, the *Herald* and *Journal*, twenty-seven SF Teachtaí Dála (TDs) were present.[4] The CI noted ironically that the Dáil 'has excited no interest, except in SF circles', presumably quite large circles in early 1919.[5] The *Messenger* lamented men in Dublin making 'declarations' while unionists were 'being heard' in Westminster. The killing of two RIC at Solohedbeg in County Tipperary on the same day as the Dáil convened caused the newspaper more concern. Force was obviously part of the republican plan to end British rule.[6] J.P. Hayden was so convinced that republicans would fail, he formed the County Roscommon Home Rule Association with John Fitzgibbon.[7] The CI reported that the forty members had 'no influence'.[8]

Ian Macpherson was appointed Irish chief secretary in January and oversaw a more stringent application of DORA. Seditious speeches and literature were targeted and arrests mounted from February, with Summerhill near Athlone, Strokestown and Elphin seeing numerous men seized, among them long-time RIC targets William Doherty, James Ryan, John Colgan and B.J. Goff.[9] Labour militancy at Strokestown, Ballaghaderreen and Roscommon town led to arrests during early spring and further unrest manifested as Labour Day, 1 May, neared. In Boyle, the 230-strong ITGWU branch instigated a lengthy strike from mid-April.[10] Michael Healy, the strike leader, was charged for 'language likely to incite riot and intimidation', with disputed reports claiming that he wanted 'employers lying in their blood on the streets'. Jasper Tully made the situation worse by printing personal insults aimed at Healy, who publicly burned a copy of the *Herald*.[11] Tully was also, however, part of the solution. Along with Count Plunkett and local clergymen, he helped broker a deal by the end of May.[12]

With the failure of Irish efforts at the peace conference, Plunkett believed that the Irish needed to shift focus.[13] At Keadue feis on 29 May, alongside Fr O'Flanagan, he acknowledged the need for sacrifice: 'if fighting we must try, then fighting we will die'. Following the Dáil's April direction to boycott the RIC, O'Flanagan proclaimed that it was a disgrace to join the police, a 'brood ... [who] deprive their fellow countrymen of their liberty'. This move to sideline the police marked perhaps the most obvious characteristic of what Charles Townshend has defined as the first of three phases in the Irish War of Independence. The low-level activity that anchored the republican approach from 1919 until the second phase emerged in 1920 was, in part, informed by recognition that the ostracization of the police would take time. The large funeral in May for Sergeant Peter Wallace, a Roscommon RIC man

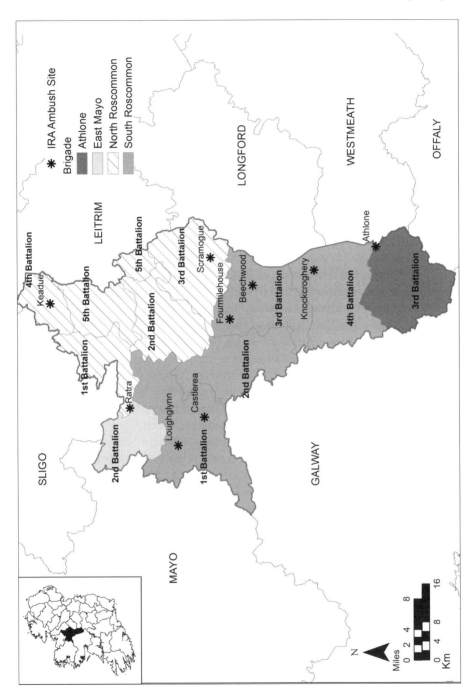

5 IRA Brigade areas and ambush sites in County Roscommon

killed by the IRA at Knocklong in Limerick, was proof that such men were still well respected.[14] However, DI Hetreed noted the effect that denunciations such as O'Flanagan's had on increasing 'the bad feeling towards the RIC'.[15] After the feis, Séamus Redican stoked animosities by posting signs around Boyle that read: 'Shoot the peelers'.[16]

SF in Roscommon were concerned at the decline in its members' activity since the formation of the Dáil, which had taken over many of the party's functions.[17] In June 1919, a North Roscommon executive meeting saw just eight out of thirty-six branches represented.[18] The *Weekly Freeman's Journal* made the turnout front page news, while the *Messenger* noted sardonically that there was 'a considerable amount of apathy [in] … the premier constituency'.[19] The *Democrat* was unable to leap to the defence of SF after the premature death of its editor Patrick Morahan but the *Herald* published the expected rebuke of the IPP press. However, Cootehall's Cumann na mBan also criticized SF. The number of active SF members had reduced markedly around Boyle according to the branch, which spearheaded the creation of the Cumann na mBan district council in Boyle.[20] Cumann na mBan's activity, even with opposition from the parents of younger women, contrasted sharply with that of SF.[21] The party hired an organizer, Michael McGrath, to combat the drift.[22] By August, with the help of Fr O'Flanagan, who was again based in Roscommon town, McGrath had achieved some success in overcoming the 'want of ardour'.[23]

Despite SF inactivity, anti-British sentiment grew when further repressive measures were introduced. In a move decried by the *Westmeath Independent* and *Herald*, DORA was used to tackle the press, one of the main promoters of the republic. Articles were monitored for sedition and the *Herald* was prevented from reporting comprehensively on the travails of the re-interned Séamus Redican.[24] Censorship could not limit the chagrin of the Crown forces in August when the expected coup of the capture of Micheál Ó Braonáin was undone. The RIC could not charge him due to the circumstantial nature of their evidence.[25] Seeing sedition around every corner, armed police attended the Pattern of Losser in Keadue on 7 September to observe Fr O'Flanagan.[26] Vigorous searches across Roscommon the following week coincided with the British proscription of Dáil Éireann.[27] Reports to IRA GHQ by both Roscommon brigades in late autumn 1919 referenced poor organization. Daniel O'Rorke, the reluctant OC of the South Roscommon Brigade, blamed ill-disciplined comrades and admitted that he needed to remain circumspect to retain his teaching job.[28] The IRA still engaged in raids, such as that on the house of Colonel Woodbrook near Ballintubber, and also sought to raise funds for the Dáil Éireann loan, a scheme of government bonds to fund the republic.[29] Patrick Hegarty's efforts to promote the scheme included a car chase, during which he and other republicans ran a gauntlet of RIC gunfire near Boyle. According to *The Globe*, the police took 'splinters out of the woodwork and wheels', but failed to stop the car.[30]

Cumann na mBan was also targeted by the Crown forces. Eithne Coyle, a Gaelic League instructor from Donegal who lived near Kilroosky, was targeted as the RIC correctly believed she was an IRA courier.[31] The Sharkey sisters' shop was revisited by the police. With the support of the *Irish Citizen*, the sisters claimed that the illegal raids had bankrupted them.[32] In a letter to the *Freeman's Journal*, they denied British claims that any injustice was righted. They were 'robbed' and whatever 'heterogeneous goods' they received back were sold by the receiver for a small fraction of their value.[33] Republican friends helped the sisters to reopen their Strokestown shop and by winter it once again had 'everything a Gael might need'.[34]

During November Dublin Castle suppressed political groups and moved to retrain and redeploy the RIC. SF, the Irish Volunteers, Cumann na mBan and the Gaelic League, as well as newspapers such as Arthur Griffith's *Nationality*, were all prohibited. The RIC in Roscommon were provided with training in the use of hand grenades at Lough Park.[35] Vulnerable rural RIC barracks, often little more than poorly fortified houses, at Ballinameen, Ballinderry, Culliagh, Cootehall, Castleplunkett and Cloonfad were closed (see map 4). The men were redeployed to Boyle, Keadue and Ballinlough.[36]

The Government of Ireland bill was introduced in December. It sought to split Ireland into two states. Lloyd George deliberately referenced Fr O'Flanagan's controversial June 1916 letter on partition when discussing the bill at Westminster.[37] The Roscommon press inveighed against the measure, which not only angered nationalists but also southern unionists, who predicted their impending abandonment by the British. The *Westmeath Independent* summarized that Lloyd George wanted to divide the nation, bleed its resources and ensure that 'England reigns supreme'.[38] Kilronan Protestant hall was burned in January in what some (albeit, not Judge Wakley who heard the case) framed as a sectarian response to the bill, which the CI related was highly unpopular.[39] Incensed by the measure, O'Flanagan trampled on a map of England during a visit to the convent school in Roscommon town.[40]

Denunciations were not limited to government legislation. In March 1920, the *Journal*, then owned and edited by John McDonnell, condemned the 'engines of repression… [that are] working more furiously than at any time in the past'.[41] Crown forces reported numerous 'fruitless' raids, acts of 'Prussianism' according to the *Messenger*, which implored people not to retaliate.[42] As part of the British strategy from January 1920 to ensure 'the troops could get directly involved', Colonel Commandant T.S. Lambert was posted to Athlone to spearhead the expansion of the British 5th Division into the west.[43] He was the region's Competent Military Authority (CMA), the officer given extraordinary powers under DORA to prosecute the war against republicans.[44]

The raids were intended to address the escalation in republican activities in Roscommon that saw Crown courts register a twofold increase in intimidation, mail theft and malicious injury in the twelve months to March 1920.[45] Additional RIC were also deployed, with some officers posted to Ballinagarde, where the judiciary who would hear the cases were accommodated.[46]

The propaganda war also intensified. The suffering of Séamus Redican, who joined 100 other republicans on hunger strike in Mountjoy in April, provided ample material. Redican had been interned for non-compliance with an order to leave Connacht and adjacent counties.[47] The prison authorities seized a letter intended for his mother, Anne, in Boyle, which described his isolation, poor health and possible martyrdom: 'Tom Ashe died; then why should I fear it if I die. You know who to avenge my death upon.' As punishment for the letter, the authorities illegally denied Redican visitations from his mother, who nevertheless attended the prison.[48] The *Irish Independent* published her emotive declaration while there that: 'because he loved Ireland better than your government, you are going to kill him'.[49] Soon after her public display, Crown forces ransacked her house in Boyle.

There was a nationwide strike to support the hunger-strikers. Driven by the ITGWU with Dáil Éireann and IRA support, the majority of the workforce in Roscommon joined the effective protest on 13 and 14 April 1920. Business owners who did not close were intimidated. Indeed, Methodist draper Robert Boles in Boyle was still being pressured in July when Count Plunkett intervened and an apology from Boles was published in the *Herald*.[50] In Castlerea, where the ITGWU was described as 'very strong', crowds with SF flags paraded under banners demanding the prisoners' release.[51] Crown forces spent the first day of the strike searching people and houses in Roscommon town. Their decision to target former members of the Connaught Rangers confirmed for one man that his war sacrifices were not worth a 'damn'.[52] The subsequent release of the hunger strikers on parole was deemed a significant republican victory.

Throughout the spring, the RIC were further marginalized. From February, when T.E. Gault-Gamble became CI, prospective RIC recruits were intimidated by republicans in Ballintubber, Kilteevan, Elphin and Strokestown.[53] Thomas Connor from Elphin was shot at and verbally abused, while in Strokestown, Pat Mannion was wounded in the leg to render him unfit for service.[54] Parents of likely recruits were targeted at Creevy, as were those of existing members near Roscommon town.[55] The *Journal* reported that two recruits 'failed to attend' for March examinations as a result of threats.[56] In the case of Hugh Cunniffe, the intimidation was persuasive. He left the RIC in April just seven days after joining, when Roscommon republicans targeted his father. Thirty-five other recruits resigned that month from across the country.[57] Work by Brian Hughes shows that the campaign to limit RIC enlistment was most effective in Roscommon, Leitrim and Cork, with sources proving that the intimidation in Roscommon continued until the truce in July 1921.[58]

The actions of the IRA at Easter 1920 further discouraged RIC recruitment and moved the war towards Townshend's second phase, which saw IRA GHQ become more central in directing activities. On the night of 3 April, Easter Saturday, as part of a nationwide offensive, police huts and barracks at Castleplunkett, Ballinameen, Ballinagare, Clogher, Bealnamulla, Carrowroe, Culliagh, Lecarrow, Cootehall and Croghan were destroyed. Apart from the last three, all were vacant. Croghan and Cootehall, though officially closed, were staffed by one sergeant each and Lecarrow was occupied by the sergeant's wife. The attacking parties, which numbered thirty at Croghan, sixty at Cootehall and twenty at Lecarrow, gave the occupants time to claim some belongings and leave.[59] Long-abandoned barracks at Gillstown and Rockfield were also burned, while, later in Easter week, so were the barracks at Athleague and Ballintubber.[60] Claims for compensation to the county council exceeded £9,000 by the third week in April.[61] The burnings contributed to Roscommon's republican activity being presented as the highest in the west and midlands (apart from Westmeath) in *An tÓglach*'s April 'War Map'.[62]

In response, the presence of the British army increased markedly. Municipal buildings in Roscommon town accommodated fifty members of the East Yorkshire Regiment and large houses were sought to billet more men.[63] Consequently, on 4 and 5 May, the IRA burned Runnamote House, the erstwhile home of Major Chichester Constable, and Southpark House, former residence of Major Balfe.[64] Some new Crown forces sought to take advantage of further destruction of barracks in May by setting a trap at Beechwood.[65] The IRA waited until July to burn it, along with the barracks in Tulsk. As map 4 indicates, rural RIC barracks were virtually absent in mid-Roscommon by autumn 1920.[66]

Inland Revenue offices were also targeted at Easter, but Roscommon republicans waited until 12 May. A gun-wielding William Black, Roscommon town's tax collector, was disarmed by three undisguised men, who were scrupulous in solely destroying income tax records.[67] The raid provided good intelligence on who continued to support the Crown institutions. Tax collectors H.J. Walker in Athlone, Patrick O'Hara of Cootehall and his colleague John McDermott were also targeted, with McDermott persuaded to cooperate when a friend was taken hostage.[68]

Spring 1920 saw the most pervasive land agitation since 1882. The absence of land purchase, poor weather and a reduced Crown forces presence in rural areas fuelled the unrest, which was most serious in Roscommon, Mayo and Galway.[69] Local initiative forced the pace, with cattle drives in Roscommon involving men, women, small boys and girls. Young men dominated, however, in part due to the fact that the lifting of emigration restrictions was by then too recent to have reduced their number. Sectarianism was not a primary motivation, although the disproportionate share of Roscommon farmland in Protestant ownership ensured many of that denomination were targeted.[70] Some, such as the Walpoles in Castlenode who were first targeted in January, tackled republican overtures head-on, opening fire alongside the RIC on a group of local men.[71] Intended to secure farmlands across south Roscommon, detachments of military left Athlone, the location of the new RIC divisional commissioner for Connacht and a depot for a new Crown forces body, the Black and Tans.[72] The *Journal* had no sympathy for large landowners. It noted that in areas like Ballynaheglish the agitation served republican and labour ends, as well as broader national and moral aims:

> The Irish Irelanders of Ballynaheglish have been industriously engaged … in clearing the way in a practical manner … to have the small farm-ers, the much-neglected labourer and the young men fixed … in the hundreds of acres of untenanted land so long devoted to the raising of the bullocks … of a … greedy crew of grass jobbers.[73]

In April and May, massive drives were staged from Athlone to Ballintubber and from Elphin to Ballaghaderreen. One at Creggs reportedly involved 1,800 people, who encountered bayonet-wielding Crown forces.[74] Allegations spread of Roscommon landholders being forced to walk naked; being beaten; having threats issued against their businesses or having graves dug on their lands. In one instance, it was reported that an uncooperative landowner was partially buried alive.[75] The threats appear to have remained just that, however. In Galway, at least four men were killed in order to induce cooperation.[76] The intimidation motif was downplayed by the *Democrat*, whereas the *Westmeath Independent* warned triumphant drivers who drove Roscommon cattle into Athlone that the army was willing to use their Lewis gun. Driving was, McDermott-Hayes wrote, 'no longer the exhilarating exercise it [once] was'.[77]

CDB properties were also the focus of attention. Ross House, near Tulsk, was burned in March, while from April, small farmers placed stock illegally on CDB lands.[78] The board's stockmasters were raided for books and brand-ing irons, with one man so frightened that he resigned.[79] Warning notices pro-moted a boycott: 'No grazing for the C.D. Board' – signed 'Rory of the Hills'.[80] The British army removed stock on CDB land at Kilmurray, near Castlerea, Castleplunkett, Killarney, Moyglass, Tulsk and Elphin, often engaging in reciprocal drives with republicans.[81] At Kilmurray, Crown forces eventually impounded 1,100 cattle and threatened to sell them unless fines were paid. The fees were forthcoming for the majority. A threat to set up two more pounds led the army to claim that the issue on CDB lands was resolved.

The RIC did not agree.[82] An unnamed Roscommon solicitor wrote to the *Irish Independent* to condemn the 'naked policy of militarism'. The problem was the CDB, not the unrest.[83]

Some landowners sought increased security. In May, the *Democrat* fuelled antagonism by reporting that certain Roscommon worthies had petitioned the military to send more troops.[84] The arrival in April of the 1st Royal Dragoons to the Pakenham-Mahon estate, near Strokestown, and in May, 200 9th Queen's Royal Lancers to Castlerea's Wills-Sandford estate seemed to prove this. The Royal Dragoons assisted the Walpoles, who had lost most of their workers after sustained IRA intimidation.[85] The deployments, which also saw additional troops in Roscommon town and Mount Talbot, were actually part of increases across Roscommon, Galway and Leitrim.[86] The *Freeman's Journal* editorialized that, although officially present 'to put down agrarian troubles', the soldiers were deployed 'to prevent a friendly settlement by agreement'.[87] The increasingly limited protection of the Crown courts in the case of arrests was further undermined by summons servers, such as Castlerea's John Conroy, being shot at and threatened.[88] The IG's report for August concluded that the reinforcements in Roscommon were too few and too late. There was 'bitter feeling towards government on the part of those who had looked to it for protection and assistance'.[89]

As reports of violence increased, the republic appeared relegated in importance. Daniel O'Rorke advised GHQ that some of his men took part, but 'as members of the community'. Reports of IRA involvement were 'manifestly false' and fabricated by landowners to malign republicanism. GHQ, which like SF regarded the land agitation as a growing threat to the republic, assured O'Rorke that it did not think 'the Volunteer force in Roscommon had run wild'.[90] The agitation needed to be controlled and, in May, the Roscommon SF executives moved to do so. They organized the first of three conferences (others were held in Galway and Dublin) to address the agitation. The Roscommon instalment saw a five-point directive devised.[91] First, SF had to lead the land agitation. Second, land issues had to be referred to a SF council for Roscommon land disputes. Third, a 'supreme commission' would make a binding decision. Fourth, the CBD would be directed to release untenanted land for fair rent. The final, contentious provision was that targeted farms had to be greater than 500 acres.[92] This framework, the first quasi-legal process for the matter, led an angry *Belfast News Letter* to suggest that the Roscommon 'Sinn Fein Presumption' made it seem as if 'the rebel organization ... alone has the right to govern'.[93]

That the directive was not widely welcomed suggested localism and socio-economic concerns trumped republicanism. In many areas, smaller farms were still targeted. After a meeting in Roscommon town, Fr O'Flanagan asserted that many did not 'understand the fundamental principle of the [SF] movement'.[94]

His disappointment was likely amplified after the death of Peter Kelly, a casualty of a dispute over a 'miserable few acres' at Aughagad, near Creggs on 23 May.[95] Graham Sennett, a Protestant Roscommon auctioneer, counselled Dáil Éireann to handle contentious cases appropriately, for then: 'Every man ... will stand by Sinn Féin and by the Republic, if we can prove that we can restore order and do justice where England could do neither, with all her tin hats.'[96] The Dáil issued protective notices to Roscommon landowners who cooperated with the republican courts. The IRA enforced the notices, while the clergy promoted the courts as the most suitable place to resolve the land issue.

Throughout the land campaign, the IRA sought weapons. A raid for arms was ordered by GHQ in May and many effortless gun seizures occurred across Roscommon. Indeed, Frank Simons and James Quigley used the same phrase in their statements to the BMH: 'it was only a matter of calling for them'.[97] Even when resistance was encountered, for example with John Beades at Rahara, it was reported that cordial negotiations led to guns being willingly handed over.[98] To prevent arms being captured by the IRA in June, the Crown forces seized sixty-four legally-held shotguns in Boyle, Strokestown and Elphin.[99] While the RIC believed republicans to be 'well supplied with revolvers', good shotguns were scarce and rifles scarcer still.[100] In June 1920 only two Lee-Enfield rifles could be bought out of republican funds in Roscommon.[101] Despite the risk of entrapment, republicans like Michael Ward purchased guns from ill-disciplined soldiers.[102] The theft of weapons from both serving and former members of the Crown forces was also fruitful. Surprisingly, purloined weapons were sometimes used to generate funds. Two separate raffles in Boyle and Ballyfarnon offered the prize of a RIC revolver and, curiously, a much sought-after rifle.[103]

Some RIC members' intolerance of police activity in Roscommon increased during July. This was in part due to the shooting in Elphin of James Hayden and George Tanner by an RIC constable believed to be drunk.[104] The *Journal* reported that a policeman named McGurk resigned after the shooting and that a second, Constable Keating, also left Elphin barracks.[105] The Elphin officers joined 250 other RIC men across Ireland who had resigned since the start of June; total resignations across Ireland for 1920 was about 1,600.[106] The resignations were welcomed by Richard Mulcahy, IRA chief of staff, who, soon after the Elphin shooting, received confirmation from Athlone that further resignations were likely if jobs were guaranteed for those leaving.[107] By September, Dáil Éireann agreed to offer policemen the inducement of a local authority job. Roscommon County Council wanted the men vetted by SF; jobs could not be given to men who went around 'shooting people' and then resigned.[108] RIC friendly with the IRA, such as John Duffy (posted variously at Athlone, Kiltoom and Roscommon town during 1920), were frequently asked to remain on so that they could provide intelligence to republicans, who often struggled with this aspect of the campaign.[109] The anticipated shortfall in Roscommon RIC numbers did not materialize. New members, including two female officers who were tasked with searching members of Cumann na mBan, more than compensated.[110]

The Elphin incident strengthened the boycott against the Crown forces. From mid-July, republicans directed traders in Beechwood, Strokestown, Castlerea, Roscommon town and Boyle to shun the police.[111] A boycott list was compiled of traders who were uncooperative. Often, the IRA acted. Two Ballaghaderreen merchants had their houses burned in July, while in Boyle and Strokestown, merchants were intimidated and denied access to fairs.[112] By August, the RIC reported that the boycott in Boyle 'was being rigorously carried out', with news of courts martial for five local Connaught Rangers as a result of the Indian Mutiny further souring relations. One, Ballymoe-born James Daly, was executed in November.[113] When the Boyle YMCA barred serving RIC members from entering, it was reported that police 'morale … is being seriously affected'. It was claimed, however, that in Boyle (and in contravention of the GHQ directive), the IRA allowed merchants to supply RIC dependants.[114] South Roscommon boycott notices also left room for interpretation:

> Notice is hereby given that all intercourse of any kind whatsoever is strictly forbidden between citizens of the Irish Republic and that portion of the army of occupation known as the R.I.C., that a general boycott of said force is ordered, and that you will cease to transact business of any sort with said force. Any person infringing this order will be included in said boycott
> – By Order Adjutant, South Roscommon Brigade.[115]

At Strokestown, Boyle and Castlerea, traders alleged that the RIC commandeered supplies but republicans were unconvinced.[116] Thomas Crawley believed that some traders, especially publicans, were taking RIC money and fabricating stories.[117] Roscommon town was considered the weakest town for implementing the boycott, with a simple RIC threat against pub licences seeing police and soldiers readmitted to the town's bars.[118] Some IRA thought the boycott ill-judged. Martin Fallon believed it 'antagonized some [RIC] … who would be good friends'.[119]

The social boycott also faced compliance issues, especially when it came to personal relationships. One Keadue man who met police socially was made parade blindfolded outside a dance in the village.[120] When Kate Loughnane of Clonfad, Ballinasloe refused to end her engagement to a policeman, the IRA threatened to shave her hair off. This was the most common punishment meted out to such women but it did not shake Loughnane, who demanded they 'cut it nicely'![121] Cumann na mBan provided intelligence on such relationships. Mary Madden indicated that these dalliances were prone to exploitation by Crown forces: 'These girls had the lives of many young men in their hands.'[122] The Roscommon IRA and GHQ were unsure about how to deal with these women. In south Roscommon in 1921, protracted indecision led to a situation where one woman's proclivity for discussing the movement of suspected IRA men with Crown forces, 'almost wiped out the brigade council'.[123] Crown forces did what they could to undermine the social boycott by targeting known organizers. William Doherty, Elphin IRA battalion commandant, was arrested on what his Strokestown RDC colleagues regarded as a 'frivolous charge', while Eithne Coyle's house was burned down.[124]

The marginalization of the RIC affected officers across the ranks. DI Hetreed, who wrote most of the Roscommon CI reports in 1920, blamed the press for promoting the ostracization. CI Gault-Gamble had stepped away from his duties in the summer of 1920 because his mental health deteriorated when the boycott intensified. At a later bankruptcy hearing, he testified that in Roscommon he had 'a terrible time of it ... I got nearly out of my mind'.[125] Undoubtedly, the stress that men like Gault-Gamble operated under was intense. RIC suicide rates in 1920, already six times that of the civil population, more than doubled in 1921.[126] Some reports claimed that Constable George Southgate took his own life in Ballaghaderreen barracks in June 1921 as a result of the pressure of the war. Officially his death was deemed accidental.[127] The death of the Auxiliary Division RIC officer known as 'One Arm' Morrison of Bangor, County Down, was undoubtedly a suicide. He was sent to Dublin from Roscommon when it became apparent that his experiences in the county in 1920 'had affected his mind'. He drowned himself in the River Liffey in August 1921.[128]

The boycott paralleled a railway strike that started in May at Dublin's dockyards. Workers refused to handle army munitions or drive trains that carried armed military. The strike spread across the country and saw stand-offs between railway staff and soldiers. In Roscommon, significant tension was seen at Athlone and Castlerea, the latter town becoming the terminus of the westbound line in June.[129] Eventually, the Midland Great Western Railway at Athlone cancelled passenger services and fired striking staff.[130] The uncertainty led many people to stockpile goods, while the delivery of newspapers and mail, both to and from Roscommon, became intermittent.[131] IRA raids on the railway services that did operate, most frequent around Ballymoe and at Kilfree junction near Ballaghaderreen, added to the disruption. The British military increased their use of courier pigeons and airplanes to deliver mail to the barracks in Athlone and Boyle, methods that continued after the strike ended in December.[132]

Until July 1920, and in line with most neighbouring counties, the Roscommon IRA had prosecuted the war using non-fatal intimidation.[133]

Thereafter, the county followed the pattern of the mid- and south-west in inflicting fatalities on the Crown forces. The first death in this new phase occurred on 11 July, when the IRA killed RIC Constable Martin Clarke near Beechwood. His death started a trend that led Roscommon to become Connacht's most violent and Ireland's seventh-most violent county during the War of Independence. Only aberrant Longford and the counties of the mid- and south-west outperformed it.[134] According to the *Herald*, Clarke was 'riddled with bullets' as he travelled from Lanesboro to Roscommon town. His colleague, P.J. Macken, was injured but managed to return to Lanesboro, unaware that a fellow police officer had assisted the IRA.[135] Three of the IRA men involved, Luke Duffy, Frank Simons and Gerald Davis, provided differing accounts of the ambush to the BMH. All referred to poor planning but only Davis asserted that Clarke's death was deliberate and this suggests that the South Roscommon IRA were still averse to fatal violence.[136] At Clarke's funeral, Fr Kielty 'alluded to the horrible work' that policemen faced, work 'the force was never intended for'.[137] The *Herald* noted that his death inspired a 'blue funk' in some RIC and 'a red rage' in others.[138] One example of that rage was the threat to hang Darrell Figgis when Crown forces raided a joint Roscommon/Leitrim meeting at Carrick-on-Shannon of the Dáil commission of enquiry into the resources and industries of Ireland.[139]

The Crown forces increased their use of repressive measures when the Restoration of Order in Ireland Act (ROIA) was passed on 9 August. The act allowed for greater coercion than DORA and provided for the broader imposition of measures such as curfews, courts martial and military inquiries into civilian deaths. As a riposte to the complaints of the *Journal* that the act gave the Crown forces the 'power of life and death over Irish civilians', the RIC ransacked its offices.[140] ROIA just post-dated the deployment of Black and Tans in Roscommon, the force which the British government hoped would take the fight to the IRA. The methods for which they became notorious were introduced first in Roscommon at Castlerea. Eight men in 'waterproof coats and ... slouched hats' beat three locals who had promoted the RIC boycott.[141] Requests for an inquiry into the assault were dismissed by Hamar Greenwood, chief secretary for Ireland, as little more than 'SF propaganda'.[142] In Boyle, two groups, one a circumspect body called 'The All-Ireland Anti-Sinn Féin Society', the other a less cautious collective styling itself the 'Black Hand Gang', intimidated republicans.[143] The latter erected notices and served missives on merchants, such as republican court adjudicator, P.J. Delahunty:

> You were warned before to prepare for death, but considering your
> wife and helpless family, we have decided to give you a chance ... if
> the boycott is not off by 12th inst., your end will be sure ... injury to
> the police or their friends will be revenged ten-fold.[144]

Rural areas near Boyle were also targeted. The press reported that at Ballinlough 'residents are pulled out of their beds … and threatened to be shot for being Sinn Féiners'.[145] James Feely was beaten and forced to swear he would leave Ireland after ending the boycott. His knowledge of the area saved him when he made a dash for freedom.[146] The Black and Tans shot pets and livestock, shaved people's heads and destroyed farm infrastructure. The *Herald* excoriated Boyle's DI Kearney for claiming that his men were not involved. The newspaper asserted that the DI had been given the name of a certain participant, one of a number of Boyle RIC 'blackguards … capable of doing it'.[147] To highlight the indiscriminate nature of the attacks, the *Herald* printed a letter from Protestant, Henry B. Sampey, who praised the 'Irish Republic' for protecting him and his (much sought after) property at Ballinlough.[148]

The intimidation was too much for some traders, who discontinued the boycott of Crown forces. At Castlerea, many traders did so without consulting the IRA, which was doubly aggrieved at the weak local implementation of the Belfast boycott.[149] Intended to disallow commercial access to Belfast goods and traders, the boycott was implemented in Strokestown and Athleague from September but Castlerea traders persisted with selling stock on hand from Belfast companies and proposed that northern cattle dealers be exempted.[150] The shortage of Belfast provisions did little to help those already discommoded by the railway strike and, as ever, support for the republic was key to both implementation and enforcement.

IRA violence in Roscommon increased from late August in response to the activity of the Black and Tans. The first Crown forces fatality since Beechwood was Sergeant Thomas Craddock, who was hated by the Athlone Brigade IRA for his bully-boy tactics. He was shot just yards from his barracks in Athlone on 22 August. Four days later, Constable William Potter was shot dead near the railway crossing at Knockcroghery.[151] His companion, Constable Michael McMahon, escaped but resigned soon afterward. At a compensation hearing into Potter's death, Judge Wakely damned republicans for 'murdering their own countrymen and ruining their own country.'[152] Potter's death led Kiltoom barracks to be abandoned. By January 1921, the number of RIC stations in Roscommon had fallen by more than half.[153] The deaths of Craddock and Potter marked the entry into the third phase of the war identified by Townshend. This was characterized by increased IRA violence and escalating, often indiscriminate, reprisals by the Crown forces.

Following Potter's death, the Black and Tans warned traders in Ballaghaderreen that 'If the boycotting of the police is not ended … within three days, the place will be burned.'[154] Any relief that locals felt when the three days passed without violence was undone on 1 September when RIC constables Edward Murphy and Martin McCarthy were ambushed and killed by

the IRA at Ratra, near Frenchpark. Thomas McDonagh, of Cloonloo, Boyle, a
captain in the IRA, also died.[155] The carefully planned attack was carried out
by the South Sligo Brigade IRA whose members entered the North
Roscommon Brigade area for the operation, one of the many cases across the
country where an IRA brigade conducted an engagement outside of its own
brigade area.[156] Black and Tans departed Ballaghaderreen for Ratra as soon as
news of the ambush broke. They returned with McDonagh's body and dis-
played it in the town square before ransacking ten business premises, including Flannery's store, which they burned down.[157] The damage totalled
£100,000. The owners of Flannery's placed a front-page advertisement in the
Freeman's Journal to confirm that their store was 'maliciously destroyed', while
Patrick Morrisroe, Catholic bishop of Achonry, wrote of the 'terror' induced in
the townspeople.[158] Questions were raised regarding the absence of a defensive
response from the East Mayo IRA Brigade which had, apparently, been ordered
not to intervene.[159] In any case, they were too poorly armed and trained to do
so. When the Ballaghaderreen republican court and the police boycott lapsed
in the weeks that followed, the Black and Tans departed.[160] However, the for-
tification of the RIC station with guns, barbed wire and blockades underlined
the continued state of tension.[161]

Just over a week after the Ballaghaderreen conflagration, military reorganization provided an opportunity for the Crown forces to retry the tactic of
ambushing the IRA at an abandoned barracks. Ballinlough and Loughglynn
barracks were closed, the former by the 9th Lancers, who secreted a detach-
ment under Lieutenant R.H. Allfrey nearby.[162] On the night of 13 September,
an IRA party intent on burning the building was ambushed. Three IRA were
killed: Captain Michael Glavey, a 38-year-old tailor, Lieutenant Michael
James Keane, a 23-year-old farmer, and Pat Glynn, the Loughglynn IRA battalion OC, who proceeded with the operation despite being warned of the
possible ambush.[163] Volunteer James Wallace was injured and subsequently
lost a leg.[164] The Crown forces were unscathed and Allfrey was awarded a
'parchment certificate' for his leadership.[165] Some 1,200 attended Glynn's
funeral at Loughglynn, where Daniel O'Rorke lauded his sacrifice.[166]

The violence caused the Roscommon gentry much concern. Sir Thomas
Stafford, a 'friend' of John French and advocate of dominion home rule,
resigned his position on the Advisory Council in protest.[167] Similarly
aggrieved, The O'Conor Don warned that government tactics were pushing
people toward the republic. Presumably, this was not anathema to him, given
that he believed that 'the Sinn Féiners are … an intelligent body … [who]
want a prosperous and happy Ireland'.[168] After efforts to organize anti-vio-
lence meetings failed, The O'Conor Don resigned his official positions and,
by October, was referring to himself as a 'moderate Sinn Féiner'.[169] Major
T.C.E. Goff's despair at his increasingly vulnerable position given not only

the violence, but the partition of the country, led him to sell his Carrowroe estate in September and end his family's 116-year association with the region. He departed for Britain.[170] Speaking at the Keadue feis at the end of that month, Fr O'Flanagan was clear. Measured republican violence was necessary: 'O'Connell repudiated physical force altogether. He made his mistake'.[171]

The three IRA deaths at Ballinlough led the South Roscommon IRA to attack the RIC barracks at Frenchpark on 2 October. The operation was led by Daniel O'Rorke, who ordered his men to seize buildings near the barracks and destroy Kilcorkery bridge to delay the arrival of Crown forces reinforcements. After an ineffective two-hour siege, the IRA abandoned the operation. Sergeant Goff, who led the RIC defence, recognized some of the IRA men involved.[172] Reprisals followed that night at Ballinagare and O'Rorke's home area of Tarmon.

In Hugh Martin's contemporaneous *Insurrection in Ireland: an Englishman's record of fact*, Ballinagare residents recounted indiscriminate reprisals.[173] Crown forces burned buildings and crops, killed livestock and stole provisions, all while roughly interrogating locals. Crown forces from Castlerea, nicknamed 'The Murder Gang', operated under Constable Moran who was known for heavy-handedness. Bombs were used to damage some buildings and the front pages of several British newspapers reported 'burning and pillage'. Their source, probably Martin, described the acts as disproportionate given what had happened at Frenchpark.[174] Again, the absence of IRA engagement was queried. One witness claimed that the attackers promised a slaughter if the IRA intervened.

While the proximate reason for the reprisal was the Frenchpark incident, lingering ill-feeling caused by the RIC boycott was key. Mary Crean of Ballinagare was disciplined by the IRA for selling milk to the Frenchpark RIC. In what the *Illustrated Police News* described as 'a new form of frightfulness', three pig rings were clamped to her buttocks on 7 August.[175] The IRA's John Haran remembered having 'no sorrow for her' given Crean's recalcitrance. The IRA men involved in the assault were deported by a republican court.[176] The British used the incident to justify their policies. Earl Curzon described the assault in visceral terms:

> Two … seized Mrs. Crean by the hands and feet, another put his hand over her mouth and the fourth fastened three pig rings … into the unfortunate woman's body … The object … was to terrorize the neighbourhood into boycotting the police.[177]

After leaving Ballinagare, the Black and Tans targeted O'Rorke. Providing strong opinions on republicanism, one Irish member at O'Rorke's house detailed the 'wickedness of Sinn Fein' before helping destroy the building.

Patrick Flynn, adjutant of the South Roscommon Brigade, was the next target. He was forced to his knees and, believing incorrectly that he was to be shot, asked for a priest. He was told: 'You're not going to have any damned priest. The priests are worse than you are and we are going to clear them out next.'[178]

Intimidation by the Crown forces spread. Roscommon town, Strokestown, Castlerea, Ballymoe and Ballintubber were all targeted, as was Drum near Athlone, where 'harrowing accounts' were heard of locals being forced at gunpoint to declare loyalty to the British monarchy.[179] Parents were taken to pressurize 'on the run' sons; the arrest of 70-year-old Michael Kearns on this pretence angering another son, a serving RIC officer, who resigned in protest.[180] The *Freeman's Journal* editorialized despairingly about the 'violence and viciousness' in Roscommon, while the Strokestown parish priest, Dean Roderick Geaty, condemned the obvious official instruction behind Crown forces supposedly unofficial 'outbursts'. He called for no retaliation after a visit from Captain Sir R.G. Peek, commanding the 9th Lancers, made clear the consequences.[181] Peek, a 'perfect gentleman', promised that his men would burn the homes of those suspected of being in the IRA.[182]

The intelligence that might have led Peek to the doors of such men was of concern to the IRA, which had already taken steps to root out Strokestown informers. Four weeks prior to Peek's visit with the dean, the IRA gave one resident the option of leaving immediately or being shot. He left.[183] Republicans moved to engage more robustly with suspected informers and by the end of 1920, three men had been kidnapped and killed by the Roscommon IRA. The first was Edward Canning, a Catholic ex-soldier whom Frank Simons, without providing much detail, confirmed was executed as a spy during the first week of November.[184] Bernard Ward was taken three weeks later. The 'habitual visitor to the police barracks in Roscommon' was drowned, his guilt inferred rather than proven. He was, however, deemed to be a 'British liability' by the Compensation Commission that sat to consider claims from the relatives of those who died in such circumstances.[185] Catholic ex-soldier, Martin Heavey, joined Ward on that list after his entire family was kidnapped at Bealnamulla near Athlone in December. The IRA executed Heavey, releasing his wife and children after 'taking them all over the country', a press exaggeration that related to moving them across Lough Ree, where Heavey's body was dumped.[186] All three men were still listed as missing the following August and their bodies were never found.[187] The three deaths were the first in a series that peaked in the spring of 1921 and led Roscommon to register more deaths of suspected informers that any other county in Connacht. Galway recorded just three, Leitrim two, Sligo one, and Mayo none at all. Only Dublin and Cork outnumbered Roscommon, with thirteen and a massive seventy-eight, respectively.[188]

The South Roscommon IRA reacted to Peek's threat by staging an ambush on Crown forces from Strokestown at Fourmilehouse on 12 October.[189] Undertaken by the Kilgefin and Kilbride companies of the 3rd Battalion under Pat Madden, the ambush targeted a lorry carrying some of those who had sacked Ballaghaderreen.[190] A donkey and cart was used to impede the truck and give the IRA time to open fire. The driver of the lorry, Galway man Constable Joyce, was one of only two uninjured when it returned to Strokestown. Constables Michael Kenny and John Crawford were killed; Constable Francis Gallagher, a 26-year-old Catholic recruit to the Black and Tans from Donegal, and Sergeant O'Connor died of their wounds. Constable O'Rahilly received non-fatal injuries.[191] Luke Duffy, one of the IRA men present, claimed that about thirty-five IRA volunteers were involved. Frank Simons recalled that the ambush was all the more impressive given that the IRA had just eight rifles. When reported to GHQ, the numbers involved were inflated by a factor of two, while some press reports doubled that figure, suggesting an intimidating 150 IRA men involved in the county's deadliest operation in 1920.[192]

Press articles both humanized and maligned the dead. A letter from Gallagher's father to Dean Geaty described the constable as 'a kind, good natured boy', who, before he died, forgave his killers and requested that reprisals did not involve innocents.[193] The *Herald* counterbalanced this by reporting that Gallagher had gained a reputation for pointing his gun at people in Ballaghaderreen, including Bishop Morrisroe and John Dillon.[194] After the military court of inquiry at Strokestown, Crown forces and supporters marched with banners: 'Sinn Feiners. Shame on you!'; 'Murdered by Irish savages.'[195] Canon Cummins expressed his sorrow at the deaths and thanked Peek for showing restraint in the aftermath. Strokestown's Reverend Hurley made the uncommon decision to censure the IRA for the 'murders'.[196] Whatever about Peek, the deployment of E Company, Auxiliary Division RIC in Boyle brought a change in approach. Auxiliary companies were highly mobile and deployed in the most disturbed areas. Their strategy in Roscommon was, as elsewhere, brutal.

Extreme personal intimidation was a favoured tactic. From mid-October, a three-week search for James Ansboro at Fuerty saw Auxiliaries repeatedly beat his 'f***ing Sinn Féiner' brother, William. On one occasion, the attack was so fierce that Ansboro reportedly begged to be shot.[197] Individuals at Rooskey, Tulsk and Arigna suffered beatings, head shavings, thefts and arson. At Arigna all of the miners were lined up for rough interrogation.[198] The Auxiliaries commandeered cars in Elphin, and demanded that the owner account for their location during the Fourmilehouse ambush.[199] At Kilteevan, Eithne Coyle's new home was ransacked. Coyle was resolute, however, and disclosed nothing of what she knew about the ambush.[200] Roscommon town was subjected to ten days of 'terror' in late October during which men were taken to Carrowroe Park where they were beaten, whipped and forced to issue 'purely voluntary' statements disowning SF and swearing allegiance to the King.[201]

Most alarming was the use of summary execution. At Ballinagare on 18 October, 33-year-old Patrick Doyle was shot dead.[202] Hamar Greenwood dismissed Doyle's death with what became a default response in such cases: Doyle was shot by a 'person or persons unknown', the military court of enquiry 'contains no charge or imputation against the forces of the Crown'.[203] The *Herald* condemned Greenwood, who 'played up to the part of a terracotta Cromwell' by defending such activity.[204] Auxiliaries killed the IRA's John (Jack) Conry near Fourmilehouse two weeks later.[205] He was robbed, 'stripped ... and shot through the head and heart'. Efforts to blame the IRA failed, as even the RIC admitted that there was no evidence that the 'extreme Sinn Feiner' was an informer.[206] Similarly, on 15 December when John James McGowan, an IRA captain, was killed near Frenchpark as a reprisal for the Ratra ambush, the CI imputed, without offering evidence, that McGowan was killed by the IRA as a spy.[207]

Statements to the BMH imply that the arrival of the Auxiliaries and an order from GHQ led to the creation of active service units (ASUs) – or flying columns – in Roscommon, a full-time mobile force of between fifteen and twenty IRA men 'on the run'.[208] Supported by members of Cumann na mBan and people in rural areas, the men set up makeshift camps, such as that of the South Roscommon Brigade on Slieve Bán.[209] ASUs promoted greater camaraderie among the IRA members involved and were intended to act as independent, mobile units that could engage Crown forces in short, sharp attacks, or assist brigades in doing so. Yet, by the time they were formed in Roscommon, Ernie O'Malley, an unpopular figure given what local men deemed to be an attitude of superiority, described how the tactics of the Crown forces had unnerved higher-ranking IRA men like James Ryan, who appeared unwilling to engage the enemy.[210] GHQ deployed Seán Connolly, an organizer with the Longford IRA, to assist in motivating the IRA in his native county. He formed a fifth battalion in the north-east of Roscommon and set up a bomb factory at Ballinameen. He also met with the senior IRA officers to plan IRA operations that would address the actions of the Crown forces.[211] IRA man Seán Leavy was impressed by Connolly's efforts to 'generally buck up the area'; there was greater organization, confidence and morale.[212]

IRA success relied in large part on convincing the wider Irish population of the perfidy of British rule. The death on hunger strike of Terence MacSwiney, the Cork lord mayor, on 25 October was influential. This was not only because of how he died but because of the British government's response to his funeral. Roscommon newspapers blackened their columns as a sign of respect but were directed by the Crown forces to print a notice

warning businesses to close on the day of MacSwiney's funeral, not in honour
of the republican martyr, but for those killed at Fourmilehouse.[213] On that
day, Crown forces in Boyle, Castlerea, Ballymoe and Ballaghaderreen forced
open shops that closed as a mark of respect to MacSwiney. In Boyle, they
beat IRA men who attempted to re-close premises.[214] The CI's assertion that
MacSwiney's death 'evoked no excitement or disorder' was not credible, especially since Greenwood received reports that, during the funeral, 'a state of
alarm existed … between Ballinasloe and Athlone … with shots fired, men
beaten and homes destroyed'.[215] Printers, including Frank Shouldice in
Ballaghaderreen, were raided for commemorative materials, while the
Westmeath Independent ceased production until February 1922 after the Crown
forces burned its printing works on 3 November.[216] Attacks on properties
peaked that month, as SF meeting halls at Kilglass and Kilmore were
destroyed, as well as the Carnadoe creamery.[217] Attacking the creamery struck
a blow at a community resource that had been championed by Fr O'Flanagan,
supported by SF and relied on by the IRA.

Controversially, the Crown forces also imprisoned two priests. At a
MacSwiney commemoration meeting of the SF North Roscommon executive
at Croghan were Drumlion curate, Fr Glynn, and his Breedogue counterpart,
Fr Roddy, arrested alongside eleven others.[218] The curates joined Fr
O'Flanagan, who had been arrested on a frivolous motor permit charge the
same month, as the only clerical arrestees in Roscommon and among the forty-
three arrested nationally during the War of Independence.[219] Visited in prison
by Bishop Coyne, the treatment of the 'universally loved and respected' men
was deemed doubly despicable by the *Herald*.[220] The IG disagreed. Their
arrest was sensible, as it 'made people believe the Government is more deter-
mined'; if priests were not safe, nobody was.[221] The curates were held for nine
weeks, a period that partly coincided with the *Herald* pulling production when
malicious damage and the railway strike led lines in the county to lie idle.[222]
The priests' courts martial in Boyle was well reported when publication
recommenced. Both were released along with three co-defendants.[223] Their
persecution led more clerics to promote anti-British feeling, which intensified
following the killing of Fr Michael Griffin in Galway shortly after the
Roscommon arrests. The sense of increased clerical vulnerability led Fr
O'Flanagan to wear a gun for a time after a November raid on his room in
Roscommon town. He believed that the Auxiliaries sought to shoot him.[224]

In late November, the Auxiliaries declared they had 'killed Sinn Féin in
Roscommon'.[225] The CI agreed; republican activity was low and the RIC boycott had 'almost died out'.[226] Republicans were undoubtedly shaken, as were
civilians. Séamus Redican's efforts to attack the Crown forces in Boyle failed,
as he was 'hunted … away' by locals who had only to look as far as the
town's workhouse to see an Auxiliary Division RIC force primed to retali-

ate.[227] The IRA continued to confront the Crown forces at Elphin, Tarmonbarry, Castlenode, Clonark, Strokestown and St John's, and even deployed mines at Emlagh, but the actions were much smaller in scale and in no case were fatalities registered.[228] The only death that did occur highlighted a tactical change, whereby an individual RIC officer was targeted. Constable Michael Dennehy was kidnapped and killed near Rooskey on 24 November. Dennehy's father was later told that his son 'was arrested on a charge of espionage, court-martialled by a duly authorized authority, found guilty and executed'.[229] Daniel O'Rorke led the operation, which forced him to abandon his teaching post and go on the run.[230] Related investigations led to the imprisonment of ASU members, Peter (Pat) Farrell and Frank (Dan) Madden, captured on Sliabh Bán when Crown forces scaled the hill from three sides.[231]

The Crown forces also arrested some of their own. Five 'English Constables', Auxiliary Division RIC, were found guilty of robbing Strokestown's Northern Banking Company branch in late December. One of a number of larcenies by members of the Crown forces in the town over Christmas, the incident highlighted not only indiscipline, but Hamar Greenwood's dishonesty. Alfred Newbould MP accused Greenwood of misleading the Commons on the issue when he asserted 'there was not a tittle of evidence against the Forces of the Crown when their implication has been notorious'.[232] Some attempted to take advantage of the indiscipline for self-enrichment. Isabelle Clarke of Roscommon town claimed that the Crown forces robbed £1,000 worth of dresses before burning her premises. It emerged that the dresses never existed and that Clarke's servant girl had burned the shop at her employer's behest.[233] The growing number of prisoners, some referred from re-emerging Crown court sessions, outstripped the capacities of the barracks at Roscommon and Boyle. Victoria Barracks in Athlone was invariably the destination for Roscommon detainees. Those who posed a greater threat were sent from there to Mountjoy or Ballykinlar camp in County Down, while some who were more resourceful escaped.[234]

There was brighter news in late 1920. Jasper Tully was uncharacteristically hopeful about efforts undertaken by Fr O'Flanagan to bring the British to the negotiating table.[235] The *Journal* paid close attention to the efforts of SF's acting president, while local authority figures in Roscommon also gave their support.[236] However, O'Flanagan's naiveté and Éamon de Valera's confirmation that the curate spoke only for SF and not Dáil Éireann ensured failure.[237] The *Herald* misread the damage that O'Flanagan did to his reputation and inaccurately stated that the curate had been 'within an ace of affecting a truce'.[238]

In the New Year the IRA sought to reinvigorate itself. The tactic of targeting individual or pairs of RIC men continued on 5 January with three operations. At Elphin, Constable Cyril R. Sharp, 'one of the bad boys of the Tans', according to the IRA's Thomas Brady, sustained non-fatal injuries, while in a second incident at Tarmonbarry Constables Sullivan and Shread were 'slightly wounded'.[239] At Strokestown, the IRA shot Sergeant Peter McArdle in the leg. Although the wound was not serious, the sergeant was unlucky enough to catch fatal pneumonia while recuperating.[240] The attacks were a co-ordinated attempt to kill numerous RIC without the risks associated with ambushing large forces. By staging the attacks in three different areas, the IRA compelled Crown forces to subdivide their response units and thereby lessened the likelihood of capture.

In what would become a trend, the Crown forces killed an IRA target almost immediately. Patrick Durr of Ballintubber, the 23-year-old IRA intelligence officer, was killed on 6 January at 3:30 a.m. He died of a 'bullet wound over the right eye, one in the heart and another in the leg'.[241] Agnes Leonard, in whose house he was hiding, testified that the killers' voices were 'not like the voices of the country people around here'. Her house was burned by the Crown forces in May.[242]

In a broader response from the CMA in Athlone to the January shootings a county-wide curfew was implemented. A reduction in motor permits and the suspension of markets were also instated at Elphin, Tarmonbarry and Strokestown.[243] The imposition of a curfew in Boyle annoyed the *Herald*, given there had been 'no outrage … in the town, or within … five miles', while its effect on Ballaghaderreen in February when imposed after a failed attack on the RIC barracks there was to make the town 'dark, deserted and still'.[244] Even quiescent Roscommon town was given localized curfew arrangements in May, though mainly due to developments outside of the town. Its citizens heeded signage that threatened severe repercussions in the event of IRA activity.[245] Confusing regional curfew variations and the requirements of lambing season led to many late night perambulators being arrested during the spring. Reinvigorated Castlerea sessions saw forty presented at one convening.[246]

The blunt nature of the curfew appeared to reduce overt IRA activity. H.C. Cole, who penned the January CI report, noted that the IRA was not especially active 'given their numbers', with the burning of the idle Ballyfarnon courthouse and a 'feeble' bombing attempt on Castlerea RIC barracks being the only notable operations after 5 January 1921.[247] The most prominent IRA action in February was an unofficial operation at Cornafulla, between Athlone and Ballinasloe. It had been unilaterally sanctioned by the leader of the Athlone ASU, James Tormey, who demanded a reprisal for the killing of his brother, Joseph, at Ballykinlar. James Tormey was the only fatality in the ambush that engaged a small RIC patrol.[248]

Complementing the curfew was the new Crown forces strategy of conducting large-scale drives and round-ups of hundreds of men at a time. In early February, 500 soldiers and RIC scoured Ballagh, Lisacul, Beechwood,

Curraghroe and Lanesboro in the south of the county, while Captain Peek rolled out the same policy further north. Numerous local politicians and priests were taken in the dragnets, which continued into the summer. Most of those arrested were quickly released once they signed the 'government undertaking renouncing allegiance to the Irish Republican Army'.[249] The promoted CI Hetreed noted a marked improvement in attitudes to the police in February as a result of the action.[250]

The round-ups also included Cumann na mBan.[251] Elizabeth Tivnan was arrested when leaving Mass at Cootehall and then interned, as were the Sharkey sisters.[252] Eithne Coyle was arrested at Kilteevan and made headlines for her approach to her trial at Kilmainham. She refused to recognize the court, read a newspaper during proceedings, made a speech in Irish at their conclusion and was sentenced to twelve months.[253] The *Daily Herald* regarded the trial as a showcase for women 'rebels', whose fortitude demonstrated why 'the authorities are at a standstill in the contest with … Cumann na mBan.'[254] Coyle, who after the war rightly advocated for Cumann na mBan to be given more credit for its work (she received a military pension), escaped in October 1921. Others such as Agnes Moran did what they could to compensate for their comrades' absences during the summer.[255]

The inconvenience to non-combatants was exacerbated by IRA efforts to hinder the Crown forces. They felled trees and telegraph poles, trenched roads and damaged railway infrastructure. Many areas, mostly in north Roscommon, became isolated; Ballaghaderreen was considered cut off by the end of February.[256] In March, Crown forces maintained telegraphic communication by introducing a 'wireless set' at Athlone and Boyle, with CI Hetreed requesting one for Strokestown.[257] In some areas, Crown forces press-ganged locals into fixing damage, while in others they added to the disruption themselves. Around Boyle, soldiers trenched roads to limit routes for republican journeys, while at Castlerea they dismantled telegraph infrastructure after repeated sabotage rendered it inoperable.[258]

The attack in Elphin on 5 January led to tit-for-tat exchanges. On 31 January Auxiliaries vandalized the Catholic church, beat male parishioners and allegedly searched the priest while he held the host.[259] The Lenten pastorals of the bishops of Elphin and Achonry reflected a deepening fear. Bishop Coyne deemed republicans as likely 'losers in an unequal struggle'. Morrisroe suggested 'the horizon of our country's future is … as black as night'.[260] In response two weeks later, the IRA attacked the well-fortified RIC barracks in Elphin in a largely futile operation. Despite damaging only the barracks gable before withdrawing, Seán Connolly deemed the attack a success given that it had 'shaken their [the RIC's] morale considerably'.[261] Colonel Lambert razed the buildings attached to the barracks in the aftermath. Mary Lenehan's public house, through which the IRA had accessed the barracks, was the first to be demolished.[262] The *Sunday Independent* claimed that the IRA had attacked the village Methodist church on the same day. B.J. Goff confirmed that Elphin had no such church and charged the newspaper with propagandizing for the British.[263]

Round-ups by the Crown forces prompted the IRA to step up action against suspected informers. The first man targeted by the IRA was Patrick Donnellan on 19 February. The IRA sought his brother, Richard, and decided to leave the Donnellan homestead 'riddled with bullets', to dissuade any would-be informers.[264] James Feely recalled that two suspected informers in Boyle, identified in RIC records as Peter and Michael Whyte, received a 'good beating ... this seemed to have a good effect on others so inclined'. Feely suggested the IRA in Boyle were quite paranoid, given the 'high percentage of military "hangers on"'.[265] Some suspected informers avoided censure, however. Patrick Higgins and Charles Flanagan from Tulsk sought sanctuary in the RIC barracks in Roscommon town when made aware of IRA intentions towards them.[266] The post offices at Boyle and Strokestown were deemed 'rotten' by republicans who were certain that staff in both were assisting the Crown forces identify IRA suspects. Unsuccessful efforts to address intelligence issues with the post office in Roscommon town saw IRA GHQ question whether the area was 'bereft of men'.[267] Action against the postman for Elphin, George Higgins, was more robust. He had to leave the county as 'life ... became unbearable', when he provided the Crown forces with the names of IRA men who robbed him in March. After spending time in protective custody at Elphin RIC barracks, he relocated to Belfast.[268] He was shot dead there by the IRA in September 1922.[269]

Execution sent the strongest message of all. On 19 February, Patrick Lyons, a 45-year-old Catholic ex-soldier, was shot dead near Ballintubber by an IRA man posing as a policeman.[270] The *Herald* reported that Lyons and Donnellan were known to travel with Crown forces patrols, but apologized when both families vehemently denied the accusation.[271] While there was room to interpret the motive behind the February incidents, from March the IRA often made direct reference to the reason for its actions. Ex-soldier and father of four Frank Elliott was shot dead on the night of 3 March. His body was left at Ballymurray railway crossing with a 'spies beware' notice in his pocket. His wife confirmed that Elliott had received an earlier warning from republicans for selling information and on the night of his death was sardonically offered £50 by IRA men. The unionist press railed against the 'spy charge as pretext', while the British army sought to buy a coffin for the impoverished Elliott family.[272]

The need to identify spies became more urgent from late March after the IRA retaliated for the execution of 26-year-old Patrick Moran at Mountjoy Gaol on 14 March. Originally from Crossna, Moran was arrested in Dublin for alleged involvement in the death of Lieutenant Ames on 21 November 1920, Bloody Sunday, when the IRA moved against intelligence officers in the capital.[273] A picture of Moran posing armed in IRA uniform, his arrest during Easter 1916 and his brother's ongoing imprisonment in Boyle convinced the authorities of his guilt, despite compelling contradictory evidence.[274] Even speeches in the House of Commons noted that 'independent witnesses ... in no way identified with Sinn Féin, testified that he was at Blackrock', rather than at the scene of the shooting on Mount Street.[275] However, Moran was probably at the Gresham Hotel on O'Connell Street engaged in a related operation, a fact that led him to refuse to escape custody with Ernie O'Malley when the opportunity arose. He believed he could not be found guilty of the specific charge laid against him given the evidence. In the event, the testimony given by lower-ranking soldiers produced a guilty verdict.[276] Novelist George Russell (Æ) made unsuccessful representations for Moran, as did Fr O'Flanagan and Dublin's Archbishop Walsh.[277] Thousands gathered outside Mountjoy on 14 March when 'as the Angelus was ringing at six o'clock [a.m.]' Moran was hanged alongside Thomas Whelan, who had been found guilty on a related charge.[278]

Moran's execution provoked dismay and anger in Roscommon. It also led the IRA to redouble efforts to resurrect the ambush strategy not seen since Fourmilehouse. On 22 and 23 March, separate ambushes claimed the lives of eight members of the Crown forces. Constables William Deveraux and James Dowling, two 'old' RIC men, were shot dead while cycling through Keadue, two miles from Moran's home. Sergeant Reilly, the lead member in the five-man cycle patrol, was wounded but survived. Failed February engagements near the same location helped refine the plan for the operation which was led by Michael Dockery and Andrew Lavin.[279] The second ambush occurred at Scramogue, near Strokestown, and caused more Crown forces fatalities than any other operation in Roscommon. It involved both the South and North Roscommon Brigades, with roughly forty men operating under Pat Madden, Luke Duffy, Frank Simons, Martin Fallon and local resident Seán Leavy.[280] Cumann na mBan members carried out reconnaissance before the IRA took up their positions and remained nearby to render first aid.[281] Intelligence correctly led the IRA to believe that the Crown forces would be transporting prisoners from Strokestown to Longford that morning. When the military tender neared the crossroads at Scramogue, the IRA opened fire. The ambush ultimately claimed the lives of six of the seven Crown forces present. The most prominent fatality was Captain Peek of the 9th Lancers.[282] Lieutenant John Tennant, a 21–year-old from Yorkshire who had been in Ireland for only a fortnight, was also shot dead. The driver, John Keenan of the Royal Army Service Corps, and RIC Constable Edward Leslie also died, the latter three days later from his wounds.[283] The IRA captured a Hotchkiss machine-gun from the only survivor, Corporal Hogben, who later refused to identify those involved.[284] The prisoners were Auxiliary Division RIC Constables James Evans and Robert Buchanan. They had been arrested for vandalising the Catholic church in Elphin in January. The IRA executed them later that day to ensure their silence and to purge any regret they might have felt for yet another failed attempt on Elphin barracks just days before the Scramogue ambush.[285] Evans was buried in a bog, Buchanan in the River Shannon.[286] The absence of IRA casualties made the operation 'a complete success' according to Leavy who had a complex view of Peek, the 'capable and vigorous soldier of an arrogant and bullying disposition'.[287] Peek's death was lamented in Tulsk and Strokestown, while the *Herald*'s descriptions of the 'best liked officer in Roscommon' fuelled republican distaste for Tully's reportage.[288] Peek's removal ceremony saw large crowds in Longford, while businesses in Strokestown remained closed until his funeral in Britain had concluded.[289]

The Crown forces responded robustly. They concentrated their enquiries for the Keadue attack in Crossna, Ballyfarnon and Arigna. Handicapped by poor knowledge of mountainous Arigna, the soldiers targeted family members of those they sought, in one case seizing a septuagenarian 'as a kind of hostage for a son of his'.[290] Ballyfarnon Cumann na mBan members Annie and Margaret Cunnane, who had sheltered the Keadue ambushers, were forced to stand outside barefoot during their interrogation by Crown forces. Bad weather did not loosen their tongues.[291] Four men from Derrymine and Crossna were arrested. One of those, Thomas Lavin, was seized at Sligo infirmary when the loss of his right hand in a grenade accident forced him to seek medical assistance.[292]

The Crown forces quickly captured men for Scramogue by focusing on Strokestown.[293] On 23 March, Pat Mullooly and Brian Nangle were arrested by Auxiliaries who beat and threatened to kill them. John Duffy recalled that only RIC intervention saved them.[294] The following day, Mullooly's brother, Michael, was killed by men who dragged him 'out to the haggard and shot' him, before drinking in his house. The military inquiry found that 'members unknown belonging to the Crown forces' had killed him, but deigned it unnecessary to examine the Auxiliaries who had participated. General Hugh Jeudwine, commander of the British 5th Division in the Curragh, demanded that the 'farcical' inquiry be reconvened.[295] Other republican suspects avoided death, but were gravely mistreated. In Strokestown demesne camp, William Mullany was beaten and starved, treatment that led to a nervous breakdown at Rath camp in the Curragh, one of a number of camps established to accommodate the growing number of men being interned.[296]

The most tragic expression of indiscipline by the Crown forces came during the Keadue investigations. On 26 March, 15-year-old Joseph Mulloy of Aughafinnegan, near Crossna was shot dead by members of the Boyle-based 1st

Battalion, Bedfordshire and Hertfordshire Regiment. Their contradictory testimony at the subsequent inquiry angered their superiors who could do little to re-frame the evidence.[297] The shots which killed Mulloy were fired by soldiers reacting to gunfire issued by 'another party of military ... operating from a different direction'.[298] His funeral on Easter Monday had thousands of mourners and an eighty-carriage cortège.[299] The deaths of innocent civilians at the hands of the Crown forces did not end with Mulloy.

In May Michael Wynne was shot dead by an army patrol that entered his house simply because the lights were on late at night.[300] The officer in charge, Lieutenant Stayner, believed that Wynne's family was to blame given that their panic unnerved the soldier that shot him. The fact that the non-political Wynne was 'somewhat lacking in intellect' appeared to further excuse his death, especially, as General Jeudwine put it, 'considering the condition of the country'. Judge Wakely reviewed the evidence at a compensation hearing and controversially insisted: 'It was a case of murder, pure and simple ... every man there should be ... tried for murder'. General Macready, commander of the British forces in Ireland, was outraged by Wakely's 'highly improper' remarks and asked the chief secretary to reprimand the judge.[301]

The following month Patrick Coyle, a 67-year-old blacksmith from Kiltoom, was killed when he attended the nearby home of Maria Murphy on business on 1 June.[302] Head Constable Michael McClean, who had been posted in Roscommon for less than a month, perjured himself repeatedly by insisting that Coyle was shot outside the house by an unidentified person. McClean eventually confessed to CI Hetreed that he had accidentally shot Coyle in the kitchen with the CI's own rifle. McClean was charged with 'involuntary manslaughter' and found not guilty. Perjury charges were not pursued.[303]

IRA paranoia peaked in April and May. At Scramogue, Edward Beirne, a 50-year-old Catholic widower and father of five, was shot dead on 5 April. His body was labelled with a notice declaring: 'Convicted Spy. Spies and informers beware of the flying column.' Beirne's 13-year-old daughter confirmed that he had been warned by the IRA to stop talking to the police. RIC Sergeant John Cawley described Beirne as being 'on very friendly terms' with his men and noted that Beirne opposed 'the Sinn Féin movement and frequently expressed his views forcibly'.[304] At Loughglynn on the same night, John Wymes, a 66-year-old ex-RIC man, and John Gilligan, a 40-year-old ex-soldier and postman, were killed. Their bodies were placed against a shed with spy notices. Gilligan's wife, Bridget, stated that her husband cried when the men, who 'spoke like other men in the locality', arrived.[305] Wymes's son, Alfred, claimed that one of the men who took his father stated: 'We'll show you the IRA isn't dead yet ... If it was the military come, ye would clap them on the back ... F*****g spies.'[306] The IRA's Thomas Crawley asserted that both men had given information when visited by IRA posing as Crown forces. Republicans drew out the men by making disingenuous inquiries for lodgings for the wife of a RIC man whose house they had burned. Wymes and Gilligan offered to assist her.[307] Both were considered British liabilities at compensation hearings.[308]

Although it is certain that some supposed informers were deemed guilty on little or no evidence, the process undertaken with regard to Patrick Egan of Castlerea showed more deliberation and highlighted the weakness of IRA intelligence-gathering in Roscommon. During April and May, incisive raids by the Crown forces around the town gave the impression of intelligence being supplied by an IRA source. Egan, the IRA's own intelligence officer, was seen in the company of the local RIC DI. Although Egan was deemed unsophisticated (the DI had used drink to loosen his tongue) the Castlerea IRA would only move if they caught him red-handed. Their own lack of sophistication ensured that Egan became aware of their suspicions and emigrated. Even when the war ended and Egan sought to return to Roscommon, it was decided that he could only do so if the IRA found enough evidence to convict him. If they failed to do so, it was decided, 'it would be better ... that he stay where he is'.[309]

The deaths of Wymes and Gilligan led to a marked escalation in violence in the Castlerea area. Indeed, people were so 'panic stricken', that even the perennial land disturbances fizzled rather than flashed.[310] On 7 April, 20-year-old Patrick Conry from Tarmon and 47-year-old James Monds of nearby Knockmurray were shot dead.[311] Although the date of their deaths makes them appear to be a reprisal by the Crown forces for Wymes and Gilligan, the evidence available is unclear. Both were shot by a group of six men who wore handkerchiefs over their faces. Unfortunately, the accents of the men were not described by witnesses. In the case of Monds, the actual target was his teenage son, William, whom the party did not shoot. Conry was viewed as a 'probable loyalist' by the military, while Monds's position as a 'respectable and inoffensive Protestant farmer' ensured that unionist newspapers saw his death as one of the 'Murders by Sinn Féin'.[312] The CI agreed and suggested that both Conry and Monds had left the IRA and sought to emigrate. He made no reference to information supplied as a more credible motive for shooting them.[313] IRA testimony and local memory strongly assert that the men were killed by the Crown forces and deliberate misdirection cannot be ruled out. IRA activity later that day certainly appeared to be a counter-reprisal.

At Castlerea, the Loughglynn IRA killed Lance-Corporal Edward Weldon of the Leicester Regiment. Sixty-year-old Mary Anne McDonagh was also killed accidentally as she stood at her front door on Patrick's Street.[314] Major Tidswell was reprimanded by Colonel Commandant

Lambert for framing McDonagh's death as inadvertent. It allowed 'Sinn Fein propaganda reports' to assert that the Crown forces killed her.[315] An angry Lambert proscribed markets and fairs in Castlerea after the deaths and set a closure time for public houses of 7 p.m.[316] Postmistress Cecilia Toolin and her colleague Joseph Downes were imprisoned for passing information to local republicans. The IRA believed that Paddy Egan led the Crown forces to Toolin.[317]

Weldon's death led to multiple round-ups by the Crown forces. During one sweep on 19 April at Loughglynn Woods, the Leicester Regiment engaged four IRA men, killing two: 19-year-old local man Stephen McDermott and 23-year-old John Bergin, a native of Nenagh. Former soldier Joseph Satchwell surrendered, while Thomas Scally escaped.[318] Lieutenant S.F. Mackay led the party that brought the bodies to Castlerea, their feet 'protruding from the back of the lorry'. Mackay asserted that Bergin had confessed to shooting Weldon and McDonagh and was primed to carry out 'several murders of RIC and military'.[319]

The *Herald*'s reportage of the escalating violence angered both sides. It publicized Andrew Wymes's view that his invalid father was a friend of the Catholic clergy and 'no spy', but a man who was 'crucified'.[320] To assist the Tullys in understanding their level of displeasure, the IRA intimidated the *Herald*'s Castlerea and Strokestown correspondents and burned one of the newspaper's delivery cars at Croghan.[321] Grasping at straws to show their republican support in the edition of 16 April, the Tullys printed a letter from Fr O'Flanagan thanking them for binding work. The same issue reported the arrest of the newspaper's Roscommon town, north Longford and Mullingar correspondents. Aggravated by the *Herald*'s failure to assert that Mary Anne McDonagh was killed by the IRA, the authorities ensured that the 30 April edition did just that. Showing consistency in its abhorrence of deaths perpetrated by both sides, the *Herald* also reported that the inquiry verdict for Loughglynn that the 'Crown forces [acted] in the execution of their duty', could not actually be established.[322]

Tully was also forced to print other British propaganda, including an interview with Colonel Stuart Forbes-Sharp of E Company, Auxiliary Division RIC. Jim Hunt of the Sligo IRA believed Forbes-Sharp to be 'a soldier who would not tolerate dirty tactics', a rather odd claim given the activities of Forbes-Sharp's subordinates. The Auxiliary commander referenced Hunt in the article and stated that his men had offered to stage a fair fight with the IRA when it was proposed by Hunt. The latter's arrest a month after the interview made this impossible.[323] Forbes-Sharp proudly proclaimed that his Auxiliaries were not 'shivering neurasthenics'; they understood the need for a 'mailed fist' outside of social settings that saw them mingle freely with Boyle citizens.[324]

Crown forces activity around Castlerea saw the South Roscommon IRA turn its attentions further east. Martin Scanlon, a 55-year-old RIC pensioner, and John McAuley, a 60-year-old sub-post office manager at Kilrooskey, were shot dead on 8 May. Their bodies were left beside a trenched road. Both had attached spy notices and the men were considered loyal to Britain.[325] Each spy notice had an addendum. In the case of Scanlon, it reflected his defiance, 'true to your colours to the last'. In the case of McAuley, it suggested a motive: 'trench'.[326] While Luke Duffy claimed that McAuley habitually helped the Crown forces, Major Tidswell asserted that it was the postmaster's move to fill in an IRA trench that proved fatal. Tidswell also made the rare claim as to who was responsible: 'Patrick Madden of Ballagh'.[327] CI Hetreed lamented the absence of 'adequate protection' for loyal men.[328] The reopening of the same trench by the IRA claimed the life of Auxiliary Constable George Redding on 29 May.[329]

It appeared that IRA action against alleged informers was effective. Hetreed noted that people in rural areas protected the IRA, which had cowed them 'into absolute silence'.[330] Increasing intimidation by the Crown forces also assisted the IRA, especially when popular figures such as Fr Malachy Brennan were the target. In separate incidents in May the Crown forces stole the priest's bicycle, ransacked his house at Mantua and threatened his sister. Lieutenant Mackay led a party that targeted Brennan's flock after one Sunday Mass. Male worshippers were beaten, while the women present were threatened for fraternizing with the IRA.[331]

In May, Michael Skelly and Pat Mullooly escaped from Victoria Barracks in Athlone while a freshly captured Michael Dockery escaped from Boyle barracks in June, in his case with the assistance of a British officer.[332] Hetreed observed that his men were 'unsettled' after the escapes as they correctly suspected complicit colleagues.[333] The redeployment of E Company, Auxiliary Division RIC from Boyle to Westport, County Mayo, in June was also welcomed by Roscommon republicans. It did not, however, mean a reduction in the strength of the Crown forces. Some 400 members of the 15th The King's Hussars and 9th Lancers were posted to Rockingham House the same week. As a precaution, the IRA burned Correal House to limit options for additional billets.[334]

The establishment in June of the southern parliament under the Government of Ireland Act had little impact on Roscommon. The *Journal* reported that: 'never before ... was interest at such a low ebb' for such an important development. The *Herald* suggested the body would 'never function' in any event.[335] SF had a walkover in nearly all constituencies. The new Mayo South–Roscommon South constituency returned Harry Boland who was joined by reluctant politician Daniel O'Rorke, as well as Mayo men William Sears and Thomas Maguire. Andrew Lavin joined Count Plunkett in

Leitrim–Roscommon North alongside James Dolan and Thomas Carter.[336] The upper house was rebuked by likely appointees Sir Thomas Stafford and Lord de Freyne, neither of whom was willing to 'exercise functions ... with any body nominated by the Lord Lieutenant'.[337]

In June the Crown forces moved against the Castlerea IRA battalion. Near Loughglynn on 2 June, 21-year-old Michael Carty was killed and his comrade Peter Shannon badly injured while hiding at the house of Frank Connor.[338] Sergeant James King, who had directed the Castlerea 'Murder Gang' since February 1921, asserted that Connor and Shannon had opened fire first, something dismissed by Gerald O'Connor, the Castlerea battalion OC. The men were shot while still in bed and the owner was not even present; it was 'simply another murder case' according to O'Connor.[339] Three weeks later, a related raid saw King and his men fatally injure John Vaughan and Edward Shannon. Vaughan's mother and sister were also beaten.[340] CI Hetreed believed the raid was 'good work', but King's actions were to have personal consequences.[341] On 12 June, American ex-naval man and Mayo resident Thomas Rush was shot dead at Lisacul. Irish sources insisted that he was robbed and 'butchered, rather than shot'. Intervention by the American consulate did little to influence Tidswell and the, by then, notorious Mackay and Stayner from arriving at the verdict of justifiable homicide. Rush, they agreed, was drilling IRA men.[342] On 1 July 30-year-old Edward Weir was killed by Crown forces at Ballintubber. Major Tidswell queried the choice of Weir given that the man had not been active in the IRA since his marriage in February.[343]

The IRA was not quiescent. On 6 June, Constable Harold Round of the Frenchpark RIC was kidnapped and drowned. The IRA also burned the abandoned former barrack building in the village.[344] On 1 July Constable Moffat of Ballaghaderreen was targeted, as were two constables near Rooskey the following day. Gunshots at Tarmonbarry on 5 July led Sergeant Patrick Smyth to prepare a signal rocket that exploded unexpectedly and claimed his life.[345]

The shots that panicked Smyth had killed Thomas McGowan. He was shot dead by members of the IRA over a land dispute, rather than McGowan's refusal to dig a trench as the CI suggested.[346] This murderous aspect to the land issue in Roscommon was an uncomfortable development that was replicated just three days later. Michael and Thomas Waldron were shot dead on 8 July with both Major Tidswell and Daniel O'Rorke confirming that land was the motive.[347] Both incidents indicated that some members of the IRA were willing to abuse their position for personal gain.

The highest-profile IRA killing in the midlands occurred on 20 June at Glasson, County Westmeath. Colonel Commandant Lambert was shot while being driven through the village after attending a social event at Killinure House. As a result of information provided by Killinure residents, the expected reprisal almost entirely destroyed the village of Knockcroghery on 21 June. The *Freeman's Journal* described the 'constant fusillades of rifle and revolver fire' that accompanied profligate arson, with numerous titles recounting how panicked residents fled to the local presbytery and church. By the time the attack concluded, only three houses remained. The villagers later sought assistance from the White Cross Fund to rebuild.[348] An absurd situation ensued whereby the British refused to set up an inquiry until the perpetrators were identified.[349] The village priest, Fr Kelly, identified them as men he recognized from Victoria Barracks. However, the RIC reported that the men could not be traced.[350]

The continued violence proved intolerable for the proprietors of the *Herald*. George Tully died of a heart attack and the effect on Jasper was obvious when he announced the suspension of publication on 2 July: 'it is impossible … to carry on … under the existing conditions of public terror and agony.'[351] The suspension did not last long. Just over a week later, news of a truce between the IRA and the British reached Roscommon. When the truce deadline of twelve noon on 11 July was made known, moves were made to settle scores around Castlerea. After an abortive ambush at Southpark that led to the capture of two IRA men, republicans moved against Sergeant King. At 9:30 a.m. the 42-year-old leader of the 'Castlerea Murder Gang' was shot dead on Patrick Street by Thomas Crawley and Edward Campion.[352] His killing, the last of the War of Independence, brought the total deaths resulting from political violence in the county since 1917 to sixty-two, the ninth highest in Ireland, just behind Galway.[353] CI Hetreed lamented the loss of a man who had 'done his duty'.[354]

The War of Independence in Roscommon, as in many parts of Ireland, took time to develop into a military conflict. As it became clear that the Peace Conference was not the route to independence, republicans considered their options. SF's lack of organization in 1919 highlighted weaknesses at a grassroots level but did not indicate increasing support for constitutional nationalism or the British administration. Repressive British policies ensured that antipathy toward Britain and its agents grew throughout 1919 and 1920. Raids, arrests and the treatment of hunger-strikers like Séamus Redican assisted in ostracizing the RIC and re-framing them as the enemy. Enforcement by the IRA ensured that the social and commercial boycott of the Crown forces was generally comprehensive. Unsurprisingly, land agitation reasserted itself in the county. The move to establish a land court system was an acknowledgment by the Dáil government that when it came to land, many in Roscommon would subordinate republicanism to localism. The drift to violent action came after the republican courts largely defused the land issue, at least in 1920. When IRA operations claimed RIC lives in July and August of that year, the British changed tactics and deployed the ill-disciplined and violent Black and Tans in Roscommon. The cycle of reprisal and counter-reprisal that began with their introduction saw the war enter a new phase that shook non-combatants and escalated violence on both sides. The use of extra-judicial killing as a tactic by the Auxiliary Division RIC after the Fourmilehouse ambush and the arrest of two priests at Croghan in October unnerved republicans. Even after Seán Connolly's intervention, moves to re-engage Crown forces were hesitant. The IRA invariably restricted itself to smaller operations against fewer enemies, a tactic better suited to the Roscommon IRA's level of training and equipment. The paranoia that tar-geted raids by the Crown forces created among the Roscommon IRA led republicans to resort to summary execution also. Suspected informers were killed, often on limited evidence. The tit-for-tat activity around Elphin between the Crown forces and the IRA culminated in the deadliest ambush in the county at Scramogue in March 1921. Paddy Moran's execution in Dublin undoubtedly motivated the IRA attacks at Keadue and Scramogue, two days of violence in Roscommon that claimed almost as many Crown forces' lives as the previous two years. The violent encounters that followed were most vicious around Castlerea, which saw a campaign that deepened personal enmities in the region. The destruction of Knockcroghery after the killing of Colonel Commandant Lambert highlighted how indiscriminate attacks by the Crown forces had become. The killing of Sergeant King on the day the truce was declared proved that tolerating the wounds inflicted by the war during a period of truce was, in some instances, too much to ask of the IRA.

8 'We may think the Treaty a rotten, compromising business': from truce to Treaty and Civil War, 1921–3

Pervasive optimism greeted the truce. In Roscommon, hostilities ceased as both sides looked forward to an agreement that would end the conflict. IRA ranks swelled and an imminent Irish republic was predicted. However, the Anglo-Irish Treaty of December 1921 disappointed many republicans. Roscommon's TDs, IRA and Cumann na mBan exemplified the divergence in opinions and confirmed there would be no smooth transition to the Irish Free State (IFS) for which the Treaty provided. From January 1922, local republicanism split between those who regarded the Treaty as a step on the road to the republic and those who saw it as a treasonous compromise. The establishment of rival groups at national level was reflected in Roscommon, as pro- and anti-Treaty sides each asserted their right to act on behalf of the Irish people. Moves in Roscommon to reinvigorate land agitation in the uncertain atmosphere were decisively discouraged in the run up to a controversial general election in June 1922 that saw Count Plunkett and Harry Boland at odds with their constituency colleagues. The election result precipitated an armed conflict in which former allies in Roscommon turned on each other for a short-lived and geographically limited conventional war. The success of the pro-Treaty side in controlling the fight in Roscommon led the anti-Treaty IRA (ATIRA) to adopt guerrilla tactics. Always on the back foot, the ATIRA concentrated its efforts on damaging infrastructure. It became increasingly unpopular in the process as the damage adversely affected the county's citizens. Roscommon County Council stepped forward to promote peace but found little support for its endeavour from a Provisional government that was creating the institutions of a new Irish state while trying to suppress the ATIRA. The introduction of draconian legislation tilted the conflict decisively in favour of the pro-Treaty side as did the support of the Roman Catholic Church. The move towards a cease-fire in Roscommon in May 1923 caused the ATIRA to maintain low-level activity redolent of a group who recognized the hopelessness of their aims. By the end of the conflict, it was apparent that the two sides in Roscommon would have to find a way to live together in the Irish Free State.

The truce halted the cycle of violence in Roscommon. While James Quigley believed that the IRA were 'only getting on our feet', Martin Fallon represented the majority, realistic view that the poorly equipped IRA were not 'in a good position to continue the fight'.[1] Monitoring of the truce in Roscommon fell to Fintan Murphy in Athlone, the region's liaison officer. He reported good adherence to the terms of the truce across the county, where it met with the 'entire approval of combatants and non-combatants alike'.[2] Sir Thomas Stafford and The O'Conor Don hoped that the pause would allow Ireland to pursue its 'legitimate aspirations'.[3]

Bonhomie prevailed in many areas. Civilians joined members of the Crown forces in swimming in the River Shannon at Athlone when the truce came into force.[4] CI Hetreed reported 'comparative peace' as farmers at Elphin and Frenchpark engaged in legal cattle drives that led parched livestock to springs at Tulsk.[5] In Boyle, members of E Company, Auxiliary Division RIC returned to holiday, something they repeated at Christmas when they stayed with 'friends'![6] Commandeered bicycles were reclaimed, while Abbey Park in Boyle was reopened to the public after firing ranges were removed. At Strokestown, IRA men saluted British soldiers when entering the town.[7] Despite some ill-feeling on the day of James King's funeral, Fintan Murphy reported that in Castlerea 'members of the RIC saunter about unarmed'.[8] From mid-July, social and sporting events recommenced, as did markets and fairs.[9] Communications began to be restored, with the much abused telegraph systems being reconnected and railway lines operating again.[10] The boycott of Belfast goods began to ease in some towns, although in Roscommon town and Boyle republicans promulgated a blacklist of shopkeepers and extended the boycott to northern banks.[11] Numerous cases listed for the county sessions were suspended, orders for internment were withdrawn, while many low risk interned republicans were released. The prison at Boyle barracks was empty by early August, while Roscommon internees at Rath camp began to return home in November.[12] At religious occasions thousands paid respects to those who had fought for Ireland's freedom. The funeral of south Roscommon's Bernard Gaffey saw 250 vehicles, 200 Cumann na mBan, hundreds of uniformed IRA, a seven-mile cortège and a congregation estimated at 7,000.[13] The reburial of John Scally of the Kilteevan IRA, who was killed at a boobytrapped trench at Beechwood on 11 May, was on such as scale that the *Journal* reported: 'Not within living memory has anything approaching the public demonstration of sympathy been witnessed in County Roscommon.'[14]

Local authority bodies reconvened. Micheál Ó Braonáin proclaimed the good work of the county council which had held meetings 'beside cocks of hay' since the spring before.[15] Daniel O'Rorke, Michael Dockery, Úna Sharkey and three others were co-opted.[16] In October, Ó Braonáin was elected chairman and Sharkey vice chair.[17]

Inevitably, there were breaches of the truce. The most controversial was the arrest for assault by the IRA of RIC Constables Pat and James Beirne. Divisional Commissioner James Wilbond believed his officers had erred but made it clear that the IRA had no jurisdiction over anyone other than their own men. Murphy's intervention led to the Beirnes being released, with reports that the men were 'none the worse for wear', helping to maintain the impression of good relations.[18] The reconvening of republican courts in Arigna, Ballinagare and Cootehall during September also breached the truce and angered the RIC.[19] However, little was done and the republican courts operated alongside the British equivalent. In one instance in October, Judge Wakely presided over petty sessions on the first floor of the Castlerea courthouse, while the republican court convened on the ground floor.[20] It was not until early 1922, when the circuit courts started in Roscommon town and Boyle, that greater clarity surrounded judicial processes in the county.[21] Numerous other minor breaches resulted in Murphy being 'snowed under' with reports and by November Captain H.J. Finlay had been appointed as the county liaison officer for Roscommon to help Murphy manage his workload.[22]

The truce was viewed as a victory by republicans. While the *Herald* described it as a 'climb down' for the British, it was not long until the *Journal* was following *An tÓglach* in criticizing the 'swelled head' IRA men, who boasted about their victory and entitlements.[23] CI Hetreed, whose final reports were devoid of the sense of injury deemed apposite by some colleagues, noted 'a good deal of bickering … as to their prowess and deeds of war' in IRA ranks.[24] In an attempt to deflate IRA egos, Fr Lavin in Tulsk told parishioners that 'Sinn Féin and the spirit of the people conquered', not just the IRA. Moves by overconfident republicans in Roscommon and adjacent counties to install council officials was a step towards clientelism. Fr Brennan halted Roscommon IRA moves to appoint their preferred magistrates for the reconvened republican courts. The priest told the IRA that their place was 'outside, guarding the walls'.[25]

During the truce, IRA ranks increased greatly and training for new recruits (again, in breach of the truce) took place from September. Short-lived and disorganized camps at Ballaghaderreen, Elphin and Runnamote were replaced by larger and comparatively better managed ones at Rockingham and Dunamon Castle.[26] Both camps registered hundreds of men, with officers at Dunamon indicating that they were training more than twice the number deemed active before 11 July.[27] Some of the additional men came as changes to IRA battalions led the South Roscommon Brigade to gain the Summerhill battalion. Formerly part of the Athlone Brigade, Summerhill's move was part of efforts to manage profligate drinking and indiscipline in Athlone.[28] Many of the rambunctious recruits were accused by the *Herald* of seeking public jobs and described as 'mushrooms of the day before yesterday' those who were an affront to 'the men who went through the heat and burden of the day'.[29] Branches of the Irish Republican Soldiers (1916–1921) and Prisoners of War Society were set up to assist veterans in securing jobs, delineating them from the new breed, whom Patrick Mullooly deemed not 'fit company for an IRA man's dog'.[30] Some of the newly enlisted IRA were stationed at the workhouses at Strokestown and Boyle in October, while others occupied Kilronan Castle.[31] Rumours of plans by the Crown forces to take the three buildings precipitated this pre-emptive IRA action.[32]

Re-engagement played on IRA minds. A report from Lanesboro in early November claimed that the RIC were being removed to 'strongholds' and trained to use a Lewis gun. The IRA were concerned that the British viewed the new IRA recruits as 'lukewarm'.[33] Republicans believed that Captain Tully, a notorious British army intelligence officer in Athlone, was monitoring Roscommon's IRA camps and assessing ways to protect Roscommon loyalists.[34] Republicans predicted a direct approach from the British: 'if the fight goes on again … all loyalists will be taken into a camp and protected … all others … will be dealt with as belligerents (shot down).'[35]

One serious issue for the South Roscommon Brigade in the event of re-engagement was the removal of Daniel O'Rorke as OC. He had been criticized on many occasions. Richard Mulcahy suggested in March 1921 that O'Rorke's 'very disappointing' reports meant that the school teacher was not on top of his brief.[36] O'Rorke was livid at 'being trampled in the mud by the HQ I lived to serve'. He charged GHQ with failing his brigade and asserted that 'there are few brigades in Ireland with similar material, similar quantity of arms and similar conditions, [that] could have done better.' O'Rorke's comrades, even his replacement Frank Simons, supported him. A GHQ officer sent to speak with O'Rorke had sympathy: 'In a tour of over 200 miles, I only saw two ambush positions and these were not the best.'[37] Despite the belief that Simons was more capable, he recommended O'Rorke be reinstated.

Any return to war hinged on ongoing political negotiations. The *Herald* was optimistic, editorializing on de Valera's 'triumphant return' from summer meetings, even with Lloyd George's 'sinister intrigues'.[38] Tully believed that the 'indomitable' Michael Collins would ensure a successful outcome in the winter.[39] Harry Boland promised that no member of Dáil Éireann would sign a document that did not secure a 'lasting and honourable peace'. His pledge was reiterated by Andrew Lavin, Fr O'Flanagan and the county council.[40]

This confidence was undermined by the outcome of negotiations in London on 6 December. The specifics of the settlement caused confusion in Boyle where newsagents were 'besieged' by people seeking the facts. The most controversial clauses of the Treaty required that an oath be sworn to the English monarch, that the British maintain ports in the proposed IFS, that a governor general for the IFS would be appointed and that the partition of Ireland would be reaffirmed. While the *Herald* printed de Valera's verdict that the Treaty was 'in violent conflict' with Irish desires, Tully supported the agreement on the basis that it 'banished the forces of the Crown from our shores'.[41] The county's other titles also printed supportive editorials, with the *Journal* reminding readers of the damage caused to Irish politics by the IPP split in the 1890s.[42] IRA members in Elphin paraded to show their support, while the release of republican prisoners ensured that the Treaty was reviewed during celebrations for the prisoners in Castlerea, Tulsk, Boyle and Ballymoe.[43] B.J. Goff reported that north Roscommon supported the agreement, as did T.J. Devine, who declared the Treaty a 'splendid charter of liberty'. Unsurprisingly, Devine's opinion did little to convince staunch republicans or Roscommon unionists; the latter remained tellingly quiet.[44] The majority of Roscommon's Roman Catholic clergy followed the national trend in being pro-Treaty. Most prominent was Canon Cummins, whose appeal directly to de Valera was published widely in both Ireland and Britain: 'While cherishing undying gratitude for your services and appreciating your position, Roscommon demands, with practical unanimity, ratification of the Treaty.'[45] Seán Mac Eoin, the newly appointed OC of the National army in the region, sensed tension and sent 'to all units an order prohibiting them from taking part in any jubilations over the reported peace'.[46] His entreaty was supported by Roscommon IRA leaders like Pat Madden, Frank Simons, Michael Dockery and Thomas Lavin, all of whom were to join Mac Eoin in the National army and bring hundreds of pro-Treaty recruits with them.[47]

Opposition to the Treaty was strong. Count Plunkett denounced it as a rehash of the Irish Convention schemes. The *Weekly Freeman's Journal* reported that, in a Dáil Éireann speech, Plunkett 'appealed to the memory of his son, and declared himself faithful to the dead who died for Ireland'. He toured his constituency to urge rejection but was 'cold shouldered' in Boyle and elsewhere.[48] B.J. Goff rounded on Plunkett and Andrew Lavin. He directed them to abstain in any Treaty vote; better 'to disenfranchise than positively misrepresent'.[49] Still in the US and not familiar with its provisions, Harry Boland initially welcomed the Treaty. He then vacillated for a week before condemning it, stating that it 'would never bring peace between Britain and Ireland'.[50] The most prominent clerical opposition in Roscommon came from Fr O'Flanagan. Speaking from America, he claimed the Treaty 'would … destroy the solidarity of the Irish movement'.[51] He was joined by Strokestown's Fr Sharkey, who deemed the measure 'a bond of slavery'.[52]

Supposedly unbiased meetings held to inform people of the Treaty's provisions were invariably dominated by pro-Treaty elements. Fr Lavin chaired a meeting in Tulsk that saw anti-Treaty attendees ejected, while at Elphin, 'ardent ratificationists' moved to assault Councillor John Colgan when he maligned the agreement. Colgan was joined by James Ryan and Úna Sharkey in opposing the Treaty in the county council. Ryan also rejected a resolution of the north Roscommon IRA in which they offered 'to serve whatever type of government was established'.[53] The North Roscommon SF executive was certain that 'rejection … would mean ruin for the country', while Dean Geaty demanded that TDs who ignored their constituents should resign.[54] SF clubs at Athlone and Ballintubber resolved in favour and were followed in Ballaghaderreen, Kilmurray and Castleplunkett.[55] The Roscommon Gaelic League was pragmatic: 'while the Treaty contained clauses not in harmony with national aspirations, it should, under present circumstances, be approved'.[56] Cumann na mBan clubs followed their organization's decision to remain faithful to the republic, albeit with a minority of dissenters.[57]

The local press assessed developments variously after a Dáil Éireann vote on 7 January 1922 saw the pro-Treaty side win by sixty-four votes to fifty-seven. Five TDs representing Roscommon voted in favour; Plunkett, Boland and Maguire voted against.[58] The majority of IRA men rejected the Treaty and deemed the Dáil division a vote of politicians, not soldiers. Although believing that there were insubstantial differences between the Treaty and de Valera's alternative Document No. 2, which sought a Treaty of Association with a modified oath and the quick reintegration of the six counties into Ireland's national parliament, the *Herald* was both strident and resigned in its analysis. Majority rule had to be observed, but the Treaty was 'a rotten, compromising business'. The *Messenger* evinced bewilderment at the strength of opposition. Hayden's editorial on 28 January smugly asserted that the Treaty vindicated Redmond's policy regarding partition and agreed with the *Westmeath Independent* that the Treaty was unexpectedly generous.[59] The Provisional government was established on 14 January. It was tasked with leading the country during the year-long transition to the IFS.

Roscommon TDs explained their position after the Dáil vote. Boland 'was in earnest when he said he stood by an Irish Republic' and that even the pro-Treaty side should acknowledge 'that the British King and governor general have no right here'.[60] Plunkett remained resolutely opposed but he cancelled a second tour of the constituency when warned by allies that he would be 'insulted'.[61] Daniel O'Rorke acted ambiguously. He opposed the Treaty but voted in favour to reflect his constituents' views.[62] He wanted to avoid more violence but would re-join the fight, if required.[63] Andrew Lavin's volte-face was framed as pragmatism. The Treaty was a step towards the republic, which was delayed but not abandoned.[64] Canon Cummins counselled both sides to come together under the presidency of 'gallant de Valera'.[65]

Ahead of the June general election, both SF executives in Roscommon adopted a pro-Treaty position, with George Geraghty and Daniel O'Rorke speaking for the Treaty at the south Roscommon meeting in opposition to Austin Stack.[66] Stack claimed that most Irish people would no longer consent to 'serve under a British Government'. O'Rorke highlighted the absence of a workable alternative to the Treaty. Micheál Ó Braonáin supported O'Rorke and, in what the *Derry Journal* believed 'a firm, dignified and self-respecting remonstrance', argued against staging fractious election meetings.[67]

The friction that Ó Braonáin sought to avoid was inevitable. At Carrick-on-Shannon in early March, Andrew Lavin outlined how he was briefly kidnapped by the ATIRA, who tried to induce him to change his mind. Instead, he strove to convince them that the republic was more likely to be achieved 'when they had their own army, [rather] than when a few men ... with an old shotgun between five, were trying to get a crack at the odd peeler'.[68] Tense exchanges in the county council saw Úna Sharkey demand the reconstitution of the voters' register. She declared it had 'British Tommies' on it, when some 'Irish people are not on it at all', a reference to eligible younger citizens who had not yet been added. Ó Braonáin opposed Sharkey's motion, which was defeated by twenty-one votes to five, proof perhaps that the pro-Treaty council recognized younger voters were more likely to support the republic.[69] O'Rorke lamented the division and asked for support in proposing that the army not take sides, lest the threat of violence undermine a fair election.[70]

When seeking evidence of pro-Treaty perfidy, Roscommon republicans believed they had to look no further than the appointment of Boyle's ex-RIC DI, John Kearney, to a role in the new Civic Guard. Numerous ex-RIC were involved in the new police force, many in senior positions, with the Kearney controversy reflecting general anger among IRA men at the appointments. Given his involvement in the arrest of Roger Casement in Kerry in 1916, the anti-Treaty side easily presented Kearney as an 'active enemy of the Republic'.[71] On the strength of Kearney's work against land grabs in Roscommon, Ballyfarnon SF claimed that his reputation for doing 'dirty work' for Britain was deserved.[72] The *Herald* deliberately misrepresented Kearney by claiming that he was a different individual to the man in Kerry in 1916. Tully noted that the former DI was actually 'on most friendly terms with Sinn Féiners', a point that oversimplified the evolution in Kearney's relationship with Roscommon republicans.[73] The issue lost much of its potency when Andrew Lavin clarified that Kearney had an unpaid position 'on a committee preparing a scheme of organization for the new police force', nothing more.[74]

The Kearney controversy highlighted an important point. In developing a new police force, the Provisional government was creating structures for the Irish state, an approach that led to Bishop Coyne's Lenten pastoral on the 'nation's resurrection'.[75] An important aspect of that resurrection was the departure of the British forces during early 1922. In January army barracks and camps at Castlerea, Drumdoe and Mount Talbot were vacated, while Boyle and Athlone followed suit in February.[76] RIC barracks at Elphin and Strokestown were flying a SF flag in early March, as was that at Castlerea, where a gun salute welcomed IRA battalion OC Gerald O'Connor.[77] Perhaps the most demonstrative handover occurred when the final 100 RIC departed Roscommon town on 24 March. Republicans destroyed a British coat of arms that adorned the barracks, while Frank Simons made a bombastic speech in which he proclaimed that the barracks would no longer 'crush out the spirit of nationality'.[78]

The creation of the Provisional government led the anti-Treaty side to establish the IRA Executive as a counterbalancing authority. Arthur Griffith sought unsuccessfully to proscribe a meeting of the Executive on 26 March, with IRA men such as Boyle's Martin Fallon not only ignoring Griffith but signing the meeting's manifesto.[79] The *Herald* condemned the 'amateur politicians' in the Provisional government and recommended an inclusive convention. According to Tully, the election needed to be deferred as, even in its preliminary stages, it was making 'war of one kind or another … inevitable'.[80]

The new political context had an effect on land agitation as Roscommon joined Leitrim, Sligo, Clare and Tipperary in reminding both pro- and anti-Treaty Irish authorities about the importance of the land.[81] The first drives occurred in the north-east of the county in March. From there, the agitation spread south to Tulsk, Lisnamult, Beechwood and Castlerea.[82] As happened elsewhere, groups of supposedly unaffiliated individuals formed at Castlerea but were deemed to be under the control of the ATIRA, which sought to harness the disruption. The Provisional government tried to suppress the unrest by directing the CDB to open up its lands, moving to introduce new land legislation and issuing warnings that indicated the government's willingness to use force, if necessary.[83] Notices erected in Roscommon town warned drivers that they would be 'dealt with as common criminals'.[84] These were only partially effective. Even after land court rulings, driving and farm seizures continued.[85] Such disregard around Boyle led James Feely to refuse bail for drivers in June.[86] In 1923 the National army set up the Special Infantry Corps, a small, short-lived section intended to target agitators.[87] It seized and sold their cattle, facilitated their arrest and assisted the Land Commission in prosecuting those who withheld rents in protest. In April, when Canon Cummins was still criticizing the 'sluggish methods' of the CDB, 300 civil bills were moved against rent defaulters in Roscommon alone.[88] The continued unrest showed that, at least according to William Sears TD, the western land problem was still 'little understood east of the Shannon' by either London or Dublin legislators. Sears indicated the importance of land in January 1923, when he described as 'fitting' that the Dáil's first 'real work of legislation' was the Land bill of 1923.[89]

The spring of 1922 also brought hostility towards Roscommon Protestants. Violence against Catholics in Belfast as part of wider unrest in the north of Ireland had put Protestants in the county on alert. Many made special efforts to publicize their abhorrence at the news from the north by placing lists of subscriptions donated to Belfast Catholics in the local press.[90] The *Herald* stated that the overt support did little to address republican opinions that many Roscommon Protestants were people 'whose condemnation of the Black and Tans only sprang to their lips in the last fortnight'.[91] The first serious attack appears to have been on the Talbots of Mount Talbot. Unionist newspapers claimed that Mrs Talbot died from a heart attack two days after republicans subjected her elderly husband to 'the pretence of a court martial … knocked [him] down some stone steps … [and] fired over his head'. In May 1922, Protestants were 'warned to leave' Ballaghaderreen, Frenchpark and Boyle, with attacks on the Boyle County Club and the Clews Memorial Hall (used as a Protestant school) deemed proof of sectarianism. The Boyle attacks were presented in the Tory press as Protestants being 'driven out from the south', a facile headline that implied that such intimidation was indiscriminate and widespread.[92] The case of Henry Sampey of Ballinlough, a friend of the republic and promoter of interfaith tolerance, shows that in certain cases, land rather than sectarianism promoted antipathetic actions.[93] While Sampey, unlike the Talbots, did not host a British army protection post on his land or engage in violent encounters during land agitation, he wished to retain his holding in the new state. This position led to the usual reaction in Roscommon: intimidation of the landowner. His support for the Provisional government meant little when land was the issue. He left for Kildare.[94] Many others departed for Dublin and Wicklow, contributing to the decline in Roscommon's Protestant population that was supplemented, among other factors, by the departure of the British army from Boyle.

The enmity towards certain Protestants was surpassed by animus against some retired RIC in Boyle. The most serious incident was the shooting dead of retired policeman, James Greer, and his ex-Auxiliary son, Thomas, on 27 May.[95] Martin Greer, a brother also in the RIC, had been shot dead in Dublin in February 1921, possibly in connection with the arrest of Paddy Moran.[96] The IRA had deemed the entire family a threat during the War of Independence, even Greer's wife, a national school principal, who directed her teachers to ask pupils about IRA activity.[97] Believed to have been involved in the shooting dead of Fr Griffin in Galway, Thomas Greer was shot eleven times.[98] In attempts to reduce tensions, the commanders of Boyle's ATIRA, Patrick Brennan, and National army, Michael Dockery, offered sympathies. The unionist press presented the 'war on the RIC' in the region as proof of 'Britain's dishonour' because it had abandoned loyal citizens.[99]

As the 1922 election approached, both sides sought to consolidate their military presence in Roscommon. ATIRA forces planned to seize Athlone barracks in late March but the unexpected return of Seán Mac Eoin prevented this. Instead, they established a post in the middle of Athlone and engaged in aggressive acts that led to the shooting dead of Brigadier George Adamson on 25 April, two weeks after the ATIRA in Dublin commandeered the Four Courts as their national headquarters. The consternation in Athlone as a result of Adamson's death saw Arthur Griffith hold a meeting in the town at which he contrasted his government's desire to build up the nation with what he alleged was the ATIRA's desire for another war with England.[100] In Boyle on 6 April 1922, the barracks was seized by the Sligo ATIRA as the headquarters of the 3rd Western Division that comprised north Roscommon, south Sligo, north Sligo, east Mayo and north Leitrim. They took the barracks after Martin Fallon switched to the pro-Treaty side following conversations with Mac Eoin.[101] The *Herald* overreacted in claiming that the Provisional government was 'practically shelved' in the region as a result.[102] The same newspaper allowed Fallon and Patrick Brennan to exchange barbs and advance incompatible claims regarding loyalties across the 3rd Western Division in the weeks that followed. As was apparent in most brigades, the rank and file IRA in Roscommon followed their OC; Fallon's defection brought the vast majority to the pro-Treaty side. Even Brennan admitted that commanders in three of the five battalions in north Roscommon, the 2nd, 3rd and 4th, were pro-Treaty. His claim that the rank and file were not was not credible.[103] William Pilkington, the Sligo IRA OC, declared an ineffective proscription of election meetings in the region to combat further conversions.[104]

Both sides sought funds. While legal fundraising was undertaken, raiding post offices and banks was lucrative. The republican police, by then a poorly-disciplined, stop-gap civil police force, was called on frequently from February to investigate such raids.[105] The most notorious bank robbery, and one of a number of high-profile raids across Ireland, saw republican police officer John Cox shot dead in Lanesboro in April. It was reported that up to £2,550 was taken by men who were later arrested by Roscommon and Longford republican police.[106] Less successful raids on banks in Roscommon town and Castlerea followed that month.[107] Only in the case of the robbery of the Bank of Ireland in Boyle was the ATIRA officially involved. The £6,000 seized was taken 'to the military barracks where a bank official was given a receipt for it'.[108] Lest raiders expand their targets, Boyle citizens quickly raised £120 to pay the republican police. People in Castlerea also did so, with raids on six nearby post offices promoting subscriptions and reflecting a nationwide trend that saw over 300 such raids.[109] By the autumn, dozens of sub-post offices from Ballintubber to Keadue and Rahara to Cootehall ceased issuing payments. This angered pensioners, who then had to find transport to the nearest large town.[110] Though undoubtedly a mix of ATIRA operations and criminal acts, the pro-Treaty side ably propagandized that the raids were part of the nexus of chaos promoted by those who sought to undermine the Treaty and peace.[111] To diminish the ATIRA further, newspapers were directed to use the pejorative term 'irregulars' when reporting on their actions. The ATIRA were depicted as a rabble.[112]

The need for better policing led the Provisional government to establish the Civic Guard in April 1922. Its roll-out proved problematic from the start, with attacks on recruiters such as Jim Hunt and H.J. Finlay ensuring that Roscommon joined Kilkenny and Clare at the forefront of anti-Civic Guard activity.[113] Exceptional dissent at the Civic Guard training depot in Kildare, among other issues, meant that it was October before Roscommon received its first deployment of fourteen men in Roscommon town and fifteen in Castlerea. James Feely was appointed as the inspector for Boyle's new recruits soon after, although his colleague in unruly Ballaghaderreen, Sligo man Joe Finnegan, had to wait until April 1923 for all of his men to be deployed.[114] While the *Journal* echoed the police commissioner Eoin O'Duffy in promoting the unarmed force as 'our police' and for all the nation's citizens, the ATIRA suggested the opposite.[115] From November, dozens of encounters from Loughglynn to Strokestown and from Kiltoom to Elphin demonstrated ATIRA antipathy and mirrored instances in numerous other counties.[116] At Loughglynn, the Civic Guard were robbed, assaulted (despite ATIRA orders to the contrary) and accused of being a 'disgrace to the name Irishmen'.[117] Although the Kiltoom police successfully repulsed an ATIRA attack in November, numerous alleged ATIRA raids in the area went unchallenged and made the Civic Guard appear impotent.[118] Similarly, at Strokestown ATIRA forces degraded the Civic Guard by robbing the guards themselves, intimidating magistrates and burning the courthouse.[119] By 1923 the Roscommon Civic Guard had been forced to consolidate at Boyle, Roscommon town, Ballaghaderreen, Castlerea, Strokestown and Elphin. Six stations seemed few but ensured a better spread of manpower than the four in Mayo or two in Sligo.[120] Intimidation continued with the burning of Elphin barracks in January, threats against the police in Boyle and an exchange of gunfire at Rooskey in March that claimed a life on both sides.[121] When the final complement of manpower and barracks had been confirmed in April 1923, it was apparent that the IFS was not providing sufficient resources.[122] When compared to the RIC in 1914, the last year of 'normal' RIC deployment, Roscommon had almost fifty per cent less men in the lower ranks of guard and sergeant (142:271) and fourteen fewer barrack locations.[123] More adequate resources were not deployed until 1924 when Roscommon, Leitrim and Galway joined some southern counties in showing improvements.[124]

The meetings held in advance of the 1922 general election were contentious. Tense scenes at Ballintubber, Castleplunkett, Cloonfad, Ballinlough and Ballinagare saw members of those regions' republican committees hector pro-Treaty speakers.[125] People often attended in limited numbers owing to fear of violence, even when the meetings were chaired by moderate clerics like

Canon Cummins.[126] Less restrained figures, like Fr Sharkey of Strokestown, did little to promote conciliation. The priest argued that the election could not validate a Treaty that was signed under duress. Count Plunkett agreed. It was 'treason against the Republic' to suggest that the election could do so, especially when the second Dáil was never prorogued and was still the de jure government of Ireland.[127] Fr Malachy Brennan dismissed both arguments. He represented the more common view and spoke with the support of the church hierarchy: the electorate was the only body that should decide on whether to accept the Treaty. The *Herald* damned the Provisional government for its 'feebleness' in allowing the enmities to fester and predicted five years of 'torture' if the same men were returned to power.[128]

Third parties endeavoured to introduce calm. Micheál Ó Braonáin was approached by the south Roscommon IFU to run as a compromise candidate. He instead recommended that farmers and labour combine on a 'common understanding', given that the labour 'peace strike' on 24 April evinced that party's desire to avoid conflict.[129] Organized labour in south Roscommon was, however, poorly positioned. Its Roscommon town branch had collapsed due to embezzlement and did not re-emerge until October 1922.[130]

News of an election pact agreed between Éamon de Valera and Michael Collins provided hope. The *Journal* printed the pact's seven points in its 27 May edition, while the *Herald* unsurprisingly declared that the Treaty was dead.[131] The most important point was that the 'present representatives' would form candidate panels and would, if re-elected, constitute a coalition government. Boland hoped that the pact would allow for a 'common platform' and SF unity.[132] He told a Roscommon town audience that the expected coalition would 'make every ounce ... out of the Treaty position' by defining a republican constitution.[133] This aspiration, among others, worried the British. They limited negotiation around the constitution and, cynically, Collins delayed releasing a draft of the agreed clauses until polling day. The constitution's restrictions on Irish autonomy were unknown to most voters by the time they cast their ballot.[134]

In most cases, existing TDs were proposed for the candidate panels. Plunkett was angered. He believed that returning three pro-Treaty TDs on the Leitrim–Roscommon North panel misrepresented the electorate. Republicans would win three of the four seats in a free vote but were instead retaining just his seat.[135] In Mayo South–Roscommon South, Daniel O'Rorke delayed the publication of a national panel with his characteristic indecision.[136] Even when he declared his candidacy, O'Rorke explained that he would reconsider his position on the Treaty if it looked likely that it would 'be the ruin of Ireland'.[137] To underscore the anti-democratic nature of the pact, competitors to the panel candidates in Roscommon were 'strongly opposed'. Although running successfully elsewhere as the Farmers' Party, the IFU withdrew a new candidate in north Roscommon and the well-known Ó Braonáin in south Roscommon. The county council chairman declared that 'Sinn Féin ... deserves the undivided support of all Irishmen'.[138] Collins undermined the pact two days before polling day by urging voters to look only to pro-Treaty candidates.[139] In seven western counties, including Roscommon, this had little effect, as thirty-four TDs were elected unopposed.[140] In the others, polling day on 16 June resulted in the anti-Treaty party losing twenty-two seats.[141]

Increased violence followed. In the days after the election result, the ATIRA in Boyle set up sentry posts, arrested Jim Hunt and tried unsuccessfully to assault Brigadier Michael Dockery of the National army.[142] On 28 June, the Provisional government attacked the ATIRA headquarters at the Four Courts in Dublin and officially started the Irish Civil War. Many fled Boyle three days later when the ATIRA attacked Boyle workhouse, the local headquarters of the National army.[143] After a short exchange of gunfire, Brigadier Dockery left the workhouse to negotiate a ceasefire. The ATIRA shot him dead but were unable to capitalize as Andrew Lavin held the workhouse until reinforcements arrived.[144] The National army then advanced on ATIRA headquarters at the town's military barracks. Although injured by the ATIRA, machine-gun fire from T.J. McNabola forced the anti-Treaty men to burn the barracks and retreat.[145] The next day, the ATIRA seized the Northern and National banks and exchanged sniper shots with government forces. The arrival of further National army reinforcements under Colonel Commandant Alec McCabe prompted a ceasefire. Most of the ATIRA then moved north, out of Boyle, with partisan press reports claiming that they mined buildings as they went.[146] ATIRA member John Kelly recalled that his superiors simply 'considered it was safer to retreat'.[147] By the evening of 3 July, Jim Hunt was released and Boyle was quiet.[148]

The violence caused Boyle's printing presses to close.[149] Consequently, many sought out national dailies to corroborate growing rumours regarding ATIRA bodies littering fields near the town.[150] When printing resumed, the *Herald* addressed the local rumour mill and thanked the National army 'for restoring ordered conditions'. It did, however, lament the accidental death of Ellen Nolan, who had been shot though her window during exchanges.[151] It was reported that the ATIRA occupied large houses near Boyle, including Rockingham, which they initially intended to use as a regional base. Persistent pressure by the National army during the first week in July convinced the bulk of the ATIRA to move north into Arigna. The mountains, caves and mines there would be their base for the remainder of the Civil War.[152]

The first weekend in July also saw the Mayo ATIRA occupy Castlerea. Among other positions, they occupied Clonalis House, one of The O'Conor Don's residences. Preparations for an expected siege led them to commandeer goods (they provided receipts), uproot railway lines, trench roads and blow up a bridge over the River Suck. The 'beleaguered city', as the *Weekly Freeman's Journal* described it, was not targeted by the National army until three weeks later when an eighteen-pounder gun, one of nine borrowed from the British, proved decisive.[153] Some 200 ATIRA were arrested and sent to the overcrowded army prison camp in the newly named Custume Barracks in Athlone. Interestingly, even *Herald* reports followed the broader pro-Treaty press in claiming that the ATIRA badly damaged Clonalis House and filled it with 'looted' goods.[154]

South Roscommon's only other engagement of note occurred at Mount Talbot, where the National army succeeded in driving the Roscommon ATIRA westwards towards Ballygar. The *Freeman's Journal* noted the arrest of Harry Burke, a prominent ATIRA engineer, who underwent a prison conversion to the pro-Treaty side.[155] In a broadly accurate recollection, Frank Simons stated that, apart from Mount Talbot, he did not 'remember a shot being fired anywhere' by the 2nd Western Division in south Roscommon.[156] With the exception of a limited and quickly reversed ATIRA incursion on 19 August and a similarly casualty free sortie in November, Roscommon town saw no Civil War violence.[157] The 'Special War edition' of the *Weekly Freeman's Journal* reported accurately that as the National army pushed ATIRA forces north and west they took towns like Frenchpark 'without firing a shot'.[158] There was some gunfire at Lanesboro, mainly from ATIRA forces attacking the town's police barracks on various occasions from August 1922 to March 1923.[159] There is no doubt that Athlone's large National army presence of over 1,000 men helped control the region. After an uneasy period in April 1922, Mac Eoin had consolidated his position both there and at Shannonbridge. The ATIRA never tried to dislodge him, even though they must have known something of the challenges he faced in securing supplies, weaponry, GHQ support and dealing with insubordination and poorly trained men.[160] Unlike Tipperary or Cork, the ATIRA in Roscommon were too few in number and too poorly supported and organized to make an impact.[161]

From late July the Roscommon ATIRA adopted guerrilla tactics redolent of those used in the War of Independence. The ATIRA who had evacuated Boyle remained in numbers in Arigna. From there, they harassed National army outposts and raiding parties that attempted to undermine anti-Treaty support networks at Ballyfarnon, the creamery at Knockvicar and at the Leitrim border, where Fr Edward Ryans, a regular visitor to Keadue, offered sustained assistance to the ATIRA Arigna brigade.[162] At Carrick-on-Shannon, government forces seized boats to limit Roscommon ATIRA action against the pro-Treaty barracks.[163] On 17 August, the National army moved into Arigna and arrested thirty, including Cumann na mBan members operating a field hospital.[164] The *Irish Independent* reported that:

> Troops ... found in a coal shed ... two wounded men, three nurses, a
> piano, six violas, one box of bacon, three bags of sugar, three bags of
> currants, three bags of soap and other commodities ... including four-
> teen beds.[165]

The arrests did not include the ATIRA leader, Sligo's Edward (Ned) Bofin,
who continued to direct small-scale attacks against the National army in
Roscommon and Leitrim, gaining a fearsome reputation in the process.[166]

Outside of Arigna, most of the Roscommon ATIRA moved towards Mayo,
the county that gave Mac Eoin most trouble.[167] They entered mainly via
Ballaghaderreen, which the ATIRA under Jim Mulrennan had taken in early
July. Comrades from Drumdoe were the first to join Mulrennan's men, who
had seized John Dillon's mansion, sabotaged communications infrastructure
and procured supplies from local merchants.[168] Others migrated there in small
groups during July, with the pro-Treaty press reporting hysterically but not
entirely untruthfully, about farms being 'plundered', clothes being stolen and
beds being commandeered.[169] Cumann na mBan's Agnes Moran supported the
ATIRA on their march and claimed that her septuagenarian father willingly
'gave his bed' to men who needed rest.[170] Patrick Brennan presented the
migrating Roscommon ATIRA as largely defeated: 'they were very fatigued ...
This we knew would end the fight as far as Roscommon was concerned.'[171]

By the end of July, the ATIRA at Ballaghaderreen had begun to move
into Mayo. The town did remain under ATIRA influence, however. The
National army was reluctant to enter because it believed ATIRA forces were
regrouping west of the town at the Mayo border. Consequently, the need for
reliable intelligence caused the army to engage in only small-scale raids under
Alec McCabe that slowly wore down ATIRA numbers. As arrests mounted,
prominent officers such as Joe O'Kelly were captured. When reporting on
O'Kelly's arrest, the *Herald* defied Provisional government instructions by
publishing his rank of adjutant.[172] The prevailing uncertainty caused
Ballaghaderreen to become a 'no man's land' during August and September,
with locals increasingly disadvantaged by the absence of markets and closure
of the town's two banks.[173]

The effect that the Civil War had on non-combatants was profound.
Many had endured hardship since the start of the First World War and had
tolerated additional stresses during the War of Independence as part of their
commitment to an independent Irish state. However, by the summer of 1922,
further disruption proved difficult to endure. The Provisional government
easily depicted the ATIRA as a disruptive, chaotic force, which was attacking
Irish life. Without doubt, damage to communications infrastructure in
Roscommon increased opposition to the ATIRA and Shaun Costello, an anti-
Treatyite from Castlerea, resigned because of the tactic:

We are not only endangering our own supply, but the supplies of the
people. While admitting that the people's verdict in the present issue
has not the force of honesty behind it ... I think their ... hostility is
pretty justifiable.[174]

Costello's point was well made but failed to persuade his comrades to adopt
different tactics. From July 1922 to October, the ATIRA in Roscommon
destroyed more than twenty road and rail bridges, dozens of railway lines, and
much telegraph infrastructure.[175] What Costello did not understand perhaps
was that the ATIRA in Roscommon resorted to such tactics because they
were ill-equipped to undertake more direct forms of anti-government militancy. They had few men, fewer weapons and limited options.

Even if civilians accepted the legitimacy of the ATIRA stratagem, the tactics used to progress it became increasingly unpopular. Initially, the railway
line at Kiltoom, between Athlone and Roscommon town, was targeted by the
ATIRA for supplies, intelligence and to disrupt National army troops using
the trains. For example, in August 1922, the ATIRA highjacked a train, emp-
tied it of people, National army soldiers and cargo, derailed it and then
dropped back to their camp on Inchcleraun island in Lough Ree.[176] However,
National army raids on the island caused desperation and, on the same line
over the next six months, a bridge was bombed twice, mines were laid near
Knockcroghery, the Dublin to Westport mail train was destroyed and the
Kiltoom station manager had his cabin burned when he successfully prevented
an unmanned train reaching Athlone.[177] Similar activity in the 'war on the railways' at Ballymoe ensured that Roscommon became a regular destination for
the National army Railway Protection Corp, which was tasked with restoring
railway security.[178] The increasingly hostile ATIRA approach was also reported
in connection with shop raids as republicans became marginalized. Civil commandeering in Strokestown in November 1922 was replaced by cash thefts and
beatings at Frenchpark and Athleague the following March.[179]

During August 1922, the county council promoted a peaceful resolution
to the Civil War. The shooting dead of Harry Boland on 31 July at Skerries,
Dublin, provided additional motivation.[180] Problems with proposed solutions
were obvious from early on with Daniel O'Rorke's call for Dáil Éireann to
reconvene prompting Denis Creaton to ask: 'From whom will they take their
instruction? From the British Government?'[181] Ó Braonáin disagreed that the
Dáil's 'bitter partisans' could be part of the solution and, with the support of
George Geraghty and the county's other local authorities, instead set about
devising 'important steps ... to have the voice of the people heard on the
matter'.[182] Writing to the *Freeman's Journal* as P.S. Mac Eachach, B.J. Goff
accused Roscommon County Council of seeking to create a smokescreen
behind which the beleaguered ATIRA would regroup. He counselled the gov-

ernment to crush the enemy.[183] Goff's opposition did not dissuade the council, especially after the lamented deaths of Griffith and, one week later,
Collins.[184] Ó Braonáin inveighed against Goff's call for the ATIRA to be
crushed and reminded the solicitor that most of the county council were pro-
Treaty. The chairman demanded that if the Provisional government under its
new president William Cosgrave sought only a military solution, they needed
to 'stand down and let others try'.[185] The council set about organizing an all-
Ireland conference with Ó Braonáin, Geraghty and James Ryan acting as the
Roscommon delegates – two pro- and one anti-Treaty attendee evincing the
balance deemed appropriate.[186] Support came from councils in Galway,
Meath, Wexford, Cavan, Louth and North Tipperary, while Kilkenny and
Clare were in the vanguard of the unenthused.[187] Ó Braonáin's namesake in
Clare reiterated many of Goff's views when responding, while the
Roscommon solicitor penned a further letter that sought to convince Ó
Braonáin to be realistic. Roscommon County Council was not in a position to
dictate; 'the National Government will not allow the like to happen'.[188]

The council's efforts came to naught. Logistics played a part. The attacks
on the railways, as well as a postal strike in September, ensured that moving
the necessary people and post was problematic.[189] While Ó Braonáin thought
Goff's assertion that the county council was buying time for the ATIRA
gained traction, in reality the release of the finalized Irish constitution was
decisive because it confirmed the move away from the republic. Goff was
thanked for his input by both sides. The Provisional government appointed
him to a remunerative magistrate post, while the ATIRA burned down his
Dublin office.[190] After the county council effort, peace resolution fatigue set
in. Local authorities in Roscommon ignored such resolutions until a proposal
from the short-lived Neutral IRA in the spring of 1923. Gerald O'Connor's
presence on the body's executive was possibly the only reason that the
Castlerea RDC did more than just mark it 'read'.[191]

In September, the new Dáil convened. Denounced by Plunkett as 'an
English-made, Partition Parliament', the inaugural 9 September session was
described by the *Journal* as 'the gravest ... on record'.[192] In his only appearance, O'Rorke demanded to know who broke the election pact, 'an agreement
... entered into before the Nation'.[193] He had hoped that a reconvened Dáil
would bring the war to a peaceful conclusion but was instead horrified as the
Herald reported three weeks later on the 'dreadful remedies' that were
enshrined in the Public Order Act.[194] Richard Mulcahy, Michael Collins's
hard-line successor as commander-in-chief of the National army, widely
advertised its most draconian provision: the execution of enemy insurgents.[195]
The quick use of that power in November shocked people across the country. George Geraghty declared that 'Ireland had gone insane'. O'Rorke
resigned his Dáil seat.[196] The new powers were complemented by the actions

of Ireland's Roman Catholic bishops. They released a pastoral letter that largely deprived ATIRA members of the sacraments of the church.[197] Denounced by Fr O'Flanagan in America, the letter drove many citizens away from the ATIRA.[198]

The IFS that came into being on 6 December 1922 quickly enforced its authority using the execution policy. At Custume Barracks in Athlone, Roscommon's Captain Thomas Hughes and four Galway ATIRA comrades were shot by a firing squad on 20 January.[199] Letters written by 21-year-old Hughes before he died showed an admirable absence of malice towards his enemies, his religious devotion and a surprising preparedness for death.[200] The executions led almost 300 prisoners in the barracks to sign a declaration rejecting the ATIRA. This was a welcome outcome for the prison authorities, who had been unequal to the task of maintaining appropriate conditions for the men.[201]

Early 1923 also saw the continuance of an effective, if rudimentary, National army ground offensive. Small ATIRA cohorts around Elphin, Kilmore, Frenchpark, Strokestown, Corrigeenroe, Cootehall and Doon had been broken up in September 1922 by Commandant Mitchell from Boyle.[202] In October the National army disrupted the ATIRA around Ballaghaderreen by shooting dead Commandant Jim Mulrennan, something they repeated in January by killing his replacement Tom Flannery.[203] Mulrennan's brother, Pat, was shot dead in Custume Barracks, Athlone soon after Jim's funeral in Ballaghaderreen. His killing prompted Count Plunkett to write to an unsympathetic Bishop Coyne to ask him to promote the humane treatment of ATIRA prisoners, over 150 of whom died in custody during the war.[204]

The ATIRA at Arigna launched unsuccessful assaults against the reduced – but still better equipped – National army forces in Boyle.[205] Richard Mulcahy wanted the threat posed by the reported 200 ATIRA around Arigna neutralized and he consented to a force of 600 soldiers from Boyle, Sligo, Carrick-on-Shannon, Longford, the Northern Command and Dublin's Portobello barracks scouring the region in February 1923. Audacious attacks in Leitrim by strong ATIRA raiding parties from Arigna made it clear that a concerted drive in the mountains was essential.[206] Although National army reports made much of the discovery of dug outs, communiqués and provisions, only five arrests were made. The commotion the operation created forewarned the ATIRA, who filtered out of the region. Fatalities occurred on both sides. National army sentry Andrew Callaghan was shot dead near Boyle, while Séamus Cull and Paddy Tymon of the ATIRA were killed when a dug-out with access to a cave was mined and gassed.[207] This led to a rumour that the National army had interred twenty-five ATIRA in a mineshaft.[208] The gruesome deaths of Cull and Tymon were deemed a stain on the National army's reputation but did not stop soldiers being active and conspicuous at the funerals of both men.[209] In protracted follow-up raids, Ned Bofin, Fr Ryans and other prominent Arigna ATIRA were arrested. The ATIRA in Arigna were then leaderless.[210]

South of Boyle, the ATIRA were less problematic. Seán Mac Eoin believed that there were just forty ATIRA active around Kilteevan, Castlerea, Elphin, Cootehall and Rockingham.[211] Drum, Kiltoom and Brideswell hosted another twenty, who continued to be motivated by the 'fear and influence ... of the female element'.[212] The influence of these women who appear, in the main, to have been individuals unaffiliated with Cumann na mBan, was addressed by Bishop Coyne in his 1923 Lenten pastoral, which followed those of his fellow bishops in condemning the ATIRA. He inveighed against republicans for operating 'without moral sanction', described their killing of Free State troops as 'murder before God' and claimed they were more interested in drinking than republicanism. He denounced:

> Half-crazed, hysterical women ... [who] devote a large portion of their time to the circulation of calumnies ... They assist in ... the slaughter of the best and bravest of Ireland's sons. They glory in ... [the] continued crucifixion of the plain people of the country.[213]

Coyne's invective mirrored that of Cardinal Michael Logue, many fellow clerics and pro-Treaty politicians and undoubtedly reduced support for the ATIRA.[214] By the late spring of 1923, train services became more regular, reports from the army's command posts in Athlone and Boyle noted greater calm, while Ballaghaderreen's banks reopened and pensions began to be paid by smaller post offices.[215] The death of Liam Lynch, national leader of the ATIRA, in April paved the way for peace negotiations between de Valera and William Cosgrave. A truce was declared for 12 p.m. on 30 April.[216] Some press reports indicated that Boyle saw the final action of the Civil War when the few ATIRA remaining in Arigna attempted to disarm and kidnap National army soldiers.[217] Republican bona fides were questioned as a result and, while government forces continued to seek out the Roscommon ATIRA, the release of fifty more ex-combatants from Custume Barracks was seen as a positive step towards promoting peace.[218] The war officially came to an end on 24 May when Liam Lynch's replacement, Frank Aiken, ordered the ATIRA to dump their arms. On 2 June the *Herald* reported 'Peace has broken out at last'.[219] The *Journal* concentrated on preparations for Corpus Christi, possibly in the hope that religious devotions would help salve the county's wounds.[220]

The five months after the truce in July 1921 saw relief, optimism and triumphalism in Roscommon. As life returned to normality, even areas that saw the worst tensions and still hosted numerous Crown forces appeared peaceful. Although in many respects the terms of the truce were not adhered to, optimism promoted tolerance as both sides kept the larger picture in view. The provisions of the Anglo-Irish Treaty undermined that optimism. Although discord among the county's TDs reflected an even split in opinions, it is certain that Plunkett and Boland represented a minority. Anti-Treaty sentiment was outweighed by abhorrence at the idea of a return to war. The indecisive Daniel O'Rorke understood that and, accordingly, voted for the Treaty as did Andrew Lavin. The support for the Treaty offered by the Roman Catholic Church proved decisive and saw Fr O'Flanagan occupy a peripheral position for the first time in his political career. From January 1922, the exodus of Crown forces and the instatement of their Irish replacements was ably portrayed as proof of the positive consequences of the Treaty. Such activity undoubtedly helped Seán Mac Eoin convince Martin Fallon to change sides and recognize, as did Andrew Lavin, that the republic could still be achieved. Moves to deal decisively with land agitators in Roscommon during 1922 showed the ongoing threat that localism posed to the new state. However, its more subdued nature also intimated that the Dublin-based legislature was trusted to deliver a more equitable solution than had Westminster. That solution probably frightened the already pressurized Protestant minority in Roscommon who were reminded that political atavisms persisted. Activity connected with the general election of June 1922 highlighted the growing enmity between the two sides which erupted after the collapse of the election pact, one that Roscommon honoured. The Civil War that followed saw only short-lived conventional warfare at Boyle and Castlerea which indicated that the ATIRA would not gain the support it required in Roscommon. Its conversion into a disparate guerrilla force scattered across the mountains at Arigna or seeking refuge in Mayo was almost predictable. Despite men like Patrick Brennan being committed to the republic, the evolution of the ATIRA war strategy made it unpopular. The dislocation of commerce and disruption of the railways denied people the normality they desired. The efforts of Roscommon County Council to force a peaceful resolution to the Civil War showed that many deemed the Provisional government's strategy divisive, brutal and short-sighted. However, the failure of the council's efforts, the government's execution policy and the reaffirmation of the Catholic Church's opposition to ATIRA activity, especially that of Bishop Coyne in Roscommon, hastened what was an inevitable republican defeat.

9 Revolution?

The period 1912–23 in Roscommon was remarkable but whether this was revolutionary is open to debate. In the main, familiar political and socio-economic desires drove behaviour that conformed to patterns established well
before the formation of Dáil Éireann, the armed conflict with Britain or the
signing of the Treaty in December 1921. Politically, the Roscommon of 1923
had much more in common with the Roscommon of 1912 than men such as
J.P. Hayden would have liked to admit. Political parties and personalities had
changed, but little had happened that could truly be described as revolutionary. Throughout those twelve years, the desire for change in Roscommon was
repeatedly restrained by a conservative localism that prioritized one issue
above all others: land.

The home rule campaign from 1912 to 1914 indicated that most in the
county were content to remain within the British imperial family. Even those
who entertained more advanced views, such as George Geraghty and Micheál
Ó Braonáin, understood that an Irish parliament subordinate to Westminster
would be accepted if it addressed the land issue. Resistance in Roscommon to
unionist efforts to derail home rule showed strong commitment to the home
rule bill (or at least its potential), local MPs and the IPP. There were few
demands for a greater measure of Irish autonomy. Indeed, after John
Redmond adopted the Irish Volunteers in May 1914, exceptional numbers
vowed to fight in the potential civil war that imperilled home rule. When the
First World War halted moves towards internecine violence, support for the
IPP in Roscommon was as strong as it had ever been.

Initially, predictions of a short war followed by implementation of the suspended Home Rule Act appeared reasonable. Roscommon nationalists and
unionists were guided by IPP politicians and the county's newspapers in supporting the war effort. However, as the conflict dragged on and the war economy exacted an unsustainable toll, many viewed the IPP in an increasingly
negative light. Due to IPP inaction, inequitable access to land in Roscommon
grew more pronounced, while food became scarce and more expensive.
Although, as in counties across Ireland, the war had a disastrous impact on
people's day-to-day lives, Roscommon's rurality ensured that the deprivation
engendered by the war, which affected urban Ireland most, was not as starkly
realized there. Even then, however, the subordination of such fundamental
issues to the war effort proved a disastrous misstep by Hayden and John
Fitzgibbon. It fell primarily to Canon Cummins and the RAEC to fight on
behalf of beleaguered small farmers pressured by IPP members who promoted
army enlistment. Roscommon's eligible male population in general was averse

to joining the army, including the Redmondite National Volunteers. The threat of conscription prompted many young men to emigrate; those prevented from doing so looked for an alternative political organization that would better represent them. The increase in Irish Volunteers membership and activity during 1915, although limited geographically and numerically, signalled growing nationalist radicalism in parts of Roscommon. The combination of the malaise that beset the UIL since the start of the war and waning IPP popularity allowed little scope for curtailing that growth or reinvigorating constitutional nationalism, even before Easter 1916.

The IPP's reaction to the 1916 Rising further undermined the party's support. Hayden, Fitzgibbon and the IPP leadership appeared powerless as the British executed the Rising's leaders and imposed repressive measures nationwide. Despite Roscommon's quiescence during Easter Week 1916, a disproportionate number of raids and arrests took place. IPP moves to save home rule by entertaining partition occasioned negative commentary on a scale that the party had never encountered in Roscommon before. With the exception of the *Messenger*, the Roscommon press represented the widely held belief that the IPP was set to betray its followers. During the autumn and winter of 1916, SF attracted more Roscommon supporters, with men such as George Geraghty and Micheál Ó Braonáin wielding greater influence. Growing SF support in Roscommon was widely acknowledged by the authorities. The first serious test of that support in February 1917 proved to be a decisive step towards the political destruction of the IPP.

Count Plunkett's victory in the Roscommon North by-election in 1917 was a pivotal moment for advanced nationalism in Ireland. It confirmed that a broader strategy of seeking parliamentary office was an effective means of undermining the British administration. The IPP was defeated by an impressive margin rather than by an impressive candidate, with the work of Fr Michael O'Flanagan proving key to Plunkett's success. Undoubtedly, the weak IPP candidate and the negligent approach of the party leadership helped. The IPP appeared as ossified and passive as advanced nationalists alleged. The by-election allowed Plunkett's supporters enhance their appeal to an electorate that was for so long under the influence of Redmondism. Canvassers did not talk of revolution, or indeed, parliamentary abstention. Instead, they relied on the poor recent record of the IPP and invoked the memory of Parnell. The involvement of young clerics, as well as young men and women in the Plunkett campaign, was important. It showed that the youth of Roscommon were inclined to think more radically than their parents and, when given the chance to vote, would reject the IPP. The Roscommon North by-election revealed many of the key indicators of Ireland's future political path and provided a springboard for further by-election victories in neighbouring Longford South and indeed across Ireland.

The period between the by-election and the general election of 1918 saw exceptional SF growth in Roscommon. By the time the impotent Irish Convention convened in the summer of 1917, it was clear that the IPP had become largely irrelevant. SF extended its grassroots, forming dozens of branches using well-established UIL structures as a framework and acknowledging older IPP legacies in the process. The comfortable continuity in reusing those structures and invoking the legacies of Emmet, Parnell and Davitt helped attract the county's moderates. So too did the involvement of clerics in branch committees and George Geraghty's assertion that SF was not a party promoting revolution. Indeed, such was the efficacy of the SF approach that when it moved to supplant the AOH in the winter of 1917, some divisions felt comfortable enough to move as a unit, bringing their finances with them. SF was the natural harbour for those seeking to demonstrate their anger with the IPP in the most politically effective way. J.P. Hayden's efforts for the IPP proved his honest devotion to its policies. However, it also exposed his lack of pragmatism. Former allies such as D.J. Kelly were able to step away from Redmond's party when its policies became undeniably unpopular.

The reinvigoration of land agitation in 1918 was the culmination of anger at four years of IPP inactivity on the land issue. It was also the first time in forty years that such widespread agitation was conducted without IPP guidance in Roscommon. Importantly, resistance to SF attempts to manage the unrest made it clear to the ascendant party that the land question would not be subordinated to the pursuit of independence in Roscommon. The more acute threat of conscription defused the agitation and brought the IPP and SF together on a common platform. However, it did not arrest the decline of the IPP, which was terminal by mid-1918. Tellingly, the boost in Irish Volunteer numbers prompted by the conscription threat was temporary in most of Roscommon. Support for an Irish revolution was limited to a minority; there was little desire to engage in armed conflict whether on the fields of Flanders or the pastures of Roscommon. As was apparent throughout the period, British strategies promoted outcomes that undermined the Crown. The German Plot arrests and the increasingly draconian use of DORA during 1918 pushed many moderates towards SF and bolstered the party's election prospects in the process.

The 1918 election result in Roscommon South was predictable; the voting simply confirmed the margin of Harry Boland's majority. Again, J.P. Hayden's earnestness was on show, but people had moved beyond home rule and the IPP; neither met the demands of the enlarged and more youthful electorate. Canon Cummins's support for Boland in 1918 was important. It confirmed that not only young curates believed that Ireland's political future was best entrusted to SF. Any allusions to a violent revolutionary strategy were masked by calls from Boland for the people to support Irish efforts to achieve independence through the Paris Peace Conference. Hayden remained a political moderate for the rest of his life – he died in 1954, and was, at the time of his death, both the last remaining prominent IPP member and the longest serving editor of any provincial newspaper in Ireland.

The establishment of Dáil Éireann in January 1919 promoted change in the Irish judicial system and local authority politics in Roscommon. The republican court system proved hugely popular, especially the land arbitration courts which limited the threat posed by the land agitation of 1920 to the republic. The alacrity with which the land courts were established showed the influence that the land agitation of the west and mid-west had; it forced the Dáil to prioritize the issue. Roscommon comprehensively supported republican parish and district courts during the summer of 1920. Again, much about them was familiar; people embraced the structures of the republican counter-state because they were not uncomfortably radical. When local elections concluded that summer, Roscommon's local authorities were almost exclusively republican. The eager councillors and guardians quickly came to understand that declarations of loyalty to Dáil Éireann, although essential for the integrity of the counter-state, greatly undermined their financial position. The unions in both Boyle and Athlone might have framed their decision to re-engage with the LGB as common-sense pragmatism; however, it was not the type of continuity that the republic could abide.

Unsurprisingly, given the reluctance to consider armed revolutionary activity, the military aspect of the War of Independence was not an early feature in Roscommon. When it became clear that the Peace Conference would not serve Irish demands, the promotion of a violent approach required groundwork. Fr O'Flanagan denounced British policy towards Ireland and repeatedly framed the RIC and British army as forces of occupation and enemies of Ireland. The ostracization of the police, in particular, was an essential step in marking them as legitimate targets in the war. Raids, arrests and propaganda surrounding hunger strikes in April 1920 all fuelled the belief that the Crown forces were malevolent. IRA enforcement ensured that the boycott of the Crown forces was comprehensive from June 1920, just before the first police fatalities in Roscommon.

When Constable Martin Clarke was shot dead at Beechwood in July, the conflict was eighteen months old; counties in the south and mid-west had already amassed a number of Crown force fatalities. The early reluctance to engage in lethal violence in Roscommon could be explained in part by the absence of good ambush positions, quality weapons, appropriately motivated commanders or, more fundamentally, the need to overcome an aversion to homicide. Crown forces fatalities increased only slowly over the autumn months as the tactics deployed by the RIC and British army became more abhorrent. Three brigades were separately responsible for the fatalities at Athlone, Knockcroghery and Ratra in August and September. Even then, the ambush at

Ratra was carried out by the South Sligo IRA, rather than a Roscommon brigade. Indeed, large swaths of the county, especially in the south, were generally quiescent during the war, with Roscommon town notable for its non-violent character throughout the entire period of 1912–23. Undoubtedly, however, the Black and Tans' response to Ratra promoted greater IRA activity in areas around Strokestown, and initiated the first instalment in Roscommon of the cycles of violence that typified the war across Ireland. The ambush at Fourmilehouse, which led to four Crown fatalities and a murderous response from the Auxiliary Division RIC that put the IRA on the back foot, was the starkest example of this in 1920. The formation of the Roscommon ASUs and the intervention of Seán Connolly were required to push the Roscommon IRA into greater offensive activity in the aftermath. Yet, even then, most operations during the winter of 1920 were both modest, in that they targeted just one or two policemen, and, with one exception, unsuccessful in killing members of the Crown forces. Anti-British sentiment was increasing, however. The death of Terence MacSwiney, the arrests of Frs Glynn and Roddy, and the comprehensive application of ROIA provisions ensured that republicans gained further support for their aims and were better motivated for the fight.

The low-level IRA activity was also influenced by the belief that some civilians in Roscommon were assisting the Crown forces. In late 1920, a paranoid IRA began to kill suspected informers. Mainly circumstantial evidence such as previous membership of the Crown forces or excessive contact with the RIC led to the deaths of Edward Canning, Bernard Ward and Martin Heavey. Greater efforts to ascertain loyalties in the spring of 1921 ensured that the evidence against men such as Frank Elliot and Edward Beirne was more convincing. Notably, the deaths of alleged informers fed the cyclical violence around Castlerea where the actions of the British army and the 'Murder Gang' under Sergeant James King made for a prolonged period of reprisal and counter-reprisal.

Another factor that contributed to the escalating violence in the spring of 1921 was the hanging of Patrick Moran. Less than a fortnight after his death on 14 March, the number of fatalities among the Crown forces in Roscommon since July 1920 almost doubled over the space of two days after ambushes at Keadue and Scramogue. Scramogue was the most ambitious operation seen since Fourmilehouse and caused more fatalities than any other, including that of the highest ranked British officer to be killed in Roscommon, Captain Peek. The brutal and undisciplined response of the Crown forces claimed the life of innocent 15-year-old James Mulloy. His death, along with those of Michael Wynne and Patrick Coyle, exposed the callous disregard many members of the Crown forces had for those caught between them and the IRA. Such disregard informed the destruction of Knockcroghery in June after the killing of Colonel Commandant Lambert and motivated the IRA to eliminate the Castlerea IRA's arch-nemesis, Sergeant James King, before the truce came into effect on 11 July 1921.

It must also be acknowledged, however, that IRA members were themselves capable of acting callously and self-interestedly. The deaths of Thomas McGowan and the Waldron brothers over land disputes proved not only that people in Roscommon would kill to increase their acreage, but that some in the IRA abused their position to do so.

The end of hostilities was embraced in Roscommon with violent encounters dropping off as soon as the truce came into force. Breaches of the terms of the truce were frequent, yet tolerated; there was too much at stake and neither side wanted a return to violence. The IRA and its supporters promoted the view that the British had been defeated, while the county's press, most notably the *Herald*, naively assured readers that another Irish victory would follow after negotiations in London. When the details of the Treaty became known, it was easy to identify those driven by ideology and those driven by realism. The opposition of Plunkett and Boland did little to promote anti-Treaty sentiment in Roscommon; most adopted the position of Andrew Lavin. The Treaty was a sensible step towards the republic, one that would allow normal life to resume more quickly. As the British Crown forces departed Roscommon for the final time, the county's newspapers all promoted acceptance of the settlement. The Treaty split in the Roscommon IRA initially saw the ATIRA in the county well situated, with Martin Fallon leading them from his Boyle base. However, his defection fatally undermined anti-Treaty support in the region and presaged a weak ATIRA military campaign in Roscommon.

The conduct of the general election of 1922 ensured that an Irish Civil War was inevitable. Roscommon was one of the few counties that honoured the election pact and voted for the promised coalition panel. The county's desire for peace ensured that the Civil War never became the vicious dogfight that was witnessed in the south and south-west. Outside of Boyle and Castlerea, there were no major skirmishes. In less than six weeks, the ATIRA was reduced to waging a guerrilla campaign that was increasingly limited, both geographically and numerically. National army operations, though often crude, were effective in corralling ATIRA forces in the Arigna mountains and around the Mayo border at Ballaghaderreen. The conduct of the campaign by the ATIRA and the propaganda deployed by the Provisional government ensured that republicans did not increase their support in Roscommon. The destruction of railway infrastructure, in particular, continued the hardships suffered by many since 1914. Ordinary Roscommon people desired normality and only the Provisional government could provide it as it established departments and made available public service jobs. The pre-eminent position of the pro-Treaty government led it to disdain the naive efforts of Roscommon County Council to usher in peace negotiations, encourage the Catholic

Church to denounce the ATIRA and carry out deeply divisive executions that claimed the life of Roscommon man Thomas Hughes in January 1923. From then until the declaration of a truce in May, the ATIRA were reduced to engaging in what were depicted as criminal acts against traders, the police and, most importantly, the people of Ireland.

The re-emergence of agrarian unrest in 1922, although more limited than in 1918 or 1920, brought back into focus Roscommon's localism, which reflected attitudes found in many western counties. Although an Irish government was now in charge, official attempts to suppress the agitation were resisted. The Provisional government and the IFS deployed tactics similar to the British in previous decades. They issued official threats and eventually sent in the army. The land issue was further complicated by the ATIRA, which used it both to foment wider unrest and to gain support among disgruntled small farmers. However, the number of such farmers was greatly diminished, even when compared to 1920. The land courts, like the land acts of 1903 and 1909, had reduced the need for such activism. Roscommon farmers were more likely to look to the Land Act (1923) and the Land Law (Commission) Act (1923) that dissolved the CDB, than the ATIRA.

During the spring and summer of 1922, land agitation in Roscommon targeted Protestant owners of large farms as it always had. Unlike previous years, however, the attacks on Protestant farmers coincided with a limited campaign against people of that denomination in particular parts of the county. Instances of land-related intimidation against owners such as the Talbots of Mount Talbot were grouped by unionist newspapers alongside instances of sectarian intimidation, such as the vandalism of Clews hall in Boyle. Presenting the action against the Talbots as sectarian was intended to promote a commonly advanced unionist thesis that the new Irish state was moving to purge non-Catholics. Census information for 1926, fifteen years after the previous census of 1911, shows that the proportionate decrease in Protestants in Roscommon at 39.5 per cent was four times the rate for Roman Catholics. However, the total reduction in Protestant numbers of 740 out of a total population decline of 10,400 in the county was undoubtedly influenced more readily by factors other than sectarian intimidation.[1] A study of Longford has noted that Protestants from that county actually migrated to Roscommon and it has advanced realistic reasons for the decline in the Protestant population that would also apply to Roscommon.[2] The withdrawal of the British army from Boyle and Athlone, the disbandment of the RIC, natural attrition, fatalities in the First World War, lower birth rates and voluntary emigration probably all exerted a greater influence than sectarianism on declining Protestant numbers in Roscommon between 1911 and 1926.

The results of the August 1923 general election showed a county still divided politically. The newly defined four-seat Roscommon constituency witnessed a turnout of 58 per cent, which was lower than the national average of 61.3. Cumann na nGaedheal, the newly-established party led by William Cosgrave, took almost 42 per cent of the vote in the county, but was closely followed by Republicans with 36.5. In what was his last election victory, Count Plunkett received the highest number of first preference votes, 5,507, but was, like all four TDs, elected without achieving the quota. He failed to regain his seat in 1927. Alongside Fr O'Flanagan, he continued to support the republic and became an increasingly marginal figure in the process. Cumann na Gaedheal's Andrew Lavin and H.J. Finlay also took seats in 1923 along with Republican Gerard Boland, Harry's brother, who represented the county for the next thirty-four years. Labour secured just 4.9 per cent of the total poll, Roscommon's rurality being key to its lack of success.[3] Jasper Tully entered the contest and received a vote total only slightly higher than that of 1917. He continued to edit the *Herald* and remained a prominent provincial voice until his death in 1938. Direct links to IPP legacies were of little benefit to Henry Fitzgibbon, the least loved son of John. Left a telling £1 in his father's will, Henry's vote total was just as unimpressive. The Farmers' Party performed poorly. Its three candidates, including Micheál Ó Braonáin, secured just a 12.2 per cent share. His decision to run alongside old-school IPP men John Drury and Edward Cline raised a few eyebrows, but was simply further proof of his prioritization of farmers' interests. Voting in the election of 1923 had concentrated on resolving the fall-out from the Civil War, rather than such local issues. Four years later the greater prominence of farmers' issues saw him elected as an Independent in June and again that September as a member of Cumann na Gaedheal.[4] He was elected to represent Roscommon on three further occasions but lost his seat in the 1943 general election.

Ó Braonáin's politics could, in part, be seen as reflecting those of Roscommon generally. Land and farming promoted political activism and often led to political success. At times, ideological considerations or national issues could shift focus, but the land was the only issue that constantly mobilized the county's citizens in their thousands and, consequently, provided long-term support for political personalities and parties. Political developments in Roscommon from 1912 to 1923 revealed the evolution of the political system, both at local and national level, rather than anything more revolutionary. Ó Braonáin obviously recognized that the IPP had gotten much right in its approach to Roscommon and he was not the only prominent advanced nationalist to do so. George Geraghty moved to emulate T.J. Devine, John Keaveny and George O'Reilly when he received what he claimed was the first auctioneers license issued by the Provisional government in January 1922.[5] He understood that to be successful in Roscommon, politically and commercially, you needed to be at the heart of the county's affairs; you needed to focus on the land.

Notes

CHAPTER ONE *County Roscommon in 1912*

1 *Roscommon Messenger (RM)*, 21 Jan. 1922.
2 *Census of Ireland 1911, County of Roscommon*, table XXIX, p. vii.
3 Ibid., table XXII, p. 79.
4 Brian Hughes, *Defying the IRA: intimidation, coercion, and communities during the Irish revolution* (Liverpool, 2016), p. 146.
5 *Census of Ireland, part two: General report with tables and appendix*, House of Commons, 1913 (Cd. 6663), p. lix.
6 *Census of Ireland 1911, County of Roscommon*, table XLI, p. 124.
7 *Emigration statistics for Ireland for the year 1912, reports and tables showing the numbers, ages, conjugal condition, and destinations of emigrants from each county and province in Ireland during the year 1912; also the occupations of the emigrants, and the number of emigrants who left each port in each month of the year*, House of Commons, 1913 (Cd. 6727), table I, p. 11, table IV, p. 15.
8 *Census of Ireland 1911, County of Roscommon*, table XXI, pp 74–8.
9 RIC County Inspector's monthly report (CI) Roscommon, Sept. 1905; May 1906 (NAI, IGCI/8; IGCI/10); *Census of Ireland 1911, County of Roscommon*, table XX, p. 69.
10 *Census of Ireland 1911, County of Roscommon*, table XX, pp 66–7, 70–2.
11 *Agricultural statistics, Ireland, 1912*, table 1, p. 23.
12 *Department of Agriculture and Technical Instruction for Ireland. Agricultural statistics of Ireland 1913. General abstracts showing the acreage under crops and the numbers and descriptions of livestock in each county and province 1912–13*, House of Commons, 1913 (Cd. 7063), pp 11, 24–5; *Agricultural statistics, Ireland, 1912*, table 17, pp 98–101.
13 Ibid., table 5, pp 34–5, table 9, pp 62–3, table 11, pp 86–7; *Agricultural statistics, 1913, general abstract*, pp 14–17.
14 Daphne Dyer Wolf, 'Two windows: the tenants of the de Freyne rent strike, 1901–1903' (PhD, Drew University, 2019).
15 *Census of Ireland 1911, County of Roscommon*, table XXIII, p. 81.
16 Michael Wheatley, *Nationalism and the Irish Party: provincial Ireland, 1910–1916* (Oxford, 2010), pp 24–5.
17 CI Roscommon, May, July, Oct. 1907 (NAI, IGCI/11; IGCI/12).
18 RIC Inspector General's monthly report (IG), Nov., Dec. 1908 (NAI, IGCI/15); CI Roscommon, Dec. 1908 (NAI, IGCI/15).
19 CI Roscommon, Feb. 1912 (TNA, CO 904/86); *Judicial statistics, Ireland, 1912*, table 6, pp 26–7.
20 David Seth Jones, *Graziers, land reform, and political conflict in Ireland* (Washington DC, 1995), pp 54, 97–9, 242.
21 www.landedestates.ie – (accessed July 2018).
22 *Department of Agriculture and Technical Instruction for Ireland. Agricultural statistics of Ireland with detailed report for the year 1908*, House of Commons, 1909 (Cd. 4940), table 1, p. 22; *Agricultural statistics, Ireland, 1912*, table M, p. 15.
23 *Agricultural statistics, Ireland, 1908*, table 1, p. 22; *Agricultural statistics, Ireland, 1912*, table M, pp 15–16.
24 *Census of Ireland 1911, general report*, table 157, p. 436.
25 Ibid., table 150, pp 424–7.
26 *Census of Ireland 1911, County of Roscommon*, table X, pp 57–9.

27 CI Roscommon, July 1911 (TNA, CO 904/84); *RH*, 6 Jan., 22 June 1912; *RJ*, 17 Aug. 1912.

28 *Census of Ireland 1911, County of Roscommon*, table XXII, pp 79–81.

29 *The Bystander*, 18 Mar. 1908.   30 *Freeman's Journal (FJ)*, 19 Aug. 1898.

31 CI Roscommon, Jan. 1901 (TNA, CO 904/72).

32 *Dublin Evening Mail*, 19 May 1902; Clancy was bishop from 1895 to 1912.

33 CI Roscommon, Sept. 1901–Mar. 1903 (TNA, CO 904/74; CO 904/75; CO 904/76; NAI, IGCI/3); *United Irish League National Directory minute book* (NLI, MS 708); CI Roscommon, July 1911 (TNA, CO 904/84).

34 *Westmeath Independent (WI)*, 22 Apr. 1911; *RM*, 12 Aug. 1911.

35 *RJ*, 6 May 1911.   36 *Weekly Freeman's Journal (WFJ)*, 2 Dec. 1911.

37 *Strokestown Democrat (SD)*, 30 Dec. 1916, 6 Jan. 1917; Paul Rouse, 'James Joseph O'Kelly', *DIB*; Owen McGee, *The IRB: the Irish Republican Brotherhood from the Land League to Sinn Féin* (Dublin, 2006), pp 38, 57, 175.

38 Paul Bew, *Conflict and conciliation in Ireland, 1890–1910: Parnellites and radical agrarians* (New York, 1989), pp 160–2, 179.

39 *Irish Times (IT)*, 3 Jan. 1912; John Bligh, 'John Fitzgibbon of Castlerea: "A most mischievous and dangerous agitator"' in Brian Casey (ed.), *Defying the law of the land: agrarian radicals in Irish history* (Dublin, 2014), pp 295–322.

40 Bew, *Conflict*, pp 179–81.

41 *RH*, 18 May 1912; Wheatley, *Nationalism*, pp 35–6, 96–8; John Bligh, 'John Fitzgibbon' in *DIB*.

42 CI Roscommon, Précis of Information, Apr. 1905 (TNA, CO 904/117); CI Roscommon, July 1905 (NAI, IGCI/8).

43 CI Roscommon, Jan., Feb., Apr. 1906 (NAI, IGCI/9).

44 CI Roscommon, Aug. 1907; Feb. 1908 (NAI, IGCI/12/13).

45 John Burke, *Athlone 1900–1923: politics, revolution and civil war* (Dublin, 2015), pp 71–3.

46 CI Roscommon, July 1911 (TNA, CO 904/84); David Fitzpatrick, *Politics and Irish life, 1913–1921: provincial experience of war and revolution* (2nd ed., Cork, 1998 [1977]), p. 82.

47 *RJ*, 4 Feb. 1899; John Cunningham, *Labour in the west of Ireland: working life and struggle, 1890–1914* (Belfast, 1995), p. 99; *WFJ*, 15 May 1920.

48 *Dublin Daily Nation*, 2 Oct. 1899.

49 CI Roscommon, Aug. 1906 (NAI, IGCI/10); Cunningham, *Labour*, pp 116–17, 121–4.

50 *SD*, 11 Oct. 1913; Cunningham, *Labour*, pp 53, 121.

51 C. Desmond Greaves, *The Irish Transport and General Workers' Union: the formative years, 1909–1923* (Dublin, 1982), p. 69.

52 *RM*, 29 June 1907.

53 *Irish Independent (II)*, 24 Sept. 1907; *RM*, 28 Sept. 1907.

54 *RM*, 5, 12 Oct. 1907.   55 CI Roscommon, Sept. 1907 (NAI, IGCI/12).

56 CI Roscommon, Oct. 1907 (NAI, IGCI/12).

57 Burke, *Athlone*, pp 60–8; McGee, *IRB*, p. 321.

58 CI Roscommon, Mar. 1908 (NAI, IGCI/13).

59 Wheatley, *Nationalism*, p. 59.   60 *Irish Citizen (IC)*, 8 June 1912.

61 Ibid., 14 Mar. 1914.   62 Ibid., 7 May 1913; 21 Feb. 1914.

63 Ibid., 14 Mar. 1914.

64 CI Roscommon, May, Sept. 1901 (TNA, CO 904/73).

65 CI Roscommon, July 1909 (TNA, CO 904/78); Matthew Davis (BMH WS 691, p. 1); Thomas Brady (BMH WS 1,008, p. 1); Andrew Keaveney (BMH WS 1,178, p. 1).

66 CI Roscommon, Nov. 1902 (TNA, CO 904/76); Timothy McMahon, *Grand opportunity: the Gaelic revival and Irish society, 1893–1910* (Syracuse, 2008), p. 241.

67 *Census of Ireland 1911, general report*, table 142, p. 291.

68 CI Roscommon, July 1905, May 1906 (NAI, IGCI/8; IGCI/9).

69 McMahon, *Grand opportunity*, pp 76–7; Diarmaid Breathnach & Máire Ní Mhurchú, *Beathaisnéis a cúig* (Baile Átha Cliath, 1997), p. 62.

70 Roscommon won the 1903 Connacht championship but were later disqualified for invalid registration. *Sport*, 19 Apr., 3 May 1902; CI Roscommon, Nov. 1903, Feb., Aug., Oct., Dec. 1904 (NAI, IGCI/4/5/6).

71 CI Roscommon, Dec. 1905, Mar., Apr. 1906, Sept. 1907 (NAI, IGCI/8; IGCI/9; IGCI/12).

72 CI Roscommon, Jan. 1912 (TNA, CO 904/86); *RJ*, 4 May 1912.

73 *Judicial statistics, Ireland 1912*, table 12, pp 38–9.

74 Ibid., *1912*, table E, pp xxxiv–xxxv.   75 Ibid., pp xiii, table 6, pp 26–7.

76 Christopher Doughan, *The voice of the provinces: the regional press in revolutionary Ireland* (Liverpool, 2019), pp 126–9.

77 Marie Louise Legg, 'Jasper Tully' in *DIB*.   78 *IT*, 10 Dec. 1909.

CHAPTER TWO *'Declare our unswerving faith': towards the home rule act, 1912–14*

1 *RM*, 6, 13, 20 Jan. 1912.   2 *FJ*, 3 Jan. 1912.

3 *United Irish League National Directory minute book* (NLI, MS 708).

4 *RH*, 3 Feb. 1912; *RJ*, 4, 11, 25 May 1912.

5 *SD*, 24 May 1913.   6 *RJ*, 21 Sept. 1912.

7 Burke, *Athlone*, p. 41.

8 CI Roscommon, Apr., May, June 1913 (TNA, CO 904/89; CO 904/90).

9 CI Roscommon, Dec. 1913 (TNA, CO 904/91); *RJ*, 24 Jan. 1914.

10 *RM*, 8 June 1912.

11 CI Roscommon, Mar., Apr. 1912 (TNA, CO 904/86).   12 *FJ*, 13 Apr. 1912.

13 *RH*, 3, 10 Feb. 1912.   14 *RJ*, 17 Feb. 1912.

15 *RM*, 18, 25 Jan. 1913.

16 Ibid., 15 Feb. 1913; *RJ*, 1 Mar. 1913.   17 *II*, 1 Mar. 1913; *WFJ*, 8 Mar. 1913.

18 *RM*, 1 Mar. 1913; *RJ*, 15 Mar. 1913.   19 *SD*, 29 Mar. 1913.

20 *RH*, 10 Aug. 1912.   21 *II*, *DDE*, 7 Aug. 1912.

22 *FJ*, 16 Aug. 1912; *RJ*, 17 Aug. 1912.   23 *IT*, 14 June 1913.

24 Ibid., 16, 20, 22 Aug. 1912. 25 *Belfast Weekly News*, 15 Aug. 1912.

26 *RM*, 2, 9 Nov. 1912.   27 Burke, *Athlone*, p. 78.   28 *RJ*, 19 Oct. 1912.

29 *SD*, 13, 27 Dec. 1913.   30 *SD*, 13, 27 Dec. 1913; *RH*, 3 Jan. 1914.

31 *Manchester Courier and Lancashire General Advertiser*, 13 Dec. 1913.

32 *Belfast Telegraph* (*BT*), 9 Dec. 1913.

33 *Weekly Irish Times* (*WIT*), 20 Dec. 1913.   34 *SD*, 27 Dec. 1913.

35 *RM*, 6, 13 Dec. 1913, 3 Jan. 1914.

36 *RM*, 20, 27 Jan., 3, 10 Feb. 1912, 21 June 1913.   37 Ibid., 16 Aug. 1913.

38 *RH*, 1 Jan., 3, 10 Feb., 5 May 1912, 2 Aug. 1913.   39 Ibid., 14 June 1913.

40 CI Roscommon, Nov. 1913 (TNA, CO 904/91).   41 *WFJ*, 20 Sept. 1913.

42 *RM*, 20, 27 Sept. 1913.   43 *RH*, 11 Oct., 1 Nov. 1913.

44 Burke, *Athlone*, pp 84–94.   45 *WI*, 18 Oct. 1913; *RJ*, 1 Nov. 1913.

46 *RH*, 29 Nov. 1913.   47 *RM*, 6 Dec. 1913.   48 *WI*, 1, 29 Nov. 1913.

49 *RH*, 6, 20 Dec. 1913.   50 Burke, *Athlone*, p. 97.

51 CI Roscommon, Mar. 1914 (TNA, CO 904/92).

52 *Irish Volunteer* (*IV*), 21 Mar. 1914.   53 *RJ*, *RM*, 14 Mar. 1914.

54 *RJ*, 28 Mar. 1914.   55 *RH*, *IT*, 14 May 1914.

56 *Aberdeen Press and Journal* (*APJ*), 28 Apr. 1914; *Exeter and Plymouth Gazette* (*EPG*), 29 Apr. 1914.

57 *RH*, 18 Apr. 1914.   58 *RJ*, 4 Apr. 1914.

59 CI Roscommon, Apr. 1914 (TNA, CO 904/93); *RJ*, 2 May 1914.

60 CI Roscommon, Apr. 1914 (TNA, CO 904/93); *RJ*, 2 May 1914.

61 *RH*, 9 May 1914; *IV*, 16 May 1914; CI Roscommon, May 1914 (TNA, CO 904/93).

62 *RH*, 16 May 1914; *WN*, 30 May 1914.

63 CI Roscommon, Mar., Apr. 1914 (TNA, CO 904/92/93); *IV*, 16 May 1914.

64 *RH*, 30 May, 6, 27 June, 4 July 1914.

65 CI Roscommon, Apr. 1914 (TNA, CO 904/93); *RM*, 25 Apr. 1914; *RH*, 23 May 1914.

66 *RH*, 30 May, 6 June 1914; CI Roscommon, July 1914 (TNA, CO 904/94).

67 *RH*, 30 May 1914.   68 *WFJ*, 30 May 1914.

69 *FJ*, 30 May, 2 June 1914.   70 *RM*, 6 June 1914.

71 *SD*, 13, 20 June, 4 July 1914.

72 Ibid., 11, 18, 25 July 1914; *IV*, 18 July 1914.

73 *SD*, 13 June, 11 July 1914; *IV*, 27 June 1914.   74 *SD*, 8 Aug. 1914.

75 *RM*, 4 July 1914.   76 CI Roscommon, June 1914 (TNA, CO 904/93).

77 *FJ*, 2 June 1914.   78 *RH*, 20 June, 1914.

79 *RJ*, 12 June 1914; *RM*, 20 June 1914.   80 *RH*, 13, 20 June, 4 July 1914.

81 *RM*, 25 July 1914; CI Roscommon, July 1914 (TNA, CO 904/94).

82 *Ballymena Weekly Telegraph* (*BWT*), 18 July 1914.   83 *RH*, 4 July 1914.

84 *RJ*, 4, 11, 25 July 1914.   85 CI Roscommon, July, Aug. 1914 (TNA, CO 904/94).

86 *RM*, 25 July 1914; *Hansard (Commons)*, 30 July 1914, vol. 65, cols. 1538–9.

87 *RJ*, 1 Aug. 1914.   88 *RH*, 1 Aug. 1914.

CHAPTER THREE *First World War to the Easter Rising, 1914–16*

1 James McConnel, *The Irish Parliamentary Party and the third home rule crisis* (Dublin, 2013), p. 298.

2 *RM*, 8 Aug. 1914.   3 *RJ*, 5 Sept. 1914.   4 *IV*, 15 Aug. 1914.

5 Michael Farry, *Sligo: the Irish Revolution, 1912–23* (Dublin, 2012), p. 21.

6 *IT*, 7 Aug., 10 Sept. 1914.   7 *RJ*, 15 Aug., 12 Sept. 1914.

8 *RH*, 29 Aug. 1914.   9 Ibid., 5 Sept. 1914.

10 *RM*, 22 Aug. 1914; CI Roscommon, Aug. 1914 (TNA, CO 904/94).

11 *RH*, 15, 29 Aug. 1914; *RM*, 29 Aug. 1914.   12 *RH*, 5 Sept. 1914.

13 *SD*, 5 Sept. 1914.   14 *RJ*, 19 Sept. 1914.   15 *WI*, 26 Sept. 1914.

16 *RM*, 19 Sept. 1914; *FJ*, 21 Sept. 1914.   17 *FJ*, 22, 24 Sept. 1914.

18 *RH*, 26 Sept. 1914.   19 *FJ*, 26 Sept. 1914.   20 *RM*, 3 Oct. 1914.

21 *IT*, 28 Sept. 1914.

22 *RH*, 10, 17, 31 Oct., 7, 14 Nov. 1914; Wheatley, *Nationalism*, pp 209–10; Conor McNamara, *War and revolution in the west of Ireland: Galway, 1913–1922* (Newbridge, 2018), pp 56–7; Marie Coleman, *County Longford and the revolution* (Dublin, 2006), pp 36–7.

23 CI Roscommon, Oct., Nov. 1914 (TNA, CO 904/95).

24 CI Roscommon, Sept. 1914 (TNA, CO 904/94).   25 *RM*, 10 Oct. 1914.

26 *RJ*, 31 Oct. 1914.   27 *RM*, *WFJ*, 31 Oct. 1914.

28 *RJ*, 5 Dec. 1914, 2 Jan. 1915.   29 *RM*, 7 Nov. 1914.

30 *RJ*, *WI*, 7 Oct. 1914; *RM*, 7 Nov. 1914.

31 *RM*, 7 Nov. 1914; *FJ*, *Northern Whig* (*NW*), 24 Nov. 1914.

32 *RM*, 14 Nov. 1914; *WFJ*, 31 July 1915.

33 *FJ*, 10 Nov. 1914; *RH*, 26 Dec. 1914.

34 *RM*, 21 Nov. 1914; *RH*, *RJ*, 28 Nov. 1914.

35 IG, Dec. 1914 (TNA, CO 904/95); *RM*, 9 Jan. 1915; *WFJ*, 30 Jan. 1915; *RJ*, 13 Feb. 1915.

36 CI Roscommon, Apr. 1915 (TNA, CO 904/96); *RJ*, 20 Mar. 1915.

37 *RH, WFJ, RJ*, 10 Apr. 1915.

38 *RM*, Nov.–Dec. 1914, 16 Jan. 1915.

39 *FJ*, 24 Feb., 3 Mar. 1915. 40 Ibid., 5 Jan. 1915.

41 *RM, RJ*, 30 Jan. 1915; CI Roscommon, Apr. 1915 (TNA, CO 904/96).

42 *FJ*, 16 Jan. 1915. 43 Wheatley, *Nationalism*, pp 232–4.

44 *RH*, 8, 15, 22, 29 Aug. 1914.

45 *WIT*, 22 Aug. 1914; *Dublin Daily Express (DDE)*, 16 Sept. 1914.

46 *FJ*, 24 Sept. 1914.

47 *RH*, 14 Nov. 1914; *Hansard (Commons)*, 23 Nov. 1914, vol. 68, cols. 817–18W; *Statement giving particulars of men of military age in Ireland*, House of Commons, 1916 (Cd. 8390), XVII.581; *Report on recruiting in Ireland, 1914–16*, House of Commons, 1916 (Cd. 8168), p. 2.

48 *RM*, 14 Nov. 1914; Burke, *Athlone*, p. 115. 49 *FJ*, 24 Sept., 11 Nov. 1914.

50 *FJ, IT*, 24 Oct. 1914. 51 *RH*, 19 Dec. 1914, 16 Jan., 20 Feb. 1915.

52 CI Roscommon, Dec. 1914, Jan. 1915 (TNA, CO 904/95; CO 904/96).

53 *DDE, IT*, 6 Oct. 1914. 54 *RJ*, 24 Oct. 1914. 55 *IV*, 31 Oct. 1914.

56 *RJ*, 24 Oct. 1914; *RH*, 24 Oct., 14 Nov. 1914.

57 *Londonderry Sentinel (LS)*, 24 Oct. 1914.

58 CI Roscommon, Oct. 1914 (TNA, CO 904/95). 59 *RM*, 24 Oct. 1914.

60 *DDE*, 10 Aug. 1914.

61 *Leitrim Advertiser*, 6 Aug. 1914; *WI*, 15 Aug., 12 Sept. 1914.

62 *II*, 9 Feb. 1915.

63 *Agricultural statistics of Ireland, with detailed report for the year 1916*, House of Commons (Cd. 112), p. iv, table H, p. 6, table 10, p. 63.

64 *RJ*, 16 Jan. 1915; *WI*, 27 Feb., 6 Mar. 1915.

65 *RM*, 19 Dec. 1914, 23 Jan. 1915; *Judicial statistics, 1915; Part I – Annual criminal statistics for the year 1915*, House of Commons (Cd. 8636), table 6, p. 23.

66 CI Roscommon, Nov. 1915 (TNA, CO 904/98).

67 *FJ*, 10 Nov. 1915; *Wicklow News Letter and County Advertiser*, 27 Nov. 1915.

68 *II*, 13 Nov. 1916. 69 *RJ*, 30 Sept. 1916. 70 *II, FJ*, 8 Apr. 1915.

71 *DDE*, 25 Mar. 1915.

72 *Agricultural statistics 1915*, p. 13, table M; *Agricultural statistics 1916*, p. 13, table M.

73 *Agricultural statistics 1915*, p. xvi.

74 *WFJ*, 9 Oct. 1915; *Agricultural statistics 1915*, pp 54–5, table 9.

75 *BWT*, 9 Oct. 1915.

76 *RH*, 13 Feb., 12, 19 June, 3, 10, 24, 31 July, 7 Aug. 1915.

77 *RM*, 27 Mar. 1915.

78 *FJ*, 15 Apr. 1915; *RM*, 24 Apr. 1915. 79 *II, FJ*, 4 Aug. 1915.

80 *RJ*, 11 Sept. 1915. 81 *DDE*, 14 Apr. 1916.

82 *DDE, Belfast News Letter (BNL)*, 2, 16 Mar. 1915. 83 *RM*, 6, Mar. 1915.

84 *RH*, 29 May 1915. 85 *FJ*, 24 May 1915; *II*, 8 June 1915.

86 CI Roscommon, July 1915 (TNA, CO 904/97). 87 *RJ, WFJ*, 17 July 1915.

88 *RM*, 17 July 1915. 89 *Dublin Evening Telegraph (DET)*, 12 July 1915.

90 *DET*, 12 July 1915; *IT*, 26 July 1915. 91 *RJ*, 14 Aug. 1915.

92 *II*, 18 Aug. 1915; CI Roscommon, Aug. 1915 (TNA, CO 904/97).

93 *RM*, 4, 11 Sept. 1915. 94 *RM, RJ*, 18 Sept. 1915.

95 *RH, RJ, RM, SD, WI*, 6 Nov. 1915.

96 *SD*, 25 Sept. 1915; *RH*, 2, 9, 16 Oct. 1915. 97 *SD*, 13 Nov. 1915.

98 *Derry Journal (DJ)*, 1 Nov. 1915; *SD*, 20 Nov. 1915.

99 *SD*, 4 Dec. 1915; Dublin Castle Special Branch files, Rev Fr M. O'Flanagan, (TNA, CO 904/211/334), pp 310, 342, 372–4.

100 CI Roscommon, Nov., Dec. 1915, Apr. 1916 (TNA, CO 904/98/99). Confusingly, he also claimed that the GAA supported the IPP; CI Roscommon, Jan. 1916 (TNA, CO 904/99).

101 *IT*, 24, 25 Mar. 1916; *Leitrim Advertiser*, 13 Apr. 1916; *Report on recruiting*, p. 4.

102 CI Roscommon, July 1915 (TNA, CO 904/97).   103 Farry, *Sligo*, p. 25.

104 Daithí Ó Corráin, 'J.J. O'Connell's memoir of the Irish Volunteers, 1914–16, 1917', *Analecta Hibernica*, 47 (2016), 31–3.   105 Burke, *Athlone*, pp 125–6.

106 *RH*, 20 Nov. 1915.

107 Ibid., 22 Jan. 1916; Patrick Cassidy (BMH WS 1,017), pp 9–10.

108 *RH*, 27 Nov. 1915; *II*, 7 Dec. 1915.

109 CI Roscommon, Dec. 1915 (TNA, CO 904/98).

110 Dublin Castle Special Branch files, J. Shouldice (TNA, CO 904/214/405), p. 53; CI Roscommon, Mar. 1916 (TNA, CO 904/99).

111 *RH*, 27 Nov., 4, 11 Dec. 1915.

112 Dublin Castle Special Branch files, Rev Fr M. O'Flanagan (TNA, CO 904/211/334), pp 310–11; 342.

113 *IV*, 11 Dec. 1915.   114 *RH, SD*, 15 Jan. 1916.   115 *FJ*, 19 Jan. 1916.

116 *RH*, 1, 15, 22 Jan., 5, 12, 19, 26 Feb. 1916.

117 CI Roscommon, Feb. 1916 (TNA, CO 904/99); *DDE*, 14 Mar. 1916.

118 *DDE*, 8 Feb. 1916; *IV*, 1 Apr. 1915; Dublin Castle Special Branch files, J. Shouldice (TNA, CO 904/214/405), p. 32.

119 *FJ*, 9 Feb., 2, 15 Mar. 1916.   120 *RJ*, 8 Apr. 1916.

121 *II*, 3 Apr. 1916.   122 *RH*, 29 Apr. 1916.

123 *RJ, RM, SD, WI*, 29 Apr. 1916.   124 *RH*, 6 May 1916.

125 *RJ*, 6 May 1916.   126 *WI*, 6 May 1916; Burke, *Athlone*, pp 131–2.

127 *RH*, 13 May, 3 June 1916; *RM*, 20 May 1916.

128 Roy Foster, *Vivid faces: the revolutionary generation in Ireland, 1890–1923* (London, 2014), pp 259–60.

129 CI Roscommon, Apr./May, May 1916 (TNA, CO 904/100).

130 *RJ*, 13, 20 May 1916.   131 *RJ*, 3 June 1916.   132 *RM*, 20 May 1916.

133 *RJ*, 20 May 1916.   134 *II*, 19 May 1916.   135 *RJ, RM*, 20 May 1916.

136 *RJ*, 29 Apr. 1916; CI Roscommon, Apr., May 1916 (TNA, CO 904/99; CO 904/100); Pension claim of Henry Joseph Feely (IMA, MSPC, 34REF46698).

137 Pension claim of Joseph Edward O'Kelly (IMA, MSPC, 34REF56091).

138 *II*, 11 May 1916.   139 *II*, 10 May 1916; *RJ*, 13 May 1916.

140 *II*, 2 June 1916; *Royal commission on the rebellion in Ireland. Report of commission*, House of Commons (Cd. 8279).

141 John Dillon to Sir Matthew Nathan, 14 Apr. 1916 (NLI, Brennan papers, MS 26008/3); *RH*, 20 May 1916.

142 *RH*, 13, 20 May 1916.

143 *SD*, 20 May 1916; *RH*, 27 May 1916; James Quigley (BMH WS 692, p. 1).

144 *Judicial statistics, 1916* p. 63 (Cd. 9066); *RJ*, 20, 27 May, 10 June 1916; *RM*, 27 May, 3 June 1916; Internment of Irish prisoners in United Kingdom (TNA, HO 313106/9/14).

145 Brendán Mac Giolla Coille, *Intelligence notes, 1913–16, preserved in the State Paper Office* (Dublin, 1966), p. 241.

146 *RM*, 27 May, 3, 10 June 1916.

147 CI Roscommon, May 1916 (TNA, CO 904/100).   148 *RJ*, 3 June 1916.

149 *RH*, 10, 17, 24 June 1916.   150 *WI*, 20 May, 10 June 1916.

151 *RH*, 27 May 1916; *II*, 29 May 1916.   152 *WI*, 10 June 1916.

153 *SD*, 24 June 1916.   154 *WFJ*, 24 June 1916.

155 *WI*, 24 June 1916; *SD*, 1 July 1916.   156 *RM*, 24 June 1916.

157 *RJ*, 22 July 1916.   158 *RM*, *RH*, 24 June, 1, 8, 15 July 1916.

159 *FJ*, 20 June 1916; Dublin Castle Special Branch files, Rev Fr M. O'Flanagan (TNA, CO 904/211/334), p. 303.

160 *RM*, 8, 15 July 1916.   161 *FJ*, 15 June 1916; *RJ*, 8, 15 July 1916.

162 CI Roscommon, June, July 1916 (TNA, CO 904/100).

163 *RH*, 17 June 1916; *RJ*, 24 June 1916.   164 *RH*, 1 July 1916.

165 *RH*, 22 July 1916.   166 *WI*, 5 Aug., 24 Sept. 1916.

167 *DDE*, 29 June, 21 July 1916; General John Maxwell to Mr Samuels commenting on … cattle drive in Ballinasloe, 11 July 1916 (NLI, Maxwell papers, MS 50,610/10).

168 *RH*, 5 Aug. 1916; *RM*, 12 Aug. 1916.   169 *RJ*, 12 Aug. 1916

170 *SD*, 29 July, 12 Aug. 1916.   171 *RH*, 29 July 1916; *NW*, 2 Aug. 1916.

172 *SD*, 29 July 1916; *RH*, 12 Aug. 1916.   173 *RH*, 5 Aug. 1916.

174 *RJ*, 12 Aug. 1916.   175 *RH*, 16 Sept. 1916.

176 *RH*, 19, 26 Aug., 23 Sept., 7 Oct., 11 Nov. 1916.

177 CI Roscommon, Nov. 1916 (TNA, CO 904/101); *II*, 5 Dec. 1916.

178 *FJ*, 26 Oct., 18 Dec. 1916.   179 *RH*, 14, 21, 28 Oct. 1916.

180 *RM*, 7 Oct., 4 Nov. 1916; *FJ*, 18, 25, 26 Oct., 1 Nov. 1916.

181 *RM*, 2, 9 Dec. 1916.   182 *FJ*, 23, 29 Dec. 1916; *WN*, 30 Dec. 1916.

183 *Yorkshire Post and Leeds Intelligencer* (*YPLI*), 30 Dec. 1916.

CHAPTER FOUR *The Roscommon North by-election, 1917*

1 *RH*, 30 Dec. 1916; *II*, 5, 13 Jan. 1917; *DDE*, 23, 25 Jan. 1917.

2 *FJ*, 5, 11 Jan. 1917; *II*, 6, 8, Jan. 1917.

3 Kevin O'Shiel (BMH WS 1,770, p. 606); Michael Laffan, *The resurrection of Ireland: the Sinn Féin party, 1916–1923* (Cambridge, 1999), pp 79–80.

4 Kevin O'Shiel (BMH WS 1,770, pp 606–7); *II*, 19 Jan. 1917.

5 *RM*, 27 Jan. 1917.   6 *FJ*, 19 Jan. 1917.

7 *BNL*, 19, 20 Jan. 1917; *DDE*, 27 Jan. 1917.   8 *DDE*, 1 Feb. 1917.

9 James Feely (BMH WS 997, p. 3); Martin Fallon (BMH WS 1,008, p. 1); Patrick Mullooly (BMH WS 755, p. 217).

10 *II*, 23 Jan. 1917; Kevin O'Shiel (BMH WS 1,770, p. 608); Michael Staines (BMH WS 944, pp 1–2); Laffan, *Resurrection*, pp 80–3.   11 *II*, 17 Jan. 1917.

12 *II*, 23 Jan. 1917.

13 Ginnell to Plunkett, 22 Jan. 1917 (NLI, Plunkett papers, MS 11,374/15).

14 Ward to Plunkett, 22 Jan. 1917 (NLI, Plunkett papers, MS 11,374/15/5); Broadside poster calling for support for Count Plunkett in the 1917 North Roscommon by-election (NLI, EPH E239).

15 *FJ*, 26, 27 Jan. 1917.   16 *FJ*, 27, 29 Jan. 1917.

17 *II*, 30 Jan. 1917; Kevin O'Shiel (BMH WS 1,770, p. 616). 18 *II*, 24 Jan. 1917.

19 *RM*, 27 Jan., 3 Feb. 1917.   20 *Western Nationalist* (*WN*), *FJ*, 27 Jan. 1917.

21 *DDE*, 2 Feb. 1917.   22 *II*, *DDE*, 30, 31 Jan. 1917.

23 *The Leader*, 3 Feb. 1917.   24 *II*, *FJ*, 1 Feb. 1917.

25 Kevin O'Shiel (BMH WS 1,770, p. 640); Laffan, *Resurrection*, p. 80.

26 *FJ*, 27 Jan. 1917.   27 *FJ*, *II*, 29, 30, 31 Jan. 1917.

28 *FJ*, 29, 30 Jan., 2, 3 Feb. 1917; *II*, 30, 31 Jan. 1917.

29 *FJ*, 29, 30 Jan., 1 Feb. 1917.   30 *II*, *FJ*, 30 Jan. 1917.

31 *FJ*, 29 Jan. 1917; Laffan, *Resurrection*, pp 81–2.   32 *II*, 3 Feb. 1917.

33 *FJ*, 26, 29 Jan., 1 Feb. 1917; *WN*, 27 Jan. 1917.

34 *RH*, 27 Jan., 3 Feb. 1917.   35 *RM*, *SD*, 3 Feb. 1917.   36 *RH*, *RJ*, 3 Feb. 1917.

37 Michael O'Flanagan to George Noble Plunkett, 27 Jan. 1917 (NLI, Plunkett papers, MS 11,374/15/6).

38 Prosecution of Reverend Father O'Flanagan, Laurence Ginnell, MP, Louis Walsh and P.J. McCrann (TNA, WO 35/95/20).

39 Kevin O'Shiel (BMH WS 1,770, pp 613–14).

40 *II*, 30 Jan. 1917.

41 *DDE*, 30 Jan. 1917; Seditious speeches, 1917, Tarmonbarry and Strokestown (TNA, WO 35/95/20).

42 *II*, 31 Jan., 1, 2 Feb. 1917.   43 *II*, 31 Jan. 1917.   44 *II*, 1 Feb. 1917.

45 Kevin O'Shiel (BMH WS 1,770, p. 629); William O'Brien (BMH WS 1,766, p. 127).

46 Address of welcome to George Noble Plunkett … on behalf of Elphin Election Committee, 2 Feb. 1917 (NLI, Plunkett papers, MS 11,402/1/26).

47 'We will not forget those members cheering' (NLI, ILB 300 p 8 (Item 64); *SD*, 26 May 1917; Fearghal McGarry, *The Rising: Ireland 1916* (2nd ed., Oxford, 2016 [2010]), p. 284.

48 *II*, *FJ*, 3 Feb. 1917; Kevin O'Shiel (BMH WS 1,770, pp 629, 614–15).

49 Kevin O'Shiel (BMH WS 1,770, pp 618–19).

50 *DJ*, 5 Feb. 1917; Jérôme aan de Wiel, *The Catholic Church in Ireland, 1914–1918: war and politics* (Dublin, 2005), p. 168.

51 *FJ*, *II*, 3 Feb. 1917; Laffan, *Resurrection*, p. 189.

52 Kevin O'Shiel (BMH WS 1,770, pp 616–17).   53 *FJ*, 1, 2, 3 Feb. 1917.

54 *RJ*, 3 Feb. 1917.

55 *BNL*, 29 Jan. 1917; *FJ*, 3 Feb. 1917; Denis Carroll, *They have fooled you again: Michael O'Flanagan (1876–1942), priest, republican, social critic* (2nd ed., Dublin, 2016 [1993]), p. 61; Tomás Flynn, *Thomas J. Devine and the election of the snows: the North Roscommon by-election of 1917* (Carrick-on-Shannon, 2016), p. 67.

56 *FJ*, 3 Feb. 1917.

57 *SD*, 3 Feb. 1917; Laurence Nugent (BMH WS 907, pp 72, 76).

58 *DJ*, 5 Feb 1917.   59 Kevin O'Shiel (BMH WS 1,770, pp 622–3).

60 *II*, 5 Feb. 1917.   61 Kevin O'Shiel (BMH WS 1,770, pp 625–6).

62 *DDE*, 6 Feb. 1917.

63 *WFJ*, 10 Feb. 1917; Dublin Castle Special Branch files, Rev Fr M. O'Flanagan (TNA, CO 904/211/334), pp 275–280.

64 *RH*, 10 Feb. 1917.   65 *II*, 6, 7, 8, 10, 12 Feb. 1917.

66 *II*, 6 Feb. 1917; *SD*, 10 Feb. 1917.   67 *The Leader*, 10 Feb. 1917.

68 *FJ*, 12 Feb. 1917.   69 *FJ*, 6 Feb. 1917.

70 *RM*, 10 Feb. 1917; *WN*, 17 Feb. 1917; *II*, 20 Feb. 1917.

71 *Enniscorthy Guardian*, *Wicklow People*, 10 Feb. 1917; *Drogheda Independent*, 17 Feb. 1917.

72 *IT*, 8 Feb. 1917.

73 *RH*, 15 Sept. 1917; Miller, *Church*, p. 350.

74 *DDE*, 6, 7 Feb. 1917; *IT*, 7 Feb. 1917; *BNL*, 6, 7, 9 Feb. 1917.

75 *Liverpool Echo*, 6 Feb. 1917; *The Daily Herald* (*DH*), 10 Feb. 1917; *Derby Daily Telegraph*, 6, 9 Feb. 1917.

76 *The Scotsman* (*TS*), 23 Mar. 1917.   77 *DJ*, 9 Mar. 1917.

78 *FJ*, 2, 3, 5, 8 Mar. 1917; *Hansard (Commons)*, 7 Mar. 1917, vol. 91, cols. 478–9.

79 *FJ*, 18 Apr. 1917.

CHAPTER FIVE *Sinn Féin growth and the 1918 general election*

1 Kevin O'Shiel (BMH WS 1,770, p. 629).

2 *Dundee Courier* (*DC*), *NW*, 16 Feb. 1917.   3 *RM*, 17 Feb. 1917.

4 Dublin Castle Special Branch files, Count Plunkett (TNA, CO 904/211/334), p. 30.

5 *YPLI*, 15 Feb. 1917.   6 *RH*, 10 Mar. 1917.

7 *RH*, 17 Feb. 1917.

8 Circular letter by George Noble Plunkett (NLI, Plunkett papers, MS 11,383/3, /11).

9 *FJ*, 4, 14 Apr. 1917; List A: Local elective authorities who adopted the circular; List B: Local authorities who have postponed consideration of the circular; List C: Local authorities who have 'taken no action' or rejected the circular (NLI, Plunkett papers, MSS 11,383/1/1, 11,383/1/17, 11,383/1/18).

10 *RJ, RM*, 31 Mar., 7, 14 Apr. 1917.

11 *RH*, 31 Mar. 1917; Strokestown Rural District Council to George Noble Plunkett, 27 Apr., 5 May 1917 (NLI, Plunkett papers, MS 11,383/12/14).

12 *RH*, 21 Apr. 1917.   13 *FJ*, 11, 19 Apr. 1917.   14 *RJ*, 21 Apr. 1917.

15 *DDE*, 20 Apr. 1917.

16 *II*, 20 Apr. 1917; Michael Laffan, 'The unification of Sinn Féin in 1917', *Irish Historical Studies*, 17:67 (1971), 361–7.

17 *WN*, 21 Apr. 1917; Carroll, *O'Flanagan*, pp 70–1.

18 For examples see: Various to George Noble Plunkett (NLI, Plunkett papers, MSS 11,383/3/24, 11,383/5/1, 11,383/7/10).

19 *RH*, 28 Apr. 1917; *II*, 7 May 1917.

20 Patrick Morahan to George Noble Plunkett, 19 May 1917 (NLI, Plunkett papers, MS 11,383/12/18).

21 *SD*, 14, 21, 28 Apr., 5, 12 May 1917.

22 *FJ*, 1, 7 May 1917; Dublin Castle Special Branch files, Rev Fr M. O'Flanagan (TNA, CO 904/211/334), pp 268–73.

23 *II*, 17 Apr. 1917.   24 *RJ*, 21, 28 Apr., 7 July 1917.

25 *RH*, 12, 19 May, 2, 16 June 1917; Pension claim of Joseph Edward O'Kelly (IMA, MSPC, 34REF56091).

26 *SD*, 19 May 1917.   27 *II*, 10 May 1917; *RM*, 19 May, 9 June 1917.

28 *RJ*, 19 May 1917.   29 *RH*, 19 May 1917.

30 Boyle Board of Guardians to George Noble Plunkett, 16 May 1916 (NLI, Plunkett papers, MS 11,383/12/16).

31 *RM*, 12 May 1917.   32 *WFJ*, 19 May 1917; *FJ*, 5 June 1917.

33 *II*, 15 May 1917.   34 *WFJ*, 16, 23 June, 14 July 1917.

35 *RH*, 2 June 1917.   36 *SD*, 23 June 1917.

37 *II, DDE*, 9 June 1917; *RJ*, 23 June 1917; *RH*, 30 June 1917.

38 *RJ, SD* 16 June 1917.   39 *RJ*, 4 Aug. 1917.

40 *SD*, 7 July 1917; *Wicklow News-Letter and Arklow Reporter*, 14 July 1917.

41 *RJ*, 14 July 1917; *WN*, 28 July, 4 Aug. 1917; Dublin Castle Special Branch files, J. Shouldice (TNA, CO 904/214/405), pp 41–2; Frank Shouldice, *Grandpa the sniper: the remarkable story of a 1916 volunteer* (Dublin, 2015), pp 222, 246.

42 CI Roscommon, May–July 1917 (TNA, CO 904/103); Laffan, 'Unification', 371–2.

43 *RM*, 23 June, 28 July, 4 Aug. 1917; *RH*, 14 July 1917.   44 *RM*, 8 Dec. 1917.

45 *SD*, 30 June 1917; *RM*, 14 July 1917; *RH*, 18 Aug. 1917.

46 *RM, WN*, 23 June 1917.   47 *RJ*, 14, 21 July 1917.   48 *WN*, 16 June 1917.

49 *RJ*, 7 July, 11 Aug. 1917; *FJ*, 9 Aug. 1917.   50 *RH, RJ*, 23 June 1917.

51 Ibid.   52 *II, DDE*, 24 July 1917.   53 *RH, RJ*, 4 Aug. 1917.

54 *FJ*, 31 July 1917; *RM*, 4 Aug. 1917.   55 *FJ*, 14 Aug., 3 Sept. 1917.

56 Sinn Féin flag at Cremully chapel (TNA, WO 35/97/4).

57 *II, IT*, 13 Aug. 1917; Press censorship, 13 Aug. 1917, Athlone (TNA, CO 904/166), p. 199.

58 *RJ*, 4, 11, 18, 25 Aug. 1917.   59 *RH, RJ*, 22, 29 Sept. 1917.

60 *DDE*, 18 Sept. 1917.   61 *II*, 2, 6, 8 Oct. 1917; *RJ*, 13 Oct. 1917.

62 *II*, 1 Oct. 1917; *WFJ*, 6 Oct. 1917.   63 *SD*, 6 Oct. 1917.

64 CI Roscommon, Sept. 1917 (TNA, CO 904/104); *RJ*, 29 Sept., 6, 27 Oct. 1917.

65 *The Bioscope*, 1 Nov. 1917. **66** *RJ*, 1, 15 Sept. 1917; *SD*, 6, 27 Oct. 1917.

67 *RJ*, 27 Oct. 1917; Laffan, 'Unification', 375–6.

68 Burke, *Athlone*, pp 153–5. **69** *RH*, 10, 17 Nov. 1917.

70 CI Roscommon, Sept.–Nov. 1917 (TNA, CO 904/104).

71 *RJ*, 20 Oct., 24 Nov. 1917; *SD*, 27 Oct. 1917; *RH*, 3, 17 Nov. 1917.

72 *RJ*, 27 Oct., 10 Nov. 1917.

73 Address of welcome from Boyle guardians to Éamon de Valera, Nov. 1917 (NLI, Plunkett papers, MS 11,402/2/4).

74 *RJ*, 24 Nov. 1917; *II*, *FJ*, 26 Nov. 1917; Civilians tried by courts martial (TNA, WO 35/97/24).

75 Dublin Castle Special Branch files, Rev Fr M. O'Flanagan (TNA, CO 904/211/334), p. 242.

76 *RH*, 1 Dec. 1917. **77** *DDE*, *II*, 27 Nov. 1917.

78 CI Roscommon, Nov. 1917 (TNA, CO 904/104); *RJ*, 1 Dec. 1917.

79 *RJ*, 1, 8, 15 Dec. 1917.

80 Press censorship, 9 Dec. 1917, Lecarrow (TNA, CO/904/166).

81 Civilians tried by courts martial (TNA, WO 35/96/5).

82 *II*, 13 Feb. 1917; *SD*, 17 Mar. 1917; Thomas Lavin (BMH WS 1,001, p. 1).

83 *RM*, 24 Feb., 7, 14, 21 Apr. 1917. **84** *RJ*, 5 May 1917.

85 *NW*, 11 May 1917; *LS*, 12 May 1917.

86 *RH*, 26 May, 2 June 1917; Ancient Order of Hibernians agenda book, 1912–81, 14 June 1917 (NAI, LOU 13/2/1–2).

87 *RH*, 19, 26 May, 9, 16 June 1917; *FJ*, 6 June 1917; *RM*, 9 June 1917.

88 *RJ*, 5 May 1917; *II*, 25 June 1917; *RH*, 1 Sept. 1917.

89 CI Roscommon, May 1917 (TNA, CO 904/102).

90 *RH*, 18 Aug., 8 Sept. 1917; *RJ*, 15 Sept. 1917.

91 Laffan, *Resurrection*, pp 186–7.

92 *RH*, *RM*, *SD*, 24 Nov. 1917.

93 *RM*, 12, 19 Jan., 9 Feb. 1918; *RH*, 5 Jan. 1918.

94 CI Roscommon, Sept., Oct. 1917 (TNA, CO 904/104); *RH*, 12 Jan. 1918.

95 *DDE*, 3, 31 Mar., 26 Apr. 1917; *Department of Agriculture and General Instruction for Ireland. Eighteenth Annual Report of the Department, 1917–18*, House of Commons, 1918 (Cd. 106), pp 27–9; 157–8.

96 *Hansard (Commons)*, 8 Feb. 1917, vol. 90, cols. 120–5; 13 Feb. 1917, vol. 90, col. 454W; *APJ*, 9 Feb. 1917.

97 *II*, 24 Feb., 22 Mar. 1917; *SD*, 31 Mar., 7, 14, 21, 28 Apr. 1917.

98 *RM*, 14 July 1917. **99** *II*, 1 Mar. 1917; *WFJ*, 10 Mar. 1917.

100 *WFJ*, 13 Jan., 16 Feb. 1917.

101 *DDE*, 27 Apr. 1917; *WFJ*, 5 May 1917; *Department of Agriculture and General Instruction for Ireland. Agricultural statistics, Ireland, 1918. General abstracts showing the acreage under crops and the numbers and descriptions of livestock in each county and province 1916–7–8*, House of Commons, 1918 (Cd. 113), p. 4.

102 *FJ*, 19, 26 Feb. 1917; Burke, *Athlone*, pp 155–6. **103** *FJ*, 11 Apr. 1917.

104 *FJ*, 26, 28 Feb., 1, 5, 26 Mar. 1918. **105** *BNL*, 21 Jan. 1918.

106 *WFJ*, 14 July 1917; *FJ*, 21 July 1917.

107 *WFJ*, 27 Oct. 1917; *Agricultural statistics 1917, vol. LII. Part I. Acreage and livestock returns of England and Wales with summaries for the United Kingdom*, House of Commons, 1918 (Cd. 9006), Table 6, p. 29.

108 *II*, 13 Dec. 1917.

109 *FJ*, 30 May, 28 July 1917. **110** *FJ*, 8 Oct. 1917.

111 CI Roscommon, Dec. 1917 (TNA, CO 904/104); *TS*, 16 Feb. 1918.

112 *RJ*, 15 Dec. 1917; *RH*, 5, 12 Jan. 1918; John Shouldice (BMH WS 679, p. 19).

113 Tony Varley, 'A region of sturdy smallholders? Western nationalists and agrarian politics during the First World War', *Journal of the Galway Archaeological and Historical Society*, 55 (2003), 141.

114 *RH*, 2, 9 Feb. 1918.   115 Civilians tried by courts martial (TNA, WO 35/96/5).

116 *Hansard (Commons)*, 21 Feb. 1918, vol. 103, cols. 892–5.

117 *RH*, 23 Feb. 1918.   118 *FJ, II*, 22, 23 Feb. 1918.

119 *BNL, FJ*, 28 Feb. 1918.   120 *FJ*, 22, 28 Feb. 1918.

121 CI Roscommon, Feb. 1918 (TNA, CO 904/105); *II*, 26, 27 Feb. 1918.

122 *Gloucestershire Echo (GE)*, 27 Feb. 1918.

123 *LS*, 21, 26, 28 Feb. 1918; *BNL, NW*, 25 Feb. 1918.

124 *II*, 26 Feb. 1918.   125 *FJ*, 5 Mar. 1918; *RH*, 9, 16 Mar. 1918.

126 *II*, 16 Feb., 7 Mar. 1918; *FJ*, 4, 27 Mar. 1918; Farry, *Sligo*, p. 39.

127 *II, BT*, 19 Mar. 1918.

128 *FJ, II*, 1 Mar. 1918; *Larne Times (LT)*, 9 Mar. 1918; *RH*, 16, 23, 30 Mar. 1918.

129 *WFJ*, 23 Mar., 13 Apr. 1918; *II*, 28, 30 Mar. 1918.

130 *RH*, 30 Mar., 25 May 1918.

131 *BNL, LS*, 26 Feb. 1918; Civilians tried by courts martial (TNA, WO 35/96/5).

132 Dublin Castle Special Branch files, J.J. Redican (TNA, CO 904/213/336B), pp 133–44.

133 *FJ*, 22, 25 Feb. 1918.   134 James Feely (BMH WS 997, pp 2–4).

135 *FJ*, 26 Feb. 1918.   136 *FJ*, 5 Mar. 1918; *RH*, 16 Mar. 1918.

137 Dublin Castle Special Branch Files, Rev Fr M. O'Flanagan (TNA, CO 904/211/334), p. 235.

138 *RH*, 23, 30 Mar., 6, 20 Apr. 1918; James Feely (BMH WS 997, pp 2–4).

139 *RH*, 9 Mar. 1918.   140 *WI*, 9 Mar. 1918; *RJ*, 30 Mar. 1918.

141 *RM*, 9, 16 Mar. 1918.   142 *FJ*, 11 Mar. 1918.

143 *RM*, 30 Mar. 1918; *RH*, 13 Apr. 1918.

144 *RH*, 13 Apr. 1918; Dublin Castle Special Branch files, J. Shouldice (TNA, CO 904/214/405), p. 75.

145 *RJ*, 27 Apr. 1918.   146 *RM*, 13, 20 Apr. 1918.

147 *II*, 9, 16 Apr. 1918; *RM*, 20 Apr. 1918.

148 CI Roscommon, Apr. 1918 (TNA, CO 904/105); *RH, RJ, RM*, 20, 27 Apr. 1918.

149 *Evening Despatch*, 16 Apr. 1918; *EPG*, 16, 23 Apr. 1918; *APJ*, 17 Apr. 1918.

150 *RJ*, 20, 27 Apr., 4 May 1918.   151 *RH*, 27 Apr. 1918.

152 *RJ*, 20, 27 Apr., 4 May 1918.

153 *II*, 24 Apr. 1918; *RJ, RM*, 27 Apr. 1918.

154 *FJ*, 6 May 1918; *Hansard (Commons)*, 9 Apr. 1918, vol. 104, cols. 1374–5.

155 *RH*, 18 May 1918.   156 *FJ*, 19 Apr. 1918; *RJ, RM*, 20 Apr. 1918.

157 *RJ*, 15, 22 June 1918; Charles Townshend, *The Republic: the fight for Irish independence, 1918–1923* (London, 2013), pp 48–9.

158 Dublin Castle Special Branch files, J. Shouldice (TNA, CO 904/214/405), p. 2; Burke, *Athlone*, pp 147–8; CI Roscommon, Jan. 1918 (TNA, CO 904/105).

159 *RH*, 4 May 1918.

160 Thomas Kelly (BMH WS 701, p. 2); Luke Duffy (BMH WS 661, p. 2).

161 Martin Fallon (BMH WS 1,121, pp 1–2).

162 Thomas Hennessy, *Dividing Ireland: World War I and partition* (London, 1998), p. 231.

163 Report on South Roscommon Brigade (IMA, Collins papers, A/0761).

164 *Birmingham Daily Post*, 10 May 1918; John Duffy (BMH WS 580, pp 8–9).

165 *NW*, 25 Apr. 1918; *DJ*, 26 Apr. 1918.

166 *RJ*, 27 Apr., 1 June, 20 July 1918; CI Roscommon Apr. 1918 (TNA, CO/904/105); Pension claim of Margaret McKeon (IMA, MSPC, 34REF62098); Pension claim of Mary Madden (IMA, MSPC, 34REF60370); Pension claim of Eileen O'Doherty (IMA, MSPC, 34REF39544); Cal McCarthy, *Cumann na mBan and the Irish revolution* (Dublin, 2014), pp 158–9.

167 *FJ*, 8, 20, 22, 29 May 1918. Bar Rahara, all districts had given over £100 (*RJ*, 18 May 1918).

168 *II*, 17 May 1918; Laffan, *Resurrection*, p. 140.   169 *RH*, 11 May 1918.

170 *WI*, 11, 25 May 1918.   171 *RM*, *RH*, 25 May, 1 June 1918.

172 *Manchester Evening News*, 18 May 1918; *The People*, 19 May 1918; *Birmingham Daily Gazette*, *Daily Mirror*, 20 May 1918.

173 *RH*, 25 May, 29 June 1918; *RJ*, *RM*, 6, 13 July 1918.

174 Sinn Féin internees (TNA, HO 144/1496/362269/135).

175 *WFJ*, 29 June 1918.

176 CI Roscommon, May, June 1918 (TNA, CO 904/106); *FJ*, 7 June 1918; *RJ*, *RM*, 15, 22, 29 June 1918; Ernie O'Malley, *On another man's wound: a personal history of Ireland's War of Independence* (Dublin, 2002 [1936]), pp 86–90.

177 Prosecution ... drilling, weapons training 1917–18 ... (TNA, WO 35/99/6).

178 *RJ*, 13 July 1918.   179 *BNL*, 15 July 1918.

180 *WFJ*, 22 June 1918; *RJ*, 20 July 1918.   181 *RH*, *RJ*, *RM*, 15 June 1918.

182 *RH*, 1 June 1918.   183 *II*, 25 May 1918; *RH*, 8, 22 June 1918.

184 *RJ*, *RM*, 22 June 1918; *Report of the proceedings of the Irish Convention*, House of Commons, 1918 (Cd. 9019), Appendix XVII, pp 140–72.

185 *RH*, 22, 29 June, 6 July 1918.   186 *RJ*, *RM*, 15 June 1918.

187 *RH*, *RJ*, 15, 22 June 1918.   188 *RJ*, *RM*, 6, 13 July 1918.

189 *BNL*, *NW*, 23 July 1918.

190 CI Roscommon, July 1918 (TNA, CO 904/106).

191 *RH*, 13, 20, 27 July, 17, 24 Aug. 1918.   192 *II*, 25, 29 July 1918.

193 *IT*, 29 July 1918.

194 *WFJ*, 17 Aug. 1918; Dublin Castle Special Branch files, Rev Fr M. O'Flanagan (TNA, CO 904/211/334), pp 215, 216–19; Carroll, *O'Flanagan*, pp 88–94.

195 *RH*, *RJ*, 31 Aug. 1918.   196 *RH*, 9 Feb. 1918.

197 *RM*, 24 Aug. 1918; *RH*, *RJ*, 31 Aug. 1918.   198 *RJ*, *II*, 10 Aug. 1918.

199 CI Roscommon, Aug. 1918 (TNA, CO 904/106); *FJ*, 24 Aug., 2, 5 Sept. 1918.

200 Sinn Féin internees (TNA, HO 144/1496/362269/135); *BNL*, 5 Sept. 1918; *RH*, 7, 14 Sept. 1918.

201 *BNL*, 10 Aug. 1918; *FJ*, *II*, 6 Sept. 1918; *RH*, 14 Sept., 19 Oct. 1918.

202 *RJ*, *RM*, 16 Nov. 1918.

203 *RH*, 28 Sept., 5 Oct. 1918; Farry, *Sligo*, p. 41.

204 *RM*, 10 Aug., 12 Oct., 9 Nov. 1918; ITGWU List of branches in chronological order (NLI, MS 7282).

205 CI Roscommon, Jan. 1919 (TNA, CO 904/108).   206 *RJ*, 19 Oct. 1918.

207 *RJ*, *RM*, 28 Sept., 2 Nov. 1918.   208 *FJ*, 18 Sept. 1918; *II*, 26, 29 Sept. 1918.

209 *RH*, 21, 28 Sept. 1918; *II*, 23 Sept. 1918.

210 Dublin Castle Special Branch files, Count Plunkett (TNA, CO 904/211/334), pp 13–14; *FJ*, 8 Nov., 5 Dec. 1918.

211 *RH*, 30 Nov. 1918. Count Plunkett, internment in the United Kingdom (TNA, HO 1458/52681/15).

212 *RM*, 28 Sept., 5, 12 Oct. 1918.   213 Ibid., 26 Oct. 1918.

214 *FJ*, 23 Nov., 13 Dec. 1918.   215 David Fitzpatrick, 'Harry Boland', *DIB*.

216 *RH*, 9 Nov. 1918; *FJ*, 5 Dec. 1918.

217 *RH*, 12, 19 Oct. 1918; Caitriona Foley, *The last Irish plague: the great flu epidemic in Ireland, 1918–19* (Dublin, 2011), p. 29.

218 *RJ, RM*, 26 Oct. 1918; *RH*, 9 Nov. 1918.   219 *RH*, 2 Nov. 1918.

220 Ibid., 9 Nov. 1918.   221 *IT*, 5, 7, Nov. 1918; *II*, 27 Nov., 2, 6, 7 Dec. 1918.

222 *RJ*, 26 Oct. 1918; *RM*, 2, 9, 16, 23 Nov. 1918; *RH*, 30 Nov. 1918.

223 *FJ*, 7 Nov. 1918; Burke, *Athlone*, p. 173; Ida Milne, *Stacking the coffins: influenza, war and revolution in Ireland, 1918–19* (Manchester, 2018), pp 60–74.

224 *II*, 25 Nov. 1918; Laffan, *Resurrection*, p. 155.

225 *RH*, 30 Nov. 1918.   226 Ibid.

227 *II*, 23 Nov. 1918; *RH*, 30 Nov. 1918; Shouldice, *Grandpa*, p. 283.

228 *RJ*, 30 Nov. 1918.   229 *RH*, 30 Nov. 1918.   230 *II*, 5 Dec. 1918.

231 *RH, RJ*, 7 Dec. 1918.   232 *RM*, 7 Dec. 1918.

233 *RM*, 30 Nov., 7 Dec. 1918.   234 *FJ*, 29 Nov., 2, 11 Dec. 1918.

235 *FJ*, 3 Dec. 1918; *II*, 11 Dec. 1918.   236 *RM, WFJ*, 23 Nov. 1918.

237 *FJ*, 19, 20 Nov. 1918.   238 *RH*, 21 Dec. 1918.

239 Ibid., 7 Dec. 1918; *Hansard (Commons)*, 14 July 1898, vol. 61, cols 1052–4; Michael Nolan, *The Parnell split in Westmeath: the bishop and the newspaper editor* (Dublin, 2018).

240 *II*, 30 Nov. 1918; *RM*, 7, 14 Dec. 1918.   241 *RH*, 14 Dec. 1918.

242 *FJ, II*, 3, 10 Dec. 1918.   243 *RM*, 7, 14 Dec. 1918.

244 *II*, 17 Dec. 1918.

245 *II*, 16 Dec. 1918; *RH, RM*, 21 Dec. 1918; Frank Simons (BMH WS 770, pp 3–4).

246 *RM, RH, RJ*, 21 Dec. 1918, 4 Jan. 1919.   247 *RM*, 21 Dec. 1918.

248 *II*, 17, 19 Dec. 1918.   249 *RJ*, 21 Dec. 1918.

250 *FJ*, 17 Dec. 1918; *RJ*, 21 Dec. 1918.   251 *RM*, 21, 28 Dec. 1918.

252 *FJ, II*, 30 Dec. 1918.   253 *RH*, 4 Jan. 1919.   254 *RH, RM*, 4 Jan. 1919.

255 *BNL*, 1 Jan. 1919; Dublin Castle Special Branch files, Count Plunkett (TNA, CO 904/211/334), p. 3.

256 *II*, 31 Dec. 1918, 1 Jan. 1919.

CHAPTER SIX *The republican counter-state, 1919—21*

1 Most was handed back. £1,070 was retained by SF with the donors' consent (CI Roscommon, Mar. 1919 (TNA, CO 904/108)).

2 *II*, 24 Jan., 12 Mar. 1919; *DET*, 4, 5 Feb. 1919; *RH*, 1, 22 Mar. 1919.

3 *RM*, 22 Mar., 5 Apr. 1919.

4 Ibid., 22 Feb. 1919; *RJ*, 17 May 1919; *FJ*, 26 May 1919.

5 *RM*, 14 June, 4 Oct. 1919; *DET*, 8 Sept. 1919.

6 *RM*, 14, 21, 28 June, 19, 27 July, 23 Aug., 27 Sept. 1919.

7 *RJ*, 25 Oct. 1919; *RM*, 25 Oct., 1, 15, 22 Nov., 6, 13 Dec. 1919.

8 *WI, RJ*, 10 Jan. 1920.   9 *II*, 7 Jan. 1920; *RM*, 10 Jan. 1920.

10 *DET*, 7 Jan. 1920.   11 *II*, 2 Feb. 1920; *RM*, 7 Feb. 1920.

12 *II, DET*, 7 Jan. 1920.   13 *II*, 9, 13 Jan. 1920; *DET*, 10 Jan. 1920.

14 Matthew Potter, *The municipal revolution in Ireland: a handbook of urban government in Ireland since 1800* (Dublin, 2011), p. 247.

15 *RJ*, 17, 24 Jan. 1920.   16 *RM*, 26 Apr., 18 Oct. 1919; *RJ*, 20, 27 Sept. 1919.

17 *RJ*, 27 Sept. 1919.   18 *RM*, 22 May 1920.   19 *RH*, 22 May 1920.

20 *RH*, 5 June 1920.   21 *BNL*, 8 May 1920; *II*, 10 May 1920.

22 *RM*, 8, 29 May 1920.   23 *SD*, 3, 10 Apr., 8 May 1920.

24 *RJ*, 5 June 1920.   25 *RH*, 5 June 1920.

26 *RM, SD*, 15 May 1920; CI Roscommon, June 1920 (TNA, CO 904/112).

27 *RH*, 5, 26 June 1920; *Roscommon Herald*; seditious comments and articles; 26 June 1920 (TNA, WO 35/111/28).

28 *II*, 24 June 1920.   29 *BNL*, 23 June 1920.   30 *II*, 23 June 1920.

31 *RJ*, 26 June 1920.   32 *RM*, 19 June 1920.

33 Ibid., 19 June, 3, 31 July 1920.   34 Ibid., *WI*, 19 June 1920.

35 Potter, *Municipal revolution*, pp 250–1.

36 *RM*, 31 July 1920; *RH*, 7, 14, 28 Aug., 18 Sept. 1920.

37 *WI*, 7, 21, Aug., 4 Sept. 1920.   38 *RJ*, 21 Aug. 1920.

39 *RJ*, 30 Sept. 1922; *FJ*, 11 Oct. 1922.

40 *RH*, 15 Feb., 19 July 1919.

41 *RJ*, 4 Sept. 1920; *WFJ*, 25 Sept. 1920.

42 Hughes, *Defying*, pp 56–66.

43 Patrick Cassidy (BMH WS 1,017, p. 17).

44 O'Higgins to Secretary, Roscommon County Council, 19 Oct. 1920; O'Higgins to Acting Chairman, Roscommon County Council, 20 Dec. 1920 (NAI, DÉLG 25/11); *RH* 15, 29 Jan. 1921.

45 *RH*, 30 Oct., 6, 13, 20 Nov. 1920; *RJ*, 4 Dec. 1920.

46 *RM*, 27 Nov., 4, 25 Dec. 1920; *FJ*, 8 Jan., 8 Feb. 1921; *RH*, 22 Jan. 1921.

47 *Pall Mall Gazette*, 23 Nov. 1920; *RJ*, 1, 22 Jan. 1921.

48 *LS*, 29 Mar. 1921.

49 Mary Daly, *Buffer state: the history of the Department of the Environment* (Dublin, 1997), p. 66; *FJ*, 8 Feb., 3 Mar. 1921.

50 *DET*, 17 Jan. 1921; *RH*, 19 Feb., 23 Apr. 1921; for Athlone union's approach see Burke, *Athlone*, pp 187–8.

51 *RH*, 22 Jan. 1921.   52 Ibid., 7, 21 May, 20 Aug. 1921; *RJ*, 28 May 1921.

53 *BT*, 11 Aug. 1921; *RH*, 13 Aug. 1921.

54 *RM*, 4 Mar. 1922; *RH*, 24 June 1922, 3 Mar. 1923.

55 *FJ*, 15 Apr., 20 May, 4 June 1921.

56 *WFJ*, 16 Apr., 24 Sept. 1921; *RH*, 7, 21, 28 May 1921.

57 *WFJ*, 27 May 1922.   58 *RH*, 6 Nov. 1920.   59 *FJ*, 1, 3 Nov. 1921.

60 *FJ*, 20 Jan. 1922.   61 *RH*, 15 May 1920; *SD*, 29 May 1920.

62 *SD*, 8 May 1920.

63 Agrarian outrages, May 1920 (TNA, CO 904/121); *RM*, 15 May 1920; *DC*, 2 June 1920.

64 *FJ*, 21 May 1920; CI Roscommon, June 1920 (TNA, CO 904/112).

65 *FJ*, 29 Apr. 1920; *II*, 10, 13 May 1920; *RM*, 29 May 1920.

66 Kevin O'Shiel (BMH WS 1,770, pp 992–3).

67 *DET*, 16 Aug. 1920; *RJ*, 21 Aug. 1920.   68 *BNL*, 29 July 1920.

69 *IT*, 23 Nov. 1966.   70 *RH*, 29 May 1920.

71 CI Roscommon, June, July 1920 (TNA, CO 904/112).

72 Reports from resident magistrates, June 1920 (TNA, CAB 27/108), quoted in Townshend, *Republic*, p. 149.

73 James Feely (BMH WS 997, p. 8); Thomas Kelly (BMH WS 701, pp 4–5); James Quigley (BMH WS 692, p. 4).

74 Thomas Lavin (BMH WS 1,001, p. 5).   75 *LS*, *II*, 22 May 1920.

76 *RH*, 22 May, 10 July 1920; *WFJ*, 12 June 1920; *RM*, 19 June 1920.

77 *RH*, 29 May, 17 July, 7, 14 Aug. 1920.   78 Ibid., 28 Aug. 1920.

79 Thomas Lennon (BMH WS 1336, pp 5–6).

80 Pension claim of Patrick Brennan (IMA, MSPC, 34REF29499).

81 *RH*, 22 May 1920.

82 *RH*, 10, 24, 31 July, 7, 14, 28 Aug., 11 Sept. 1920; *Hansard (Commons)*, 25 Oct. 1920, vol. 133, col. 1380W.

83 *RM*, 19 June 1920.

84 *RH*, 10, 17 July, 18 Sept. 1920; *RM*, 25 Sept., 20 Nov. 1920.

85 *WI*, 10 July 1920.   86 *The Globe* (*TG*), 16 July 1920; *RH*, 17 July 1920.

87 *WFJ*, 10 July 1920; *RH*, *FJ*, 31 July 1920; Outrages against police, Aug. 1920 (TNA, CO 904/149); Compensation claim of Seán Hunt (IMA, 1P48).

88 *WFJ*, 10 July 1920; *DET*, 20 Aug. 1920.

CHAPTER SEVEN *The War of Independence in Roscommon, 1919–21*

1 *DJ*, 6 Jan. 1919; *RH*, 11 Jan. 1919.   2 *FJ*, 21 Jan. 1919.

3 *II*, 24 Jan., 7, 18 Mar. 1919; Sinn Féin Internees (TNA, HO 144/1496/362269/179); Frank Shouldice and George Geraghty, 'The break-out from Usk Jail in Wales by four "German Plot" prisoners' in Florence O'Donoghue (ed.), *Sworn to be free: complete book of IRA jail-breaks, 1918–21* (Tralee, 1971), pp 25–34.

4 *RH*, *WI*, *RJ*, 25 Jan. 1919.

5 CI Roscommon, Jan. 1919 (TNA, CO 904/108).

6 *RM*, 11, 25 Jan. 1919.

7 *II*, *FJ*, 27 Jan. 1919; *RM*, 1 Feb 1919.

8 CI Roscommon, Jan. 1919 (TNA, CO 904/108).

9 *II*, *DET*, 13 Jan. 1919; *RH*, *RM*, 1, 8 Feb. 1919; *WFJ*, 8, 29 Mar., 19 Apr. 1919; Dublin Special Branch files, B.J. Goff (TNA, CO/904/202/165), pp 6–10.

10 *II*, 12 Apr. 1919; *RH*, 5 May 1919.

11 *RM*, 19, 26 Apr. 1919; *II*, 27 May 1919.

12 *RH*, 17, 31 May 1919; Flyer detailing the terms for the cessation of an Irish Transport and General Workers' Union strike in Boyle, County Roscommon, 26 May 1919 (NLI, William O'Brien papers, MS 15,670/10).

13 *RH*, 31 May 1919.

14 *II*, 17, 19 May 1919; John O'Callaghan, *Limerick: the Irish Revolution, 1912–23* (Dublin, 2018), pp 75–7.

15 Dublin Castle Special Branch files, Rev Fr M. O'Flanagan (TNA, CO 904/211/334), pp 154, 149.

16 Dublin Castle Special Branch files, J.J. Redican (TNA, CO 904/213/336B), p. 72; *RH*, 28 June 1919.   17 Laffan, *Resurrection*, pp 305–7.

18 The CI was recording seventy branches with almost 5,300 members (CI Roscommon, July 1919 (TNA, CO 904/109).

19 *FJ*, 11 June 1919; *RM*, *RH*, 14 June 1919.

20 *RH*, 24 May, 7 June 1919.   21 Brigid O'Mullane (BMH WS 450, pp 2–3).

22 *RH*, 7 June, 19 July 1919.

23 *RH*, *II*, 9 Aug. 1919; CI Roscommon, Aug. 1919 (TNA, CO 904/109).

24 Dublin Castle Special Branch files, J.J. Redican (TNA, CO 904/213/336B), p. 160; *RH*, 14 June, 30 Aug. 1919.

25 *RJ*, 16 Aug. 1919.

26 *FJ*, 10 Sept. 1919; Dublin Castle Special Branch files, Rev Fr M. O'Flanagan (TNA, CO 904/211/334), pp 38–9.

27 *WI*, *IT*, 13 Sept. 1919; *RH*, *RM*, 20 Sept. 1919.

28 Michael Collins to Commandant North Roscommon Brigade, 14 Oct. 1919, Reports from IRA North Roscommon Brigade, 1919; Daniel O'Rorke to Michael Collins, 15 Dec. 1919, Reports from IRA South Roscommon Brigade, 1919 (IMA, Collins papers, A/0364).

29 *II*, 20 Sept. 1919; Raid for arms on house of Col. Kirkwood (TNA, WO 35/108/12).

30 Patrick Hegarty (BMH WS 1,606, pp 15–17). After Mayo, Roscommon was the second highest Connacht contributor per person. By September 1920, the southern constituency

handed over £4,667, the north £4,606 (Dáil Éireann Loan: nett amounts received at head office as on 27 September 1920 (NLI, ILB 300, p. 2 (Item 46)); *TG*, 17 Nov. 1919.

31 *WFJ*, 29 Nov. 1919; Mrs Bernhard O'Donnell (BMH WS 750, p. 3); Pension claim of Eithne Coyle (IMA, MSPC, 34REF60256).

32 *IC*, 6 Sept. 1919.

33 *FJ*, 17 Nov. 1919; Prosecution of Winifred and Lena Sharkey (TNA, WO 35/102/28).

34 *DH*, 24 Nov. 1919.   35 *FJ*, 15 Dec. 1919.   36 *RH*, 15, 22 Nov. 1919.

37 *Hansard (Commons)*, 22 Dec. 1919, vol. 123, cols. 1173–4; *APJ*, *BNL*, 23 Dec. 1919.

38 *WI*, 27 Dec. 1919, 3 Jan. 1920. The Roscommon North constituency joined Leitrim and Roscommon South joined Mayo South. Each would send four representatives to a Dublin parliament and one to Westminster (*II*, 28 Feb. 1920).

39 *RM*, 3 Jan. 1920; CI Roscommon, Jan., Feb. 1920 (TNA, CO 904/111).

40 Dublin Castle Special Branch files, Rev Fr M. O'Flanagan (TNA, CO 904/211/334), pp 27–33.

41 *RJ*, 21 Feb., 6 Mar. 1920; *II*, 2, 9 Mar. 1920.

42 CI Roscommon, Feb. 1920 (TNA, CO 904/111); *RM*, 31 Jan. 1920.

43 *Record of the rebellion in Ireland in 1920–21 and the part played by the military in dealing with it*, Rebellion in Ireland: historical record (TNA, WO 141/93/79/Irish/966), pp 9, 18, 23, 83.

44 A CMA was appointed in Boyle in February 1921 (*Record of the rebellion*, pp 48, 90).

45 *II*, 19 Mar. 1920.   46 *BNL*, 22 Mar. 1920.

47 CI Roscommon, Feb. 1920 (TNA, CO 904/111).

48 Dublin Castle Special Branch files, J.J. Redican (TNA, CO 904/213/336B), pp 26–9, 49–58.

49 *II*, 16 Apr. 1920.

50 *RH*, 17 July 1920; Outrages against police, July 1920 (TNA, CO 904/148).

51 *SD*, 3 Jan. 1920; *RM*, 24 Apr. 1920.

52 *RJ*, 17 Apr. 1920; *RM*, 17, 24 Apr. 1920.

53 *RM*, *LS*, 7 Feb. 1920; Record of activities in A Coy area (Boyle), 1st Battalion, North Roscommon Brigade (IMA, MSPC, A/31/(4)).

54 Seán Leavy (BMH WS 954, p. 4); CI Roscommon, Feb. 1920 (TNA, CO 904/111); *SD*, 14 Feb. 1920; *II*, 2 Mar. 1920; *RM*, 3 Apr. 1920; Outrages against police, May 1920 (TNA, CO 904/148).

55 *DJ*, 13 Feb. 1920; *BNL*, 24 July 1920; Frank Simons (BMH WS 770, p. 4).

56 *RJ*, 6 Mar. 1920.

57 Outrages against police, Apr. 1920 (TNA, CO 904/148); *LS*, 27 Mar. 1920; *RM*, 3 Apr. 1920.

58 Hughes, *Defying*, pp 28–30; Outrages against police, June–Aug. 1920, Jan.–July 1921 (TNA, CO 904/148; CO 904/149; CO 904/150).

59 *II*, 5, 6 Apr. 1920; *RM*, *SD*, 10 Apr. 1920; *DET*, 25 May 1920.

60 *BNL*, 6, 7, 12 Apr. 1920; *RJ*, *RM*, 17 Apr. 1920.

61 *SD*, 17 Apr. 1920.   62 *An tÓglach*, 1 May 1920.   63 *RM*, 17 Apr. 1920.

64 Ibid., 8 May 1920; Outrages against police, May 1920 (TNA, CO 904/148).

65 *WFJ*, 8 May 1920; *II*, 14 May 1920.

66 *DET*, 21 July 1920; *LS*, 31 July 1920.

67 *RM*, *RJ*, 15 May 1920; Commandant South Roscommon IRA to Adjutant General, IRA, 21 May 1920, IRA South Roscommon Brigade (IMA, Collins papers, A/0525).

68 *RH*, 15 May 1920; James Feely (BMH WS 997, p. 6); Burke, *Athlone*, p. 193.

69 Fergus Campbell, *Land and revolution: nationalist politics in the west of Ireland, 1891–1921* (Oxford, 2005), pp 246–57.

70 *FJ*, *LS*, 22 Apr. 1920.   71 *SD*, 24 Jan., 7 Feb., 1 May 1920.

72 *Record of the rebellion*, pp 9, 18–19.   73 *RJ*, 17 Apr. 1920.

74 Burke, *Athlone*, pp 189–91; *DH*, *LS*, 5 Apr. 1920; *RM*, 10, 17 Apr., 15 May 1920.

75 *BNL*, 7 Apr. 1920; *DJ*, 9 Apr., 7 May 1920; *WFJ*, 22 May 1920; Kevin O'Shiel (BMH WS 1,770, pp 991–2).

76 Campbell, *Land*, pp 251–4. 77 *WI*, 10 Apr. 1920.   78 *WFJ*, 27 Mar. 1920.

79 Agrarian outrages, May 1920 (TNA, CO 904/121); *RM*, 5, 12 June 1920.

80 *BNL*, 6 May 1920; Agrarian outrages, Aug. 1920 (TNA, CO 904/121).

81 *LS*, 29 Apr., 22 June 1920; *DET*, 26 May, 5 June 1920; CI Roscommon, June 1920 (TNA, CO 904/112).

82 *Record of the rebellion*, pp 20–1; CI Roscommon, July, Oct., Dec. 1920 (TNA, CO 904/112/113).

83 *II*, 8, 16 June 1920.   84 *SD*, 8 May 1920.

85 Agrarian outrages, May, June 1920 (TNA, CO 904/121); *RM*, 5 June 1920; *Record of the rebellion*, p. 23.

86 *DC*, 15 May 1920; *RH*, 5 June 1920.   87 *FJ*, 5 Aug. 1920.

88 *II*, 31 Jan. 1920; *WFJ*, 31 July 1920; *DET*, 30 Sept. 1920.

89 IG, Aug. 1920 (TNA, CO 904/112).

90 Commandant South Roscommon Brigade, IRA to Adjutant General, IRA, 9 May 1920; Adjutant General, IRA to Commandant South Roscommon Brigade, IRA, 12 May 1920, IRA South Roscommon Brigade (IMA, Collins papers A/0525).

91 *SD*, 22 May 1920; Campbell, *Land*, pp 255–6.

92 *II*, 18 May 1920; *RJ*, *WIT*, 22 May 1920. 93 *BNL*, 17 May 1920.

94 *RJ*, 29 May 1920.   95 *II*, 24, 26 May 1920.

96 Kevin O'Shiel (BMH WS 1,770, pp 975–7).

97 Frank Simons (BMH WS 770, p. 7); James Quigley (BMH WS 692, p. 5).

98 *BNL*, 5 May 1920; *RH*, 29 May 1920; Activities of Kilteevan Company, South Roscommon Brigade IRA (IMA, MSPC, A/27).

99 Brigade Commandant North Roscommon IRA to Adjutant General, IRA, 29 June 1920, IRA North Roscommon Brigade (IMA, Collins papers, A/0524).

100 CI Roscommon, Feb. 1920 (TNA, CO 904/111); Thomas Lavin (BMH WS 1,001, p. 5).

101 Townshend, *Republic*, p. 183.

102 Prosecution of Michael Ward (TNA, WO 35/111/21); *DJ*, 31 Mar. 1920.

103 *LS*, 6 Nov. 1920, 17 Feb. 1921; Seamus Ryan, Commandant North Roscommon IRA to Chief of Staff, IRA, 8 June 1920, IRA North Roscommon Brigade (IMA, Collins papers, A/0524).

104 *RH*, *RJ*, 17 July 1920; James Feely (BMH WS 997, p. 7).

105 *RJ*, 10, 17 July 1920.

106 *Hansard (Commons)*, 15 July 1920, vol. 131, col. 2624W; Fitzpatrick, *Politics and Irish life*, p. 35.

107 OC Athlone Brigade IRA to Richard Mulcahy, 20 July 1920 (UCDA, Richard Mulcahy papers, P7/A/40).

108 *RJ*, *RH*, 11, 18 Sept. 1920.

109 John Duffy (BMH WS 580, pp 10–11).

110 *RM*, 31 July 1920; *Hansard (Commons)*, 9 Aug. 1920, vol. 133, cols. 24–5.

111 Outrages against police, July 1920 (TNA, CO 904/148); *RH*, 17 July 1920; D.M. Leeson, *The Black and Tans: British police and auxiliaries in the Irish War of Independence* (Oxford, 2012), p. 209; Pension claim of Patrick Brennan (IMA, MSPC, 34REF29499).

112 North Roscommon Commandant, IRA to Adjutant General, IRA, 4 July 1920, IRA North Roscommon Brigade (IMA, Collins papers, A/0524).

113 Outrages against police, July 1920 (TNA, CO 904/148); *RH*, 4 Mar. 1922.

114 Outrages against police, July, Aug. 1920 (TNA, CO 904/149).

115 *DET*, 23 July 1920.

116 *RM*, 24 July 1920; Frank Simons (BMH WS 770, p. 4).

117 Sgt. T. Crawley (BMH WS 718, p. 5).

118 *RH*, 29 May, 10 July 1920; CI Roscommon, July 1920 (TNA, CO 904/112).

119 Martin Fallon (BMH WS 1,121, p. 23).

120 Outrages against police, Sept. 1920 (TNA, CO 904/149).

121 Outrages against police, Aug. 1920 (TNA, CO 904/149); *BNL*, 3 Sept. 1920.

122 Pension claim of Mary Madden (IMA, MSPC, 34REF60370).

123 Commandant South Roscommon Brigade to unnamed, 4 Mar. 1921, IRA South Roscommon Brigade (IMA, Collins papers, A/0761).

124 CI Roscommon, June, July 1920 (TNA, CO 904/112); *RJ*, 17, 31 July 1920; *RH*, 7 Aug. 1920; Pension claim of Eithne Coyle (IMA, MSPC, 34REF60256).

125 *DET*, 24 Aug. 1921.

126 Pádraig Óg Ó Ruairc, *Truce: murder, myth and the last days of the Irish War of Independence* (Cork, 2016), p. 49.

127 *RH*, 11 June 1921; Military court of inquiry on Constable George Southgate (TNA, WO 35/159A/33).   128 *FJ*, 12 Aug. 1921.

129 CI Roscommon, June 1920 (TNA, CO 904/112); *TG*, 21 June 1920.

130 *RM*, 3 July, 7 Aug., 23 Oct., 11 Nov. 1920; CI Roscommon, Aug., Oct., Nov. 1920 (TNA, CO 904/113).

131 *WFJ*, 15 May, 3 July, 7 Aug. 18, 25 Dec. 1920.

132 *RH*, 30 Oct. 1920, 4 June 1921; *Record of the rebellion*, p. 19.

133 Joost Augusteijn, 'Military conflict in the War of Independence' in John Crowley, Donal Ó Drisceoil & Mike Murphy (eds), *Atlas of the Irish Revolution* (Cork, 2017), p. 352; Conor McNamara, 'Connacht' in Crowley et al. (eds), *Atlas of the Irish Revolution*, p. 601.

134 Peter Hart, 'The geography of revolution in Ireland, 1917–1923', *Past and Present*, 155 (May, 1997), 47; Fitzpatrick, 'The geography of the War of Independence' in Crowley et al. (eds), *Atlas of the Irish Revolution*, pp 537–8.

135 *RH*, *DET*, 17 July 1920; Michael Joseph Ryan (BMH WS 633, pp 21–2); Frank Simons (BMH WS 770, pp 7–9); Moneen ambush, 11 July 1920, Brigade activity reports of South Roscommon Brigade (IMA, MSPC, A/27).

136 Luke Duffy (BMH WS 661, pp 6–8); Frank Simons (BMH WS 770, pp 8–9); Gerald Davis (BMH WS 718, pp 3–4).

137 *RH*, *RM*, 24 July 1920.   138 *RH*, 31 July 14, 28 Aug. 1920.

139 *BNL*, 22 July 1920; Michael Ó Laoghaire (BMH WS 797, p. 57).

140 *DJ*, 23 Aug. 1920; *RJ*, 28 Aug. 1920.

141 *RH*, *RM*, 7 Aug. 1920.   142 *YPLI*, *NW*, 3 Aug. 1921.

143 John Borgonovo, *Spies, informers and the 'Anti-Sinn Féin Society': the intelligence war in Cork city, 1920–1921* (Dublin, 2007), pp 7–10, 18.

144 *RH*, 14 Aug. 1920.   145 *RH*, *RM*, *RJ*, 21 Aug. 1920.

146 James Feely (BMH WS 997, p. 9).   147 *RH*, 21, 28 Aug. 1920.

148 *RH*, 14 Aug. 1920.   149 *IT*, 18 Aug. 1920; *DET*, 24 Sept. 1920.

150 *DET*, 25 Sept. 1920.   151 *DET*, *TG*, 27 Aug. 1920.   152 *RJ*, 13 Nov. 1920.

153 John Duffy (BMH WS 1,770, pp 5–6); *DET*, 6 Sept. 1920; CI Roscommon, Aug. 1920 (TNA, CO 904/112); David Leeson, 'The Royal Irish Constabulary, Black and Tans and Auxiliaries' in Crowley et al. (eds), *Atlas of the Irish Revolution*, p. 377.

154 *RM*, *RH*, 28 Aug. 1920.

155 Outrages against police, Sept. 1920 (TNA, CO 904/149); *RH*, *RJ*, *RM*, 4 Sept. 1920; Compensation claim from the family of Thomas J. McDonagh (IMA, MSPC, 1D68).

156 Jim Hunt (BMH WS 905, pp 7–10); Thomas Lavin, 'The ambush at Teevnacreeva' in Michael O'Callaghan, *For Ireland and freedom: Roscommon and the fight for independence, 1917–1921* (2nd ed. Cork, 2012 [1964]), pp 60–8.

157 *RM, RH*, 11 Sept. 1920; *Hansard (Commons)*, 5 Nov. 1920, vol. 134, cols. 768–9.

158 *FJ*, 7 Sept. 1920; Brian Heffernan, *Freedom and the fifth commandment: Catholic priests and political violence in Ireland, 1919–21* (Manchester, 2014), p. 216.

159 Work in connection with attempt to prevent burning of Ballaghaderreen, Brigade activity reports of East Mayo 5th Brigade (IMA, MSPC, A/33).

160 *DET*, 18 Oct. 1920; Leeson, *Black and Tans*, p. 160.

161 *RH*, 25 Sept., 2 Oct. 1920.

162 *DET*, 31 Aug. 1920; *RH*, 4 Sept. 1920; *Record of the rebellion*, pp 34, 39.

163 *RJ*, 18 Sept. 1920; Claim for dependants' allowance from the family of Patrick Glynn (IMA, MSPC, 1D45); Claim for dependants' allowance from the family of Michael James Keane (IMA, MSPC, 1D54); Claim for dependants' allowance from the family of Michael Glavey (IMA, MSPC, DP1763).

164 Pension claim of James Wallace (IMA, MSPC, 34REF4404).

165 *Record of the rebellion*, pp 37, 116. 166 *RM*, 25 Sept. 1920.

167 *TG*, 11 Aug. 1920. 168 *RJ, RH*, 28 Aug. 1920. 169 *FJ*, 6 Sept. 1920.

170 *Irish Society*, 18 Sept. 1920; *RM*, 25 Sept. 1920. 171 *WFJ*, 2 Oct. 1920.

172 *RH, RM*, 9 Oct. 1920; Outrages against police, Oct. 1920 (TNA, CO 904/149); Brigade activity reports of Castlerea Brigade, 2nd Western Division (IMA, MSPC, A/25 (1)).

173 Hugh Martin, *Insurrection in Ireland: an Englishman's record of fact* (London, 1921), pp 106–15.

174 *BNL, GE*, 4 Oct. 1920; *RH*, 9 Oct. 1920.

175 Outrages against police, Aug. 1920 (TNA, CO 904/149); *Illustrated Police News*, 26 Aug. 1920; *RH*, 4 Sept. 1920.

176 John P. Haran (BMH WS 1,458, p. 6); *BNL*, 8 Sept., 21 Oct., 21 Dec. 1920.

177 *Hansard (Commons)*, 20 Oct. 1920, vol. 42, cols. 35–7.

178 *RH*, 9 Oct. 1920; Leeson, *Black and Tans*, pp 204–5.

179 *II, DET*, 11 Oct. 1920; Burke, *Athlone*, p. 199.

180 *Nottingham Journal*, 12 Oct. 1920. 181 *FJ*, 5 Oct. 1920.

182 *RM, II*, 9 Oct. 1920. 183 *WFJ*, 11 Sept. 1920.

184 Ernie O'Malley Notebooks (UCDA, P17b/107), p. 137

185 Luke Duffy (BMH WS 661, p. 31); Ó Ruairc, *Truce*, pp 119–21.

186 CI Roscommon, Jan. 1921 (TNA, CO 904/114); *BNL*, 8 Jan. 1921; Courts martial of civilians (TNA, WO 35/208); *RH*, 14 May, 4 June 1921; Treatment of Irish political prisoners in England (TNA, HO 144/1734/376829/221); Pension claim of Patrick Redington (IMA, MSPC, 34REF47624).

187 *IT*, 21, 22 Aug. 1921.

188 Pádraig Óg Ó Ruairc, '"Spies and informers beware?": IRA execution of alleged civilian spies during the War of Independence' in Crowley et al. (eds), *Atlas of the Irish Revolution*, p. 433.

189 CI Roscommon, Oct. 1920 (TNA, CO 904/113).

190 Brigade activity report of the South Roscommon Brigade IRA (IMA, MSPC, A/27); O'Callaghan, *For Ireland*, pp 87–9.

191 *RM*, 23 Oct. 1920.

192 Luke Duffy (BMH WS 661, pp 8–9); Frank Simons (BMH WS 770, pp 10–13); Brigade activity report of the South Roscommon Brigade IRA (IMA, MSPC, A/27); *RH*, 16 Oct. 1920.

193 *BNL*, 13, 14 Oct. 1920; *RM*, 30 Oct. 1920. 194 *RH*, 16 Oct. 1920.

195 *BT*, 15 Oct. 1920; *RH*, 16 Oct. 1920. 196 *RJ, RM*, 23, 30 Oct. 1920.

197 *RJ*, 11 Feb. 1922.   **198** *RH*, 23 Oct., 20 Nov. 1920.
199 *DET*, 21 Oct. 1920; *WFJ*, 6 Nov. 1920.
200 Pension claim of Eithne Coyle (IMA, MSPC, 34REF60256).
201 *RJ*, 6 Nov. 1920; *WFJ*, 18 Feb. 1922.
202 *FJ*, 20 Oct. 1920; Courts of inquiry in lieu of inquest (TNA, WO 35/162).
203 *Hansard (Commons)*, 27 Oct. 1920, vol. 133, cols. 1734–5.
204 *RH*, 23 Oct. 1920.
205 *FJ*, 5 Nov. 1920; *RH*, 20 Nov. 1920; James Quigley (BMH WS 692, pp 7–8).
206 *RJ*, *RM*, 6 Nov. 1920; CI Roscommon, Nov. 1920 (TNA, CO 904/113); Court of inquiry in lieu of inquest (TNA, WO 35/162).
207 CI Roscommon, Dec. 1920 (TNA, CO 904/113); Death of John McGowan (TNA, WO 35/154/53); *WFJ*, 1 Jan. 1921.
208 CI Roscommon, Oct. 1920 (TNA, CO 904/113); Luke Duffy (BMH WS 661, p. 10); Frank Simons (BMH WS 770, p. 14); Andrew Keaveney (BMH WS 1178, p. 6).
209 Pension claim of Margaret Cunnane (IMA, MSPC, 34REF39294); Martin Fallon (BMH WS 1121), p. 7; James Quigley (BMH WS 692, p. 6); Pension claim of Teresa McDermott (IMA, MSPC, 34REF60035).
210 Ernie O'Malley, *Rising out* (Dublin, 2007), pp 82–3; Seán Glancy (BMH WS 964, p. 5); Thomas Lavin (BMH WS 1,001, p. 6); Thomas Brady (BMH WS 1,008, pp 6–7).
211 O'Malley, *Rising out*, pp 96–7, 113.
212 Seán Leavy (BMH WS 954, p. 11).   **213** *RH*, 6 Nov. 1920.
214 *RH*, 30 Oct., 6, 13 Nov. 1920; Summary of major operations of 1st Battalion, North Roscommon Brigade up to 11 July 1921, Brigade activity report of the North Roscommon Brigade, 3rd Western Division IRA (IMA, MSPC, A/31 (4)).
215 CI Roscommon, Oct. 1920 (TNA, CO 904/113); *IT*, 6 Nov. 1920.
216 CI Roscommon, Dec. 1920 (TNA, CO 904/113); Shouldice, *Grandpa*, pp 305–8; Burke, *Athlone*, pp 199–200, 204–5.
217 *FJ*, 29 Nov. 1920; Leeson, *Black and Tans*, pp 161–2.
218 Prosecution of … 17 October, 1920, Croghan, County Roscommon (TNA, WO 35/131/14).
219 *RH*, 16, 30 Oct., 27 Nov 1920; Heffernan, *Freedom*, pp 258–9.
220 *RH*, 27 Nov. 1920.   **221** IG, Nov. 1920 (TNA, CO 904/113).
222 CI Roscommon, Nov. 1920 (TNA, CO 904/113); *RH*, 8 Jan. 1921.
223 *WFJ*, 22 Jan. 1921.
224 *FJ*, 8 Nov. 1920; Vera McDonnell (BMH WS 1,050, pp 5–7); Carroll, *O'Flanagan*, p. 127.
225 *RJ*, *RM*, 27 Nov. 1920.
226 CI Roscommon, Oct. 1920 (TNA, CO 904/113); IG, Nov. 1920 (TNA, CO 904/113); *RH*, *RM*, 2, 9 Oct. 1920.
227 IG Report, Nov. 1920 (TNA, CO 904/113).
228 CI Roscommon, Nov. 1920 (TNA, CO 904/113); *DET*, 8 Feb. 1922; *RJ*, *RM*, 18 Feb. 1922; Brigade activity report of the North Roscommon Brigade, 3rd Western Division IRA (IMA, MSPC, A/31 (1)); Pension claim of Patrick Flynn (IMA, MSPC, 34REF130).
229 Outrages against police, Nov. 1920 (TNA, CO 904/149); *DET*, 25 Nov. 1920, 16 May 1922; Pension claim of Denis McGuire (IMA, MSPC, 34REF54274).
230 Report on South Roscommon Brigade (IMA, Collins papers, A/0761/III).
231 *BNL*, *DJ*, 3 Dec. 1920; Civilians tried by court martial (TNA, WO 35/131/4); Compensation claim of Francis Madden (IMA, MSPC, 24SP7197).
232 CI Roscommon, Dec. 1920 (TNA, CO 904/113); *Hansard (Commons)*, 1 Mar. 1921, vol. 138, cols. 1735–6; Leeson, *Black and Tans*, pp 83–4, 160, 198.
233 *FJ*, 4 May, 12 Dec. 1921.   **234** *RH*, 8 Jan., 26 Mar. 1921.
235 *RH*, 8, 15 Jan. 1921.   **236** *RJ*, 11, 18, 25 Dec. 1920, 15 Jan. 1921.

237 *RM*, *DET*, 11 Dec 1920; O'Carroll, *O'Flanagan*, pp 128–32; Michael O'Flanagan, Roscommon, to David Lloyd George (Parliamentary Archives, Lloyd George Papers, LG/F/95/2/71, LG/F/95/2/64, LG/F/95/2/69).

238 *RH*, 19 Feb. 1921; Patrick Murray, *Oracles of God: the Roman Catholic Church and Irish politics, 1922–37* (Dublin, 2000), pp 156–60.

239 Thomas Brady (BMH WS, 1,008, p. 10); Seán Leavy (BMH WS, 954, pp 8–9); Martin Fallon (BMH WS 1,121, p. 8); Brigade activity report for the North Roscommon Brigade IRA (IMA, MSPC, A31/1); *NW*, 7, 10 Jan. 1921; CI Roscommon, Jan. 1921 (TNA, CO 904/114).

240 Outrages against police (TNA, CO 904/150); *EPG*, 10 Jan. 1921; Courts of inquiry in lieu of inquest (TNA, WO 35/154); Seán Leavy (BMH WS 954, pp 8–9); Martin Fallon (BMH WS 1,121, pp 11–12).

241 *NW*, *BNL*, 8 Jan. 1921; *FJ*, 11 Jan. 1921; Compensation claim of Durr family (IMA, MSPC, MD7477).

242 Military court of inquiry on Patrick Durr (TNA, WO 35/149A); *DET*, 11 May 1921.

243 *FJ*, 26 Jan. 1921; *RH*, 29 Jan. 1921.

244 *RH*, 29 Jan., 19 Feb., 12 Mar. 1921; Abortive attack on Ballaghaderreen RIC barracks, Brigade activity report for the East Mayo 5 Brigade (IMA, MSPC, A/33).

245 *SDT*, 1 Feb. 1921; *FJ*, 31 Mar., 18 May, 15 June 1921.

246 CI Roscommon, Jan., Feb., Mar. 1921 (TNA, CO 904/114); *WFJ*, 11 June, 9 July 1921.

247 CI Roscommon, Jan. 1921 (TNA, CO 904/114); *RH*, 5 Feb. 1921.

248 Military court of inquiry on James Tormey (TNA, WO 35/160/18); Burke, *Athlone*, p. 209.

249 *RH*, 5, 12, 19 Feb., 12 Mar., 30 Apr., 4, 18 June 1921.

250 CI Roscommon, Feb. 1921 (TNA, CO 904/114).

251 *DJ*, 9 Feb. 1921; *RH*, 19 Feb. 1921; *Record of the rebellion*, p. 45.

252 *FJ*, 25 Jan. 1921; *LS*, 26 May 1921; Pension claim of Thomas Dunne (IMA, MSPC, 34REF40202); Pension claim of Elizabeth Tivnan (IMA, MSPC, 34REF50591); Pension claim of Eileen O'Doherty (IMA, MSPC, 34REF39544).

253 *RJ*, *RH*, 5, 12 Mar. 1921; Courts martial of civilians (TNA, WO 35/208); Pension claim of Eithne Coyle (IMA, MSPC, 34REF60256).

254 *DH*, 2 May 1921.

255 Eithne Coyle (BMH WS, 750, pp 10–12); Pension claim of Bridget Agnes Flynn (IMA, MSPC, 34REF41073).

256 *Record of the rebellion*, p. 42; *SDT*, 1 Feb. 1921; *RH*, 12 Feb. 1921; *BT*, 12 Mar., 9 May 1921.

257 *RH*, 29 Jan., 19 Feb., 12 Mar. 1921; *Record of the rebellion*, p. 47; CI Roscommon, Mar. 1921 (TNA, CO 904/114).

258 *RH*, 16 Apr. 1921; *SDT*, 3 May 1921; *RJ*, 16 July 1921.

259 *Hansard (Commons)*, 24 Feb. 1921, vol. 138, cols. 1153–4, 3 Mar. 1921, vol. 138, cols. 1981–2; *RH*, 5 Mar. 1921.

260 *RH*, 12 Feb. 1921.

261 Seán Connolly to IRA Director of Intelligence, 14 Feb. 1921 (IMA, Collins papers A/0760); *DET*, 12 Feb. 1921; *RJ*, 19 Feb. 1921; Brigade activity report for the South Roscommon Brigade IRA (IMA, MSPC, A/27); Brigade activity report for the North Roscommon Brigade IRA (IMA, MSPC, A31/1).

262 *Record of the rebellion*, p. 103.   263 *FJ*, 21 Feb. 1921.

264 CI Roscommon, Feb. 1921 (TNA, CO 904/114); *FJ*, *BNL*, 22 Feb. 1921; *RH*, 26 Feb. 1921.

265 James Feely (BMH WS 997, p. 11); Outrages against police, Mar. 1921 (TNA, CO 904/150).

266 Outrages against police, Apr. 1921 (TNA, CO 904/150); OC South Roscommon Brigade IRA to IRA Director of Intelligence, 20 Sept. 1920 (IMA, Collins papers, A/076I).

267 Seán Connolly to IRA Director of Intelligence, 14 Feb. 1921, IRA North Roscommon Brigade (IMA, Collins papers, A/0760); IRA Director of Intelligence to OC South Roscommon Brigade IRA, 3 Mar. 1921; IRA Director of Intelligence to OC South Roscommon Brigade IRA, 11 Apr. 1921; OC South Roscommon Brigade IRA to IRA Director of Intelligence, 25 Apr. 1921 (IMA, Collins papers, A/076I).

268 *RJ*, 19 Feb., 5 Mar. 1921; *BWT*, 18 June 1921; Athlone Division: List of Crown witnesses now in police barracks (IMA, Collins papers, A/076I).

269 Acting OC South Roscommon Brigade IRA to IRA Director of Intelligence, 13 Oct. 1921 (IMA, Collins papers, A/076I); *BT*, 2, 6 Sept. 1922.

270 *FJ*, 22 Feb., 4 Apr. 1921; Military court of inquiry on Patrick Lyons (TNA, WO 35/153A/59).

271 *RH*, 12 Mar., 9 Apr. 1921.

272 *BNL, DET*, 5 Mar. 1921; *RJ, BWT*, 12 Mar. 1921; CI Roscommon, Mar. 1921 (TNA, CO 904/114); Military court of inquiry on Francis Elliott (TNA, WO 35/149B/9).

273 *RH*, 19, 26 Feb., 5, 12 Mar. 1921; Courts martial case register (TNA, WO 35/135).

274 Daily raid reports (TNA, WO 35/80/96); Compensation claim for the Moran family (IMA, MSPC, WDP7559P).

275 *Hansard (Commons)*, 3 Mar. 1921, vol. 138, col. 1611; *DET*, 10 Mar. 1921.

276 Civilians tried by courts martial (TNA, WO 35/130/5).

277 *RH, RJ*, 19 Mar. 1921; May Moran, *Executed for Ireland: the Patrick Moran story* (Cork, 2010).

278 *RH*, 19 Mar. 1921; Court of inquiry in lieu of inquest (TNA, WO 35/147B/21).

279 Outrages against police, Mar. 1921 (TNA, CO 904/150); Seán Glancy (BMH WS 964, pp 10–11); Thomas Lavin (BMH WS 1,001, p. 9); Keadue ambush in March 1921, Brigade activity report for the Arigna Brigade IRA (IMA, MSPC, A30); Military court of inquiry on Constables William Devereux and James Dowling (TNA, WO 35/149A/14).

280 Luke Duffy (BMH WS 661, pp 19–20); Frank Simons (BMH WS 770, pp 24–5); Seán Leavy (BMH WS, 954, pp 12–14); Martin Fallon (BMH WS 1,121, pp 12–16); Scramogue ambush March 23 1921, Brigade activity report for the South Roscommon Brigade IRA (IMA, MSPC, A/27); Compensation claim of Madden family (IMA, MSPC, 24SP7439).

281 Pension claim of Teresa McDermott (IMA, MSPC, 34REF60035); Pension claim of Rita Duignan (IMA, MSPC, 34REF59552).

282 *FJ, IT*, 24 Mar. 1921; Outrages against police, Mar. 1921 (TNA, CO 904/150).

283 *YPLI*, 25, 28 Mar. 1921; Military court of inquiry on Constable Edward Leslie (TNA, WO 35/153A/38).

284 Luke Duffy (BMH WS, 661, p. 24); Patrick Mullooly (BMH WS 955, p. 20); *RJ*, 18 June 1921.

285 *RJ*, 26 Mar. 1921; Sean Glancy (BMH WS 964, p. 18); Compensation claim of Andrew Lavin (IMA, MSPC, W24SP4060).

286 Luke Duffy (BMH WS, 661, p. 23); Frank Simons (BMH WS 770, p. 25); Seán Leavy (BMH WS, 954, pp 18–19); Martin Fallon (BMH WS 1,121, p. 18); Leeson, *Black and Tans*, pp 150–1.

287 Seán Leavy (BMH WS, 954, pp 14, 17).

288 *FJ*, 24 Mar. 1921; *RH*, 2 Apr. 1921.

289 *RH*, 2 Apr. 1921; *Army and Navy Gazette*, 9 Apr. 1921.

290 Civilians tried by courts martial (TNA, WO 125/39); *RH*, 2 Apr. 1921.

291 Compensation claim of Annie Cunnane (IMA, MSPC, DP5698).

292 *DJ*, 28 Mar. 1921; Thomas Lavin (IMA 653/56); Pension claim of Annie Cunnane (IMA, MSPC 34REF57691).

293 Military operations and enquiries (TNA, WO 35/89); *Record of the rebellion*, p. 52.

294 John Duffy (BMH WS, 580, pp 17–18); Patrick Mullooly (BMH WS 1,086, pp 34–50); CI Roscommon, Mar. 1921 (TNA, CO 904/114).

295 Court of inquiry in lieu of inquest (TNA, WO 35/162); Military court of inquiry on Michael Mullooly (TNA, WO 35/155A); *RJ*, 18 June 1921.

296 *RJ*, 11 Feb. 1922; O'Callaghan, *For Ireland*, p. 145.

297 *FJ*, 29 Mar. 1921; *Record of the rebellion*, p. 47; Courts of inquiry in lieu of inquest: register of cases (TNA, WO 35/162).

298 Military court of inquiry on Joseph Mulloy (TNA, WO 35/155A/57).

299 *RH*, 2 Apr. 1921.

300 Military operations and inquiries (TNA, WO 35/89); *DET*, 9, 10 May 1921.

301 Military court of inquiry on Michael Wynne (TNA, WO 35/159B/39).

302 *RJ*, 11 June 1921; Outrages against police, June 1921 (TNA, CO 904/150).

303 Prosecution of Head Constable Michael McLean (TNA, WO 35/127/30).

304 *RJ*, 9 Apr., 11 Feb. 1922; Military court of inquiry on Edward Beirne (TNA, WO 35/146B/5); Courts of inquiry in lieu of inquest: register of cases (TNA, WO 35/162).

305 *FJ*, 8 Apr. 1921; Deaths of John Gilligan and John Wymes (TNA, WO 35/149B/23).

306 Military court of inquiry on John Wymes (TNA, WO 35/159B/38).

307 Outrages against police, Feb. 1921 (TNA, CO 904/150); *RH*, 9 Apr. 1921; Andrew Keaveney (BMH WS 1,178, p. 6).

308 Thomas Crawley (BMH WS 718, pp 14–15); Ó Ruairc, *Truce*, p. 121.

309 OC South Roscommon Brigade IRA to IRA Director of Intelligence, 22 Jan. 1921; OC South Roscommon Brigade IRA to IRA Director of Intelligence, 8 Mar. 1921; OC South Roscommon Brigade IRA to IRA Director of Intelligence, 23 Mar. 1921; Daniel O'Rorke to IRA Adjutant General, 27 Oct. 1921; IRA Deputy Chief of Staff to IRA Director of Intelligence, 9 Nov. 1921 (IMA, Collins papers, A/076I).

310 Roscommon lagged behind Tipperary, Clare, Galway and Kerry (Agrarian outrages, Apr., May, June, July, Sept. 1921 (TNA, CO904/121)).

311 *RH*, 9, 16 Apr. 1921.

312 Courts of inquiry in lieu of inquest: register of cases (TNA, WO 35/162); *NW*, 9 Apr. 1921; *BWT*, 16 Apr. 1921.

313 CI Roscommon, Apr. 1921 (TNA, CO 904/115).

314 *RH*, *RJ*, 16 Apr. 1921; Andrew Keaveney (BMH WS 1,178, p. 12).

315 Military court of inquiry on Mary-Anne MacDonagh (TNA, WO 35/154/36); Thomas Crawley (BMH WS 718, p. 10); *RH*, 7 May, 18 June 1921.

316 *RJ*, 30 Apr., 7 May 1921.

317 OC South Roscommon Brigade IRA to IRA Director of Intelligence, 8 Mar. 1921 (IMA, Collins papers, A/076I).

318 *FJ*, *NW*, 20 Apr. 1921; Attack by enemy soldiers at Loughglynn Demesne, April 1921, Brigade activity report for the Castlerea Brigade, 2nd Western Division (IMA, MSPC, A25/1).

319 *RH*, 23 Apr. 1921; Military court of inquiry on Stephen W. McDermott and John Bergin (TNA, WO 35/154/32).   320 *RH*, 9 Apr. 1921.

321 *RJ*, *RH*, 16 Apr. 1921; *FJ*, 20 Apr. 1921. 322 *RH*, 30 Apr. 1921.

323 Jim Hunt (BMH WS 770, p. 17); *RH*, 21, 28 May 1921.

324 *RH*, 30 Apr. 1921.

325 *FJ*, 3 May 1921; Courts of inquiry in lieu of inquest: register of cases (TNA, WO 35/162).

326 *FJ*, 10, 11, 21 May 1921.

327 Luke Duffy (BMH WS 661, pp 28–30); Military court of inquiry on Martin Scanlon, ex-RIC (TNA, WO 35/159B/1).

328 CI Roscommon, June 1921 (TNA, CO 904/115).

329 Outrages against police, May 1921 (TNA, CO 904/150).

330 CI Roscommon, May 1921 (TNA, CO 904/115).

331 *FJ*, 24 Jan. 1922; *RJ*, 4 Feb. 1922.

332 *RJ*, 21, 28 May, 4 June 1921; Internment camps and prisons (TNA, WO 35/141); Pension claim of Patrick Brennan (IMA, MSPC, 34REF29499); Compensation claim of George Meadlarklan (IMA, MSPC, B380).

333 CI Roscommon, June 1921 (TNA, CO 904/115).

334 *DET*, 15 June 1921.   335 *RJ*, *RH*, 21 May 1921.

336 *FJ*, 11 May 1921.

337 *RH*, 7, 21 May 1921.

338 Outrages against police, June 1921 (TNA, CO 904/150); *FJ*, 3, 23 June 1921; Compensation claim of Carty family (IMA, MSPC, 1D420).

339 Brigade activity report for the Castlerea Brigade, 2nd Western Division (IMA, MSPC, A/25(1)); South Roscommon Brigade, Death of Michael Carty, Loughglynn (IMA, Collins papers, A/076I); Civilians tried by courts martial (TNA, WO 35/131/47).

340 *RJ*, 25 June 1921; Outrages against police, June 1921 (TNA, CO 904/150); Batt I, South Roscommon Brigade, 9 July 1921, Shooting of John Vaughan and Edward Shannon (IMA, Collins papers, A/076I); Military court of inquiry on Edward Shannon and John Vaughan (TNA, WO 35/160/6); Compensation claim of Shannon family (IMA, MSPC, 3MSRB286); Compensation claim of Vaughan family (IMA, MSPC, 1D121).

341 CI Roscommon, June 1921 (TNA, CO 904/115).

342 OC South Roscommon Brigade IRA to IRA Director of Intelligence, 9 July 1921 (IMA, Collins papers, A/076I); Military court of inquiry on Thomas Rush (TNA, WO 35/158/48); Martin and Bridget Rush to Count Plunkett, 16 July 1921 (NLI, Plunkett papers, MS 11,374/22/12).

343 Courts of inquiry in lieu of inquest: register of cases (TNA, WO 035/163); Military court of inquiry on Edward Weir (TNA, WO 35/160/55); *WFJ*, 15 July 1922.

344 *FJ*, 21 June 1921; Brigade activity report for the North Roscommon Brigade IRA (IMA, MSPC, A31/1); Special advances to widows of members of the Royal Irish Constabulary murdered on duty (TNA, HO 144/22334/D304/1920).

345 Outrages against police, July 1921 (TNA, CO 904/150); Courts of inquiry in lieu of inquest (TNA, WO 35/163).

346 CI Roscommon, July 1921 (TNA, CO 904/116); *NW*, 6 July 1921; Seán Leavy (BMH WS 954, p. 23).

347 *DET*, 9 July 1921; Military court of inquiry on Michael Waldron and Thomas Waldron (TNA, WO 35/159B/24).

348 CI Roscommon, June 1921 (TNA, CO 904/115); *RH*, *RJ*, 25 June 1921.

349 *Hansard (Commons)*, 23 June 1921, vol. 143, cols. 1531–3.

350 *FJ*, 24 June, 29 Oct., 1 Nov. 1921.

351 *RH*, 2 July 1921.

352 *RJ*, 16 July 1921; Military operations and inquiries (TNA, WO 35/89); Brigade activity report for the Castlerea Brigade, 2nd Western Division (IMA, MSPC, A25/1); Thomas Crawley (BMH WS 718, p. 13).

353 Eunan O'Halpin and Daithí Ó Corráin, *The dead of the Irish Revolution* (London, 2020), p. 543.

354 CI Roscommon, July 1921 (TNA, CO 904/116).

CHAPTER EIGHT *From truce to Treaty and Civil War, 1921–3*

1 James Quigley (BMH WS 692, p. 14); Martin Fallon (BMH WS 1,121, p. 20).
2 *RJ, RH*, 23 July 1921.　　　3 *DJ*, 18 July 1921.　　　4 *RJ*, 16 July 1921.
5 CI Roscommon, July 1921 (TNA, CO 904/116); *FJ*, 9 July 1921.
6 *RH*, 31 Dec. 1921.　　　7 *NW*, 16 July 1921; *WFJ*, 23 July 1921.
8 Police reports 1921, Roscommon (TNA, CO 904/155); *RH, RJ*, 23, 30 July 1921.
9 *WFJ*, 23 July 1921; *Record of the rebellion*, p. 57.
10 *RH*, 3 Dec. 1921.
11 Police reports 1921, Roscommon (TNA, CO 904/155); *RJ*, 16 July 1921.
12 Internment camps and prisons (TNA, WO 35/140); *RH*, 6 Aug. 1921; *FJ*, 9 Dec. 1921.
13 *RH*, 6 Aug. 1921; *RJ*, 20 Aug. 1921.
14 Brigade activity report for the South Roscommon Brigade IRA (IMA, MSPC, A/27); *RJ*, 3 Sept. 1921; Compensation claim of John Connor (IMA, MSPC, 1P167).
15 *BT*, 11 Aug. 1921; *RH*, 13 Aug. 1921.
16 *WFJ*, 27 Aug. 1921; *RH*, 15 Oct. 1921.
17 *RH*, 15 Oct. 1921.
18 *LS*, 20 Sept. 1921; Outrages against the police, Sept. 1921 (TNA, CO 904/150); Police reports 1921, Roscommon (TNA, CO 904/155).
19 Police reports 1921, Roscommon (TNA, CO 904/155).　　　20 *FJ*, 27 Oct. 1921.
21 Cahir Davitt (BMH WS 993, pp 78–80).
22 *RH*, 23 July, 12 Nov. 1921; *Record of the rebellion*, p. 57.
23 *RH*, 30 July 1921; *RJ*, 12 Nov. 1921
24 CI Roscommon, Sept. 1921 (TNA, CO 904/116).　　　25 *RH*, 3 Dec. 1921.
26 CI Roscommon, Sept. 1921 (TNA, CO 904/116); Police reports 1921, Roscommon (TNA, CO 904/155); Report of training instruction tour, North Roscommon Brigade, Nov. 1921 (IMA, Collins papers, A/076O).
27 Police reports 1921, Roscommon (TNA, CO 904/155).
28 Report on South Roscommon Brigade (IMA, Collins papers, A/076I).
29 *RH*, 14 Jan. 1922.
30 *RH*, 4, 25 Mar., 22 Apr. 1922; Patrick Mullooly (BMH WS 1,086, p. 63).
31 *RJ*, 19 Nov. 1921; *RH*, 5, 26 Nov. 1921.
32 Police reports 1921, Roscommon (TNA, CO 904/155).
33 Vice Commandant South Roscommon IRA to IRA Director of Intelligence, 5 Nov. 1921 (IMA, Collins papers, A/076I).
34 Intelligence officer, South Roscommon IRA to IRA Director of Intelligence, 8 Nov. 1921 (IMA, Collins papers, A/076I).
35 Vice Commandant South Roscommon IRA to IRA Director of Intelligence, 21 Nov. 1921 (IMA, Collins papers, A/076I).
36 Richard Mulcahy to OC South Roscommon Brigade IRA, 4 Mar. 1921 (UCDA, Mulcahy papers, P7/A/17).
37 Report on South Roscommon Brigade IRA (IMA, Collins papers, A/076I).
38 *RH*, 6 Aug. 1921.　　　39 Ibid., 30 July 1921.
40 *WFJ*, 17 Sept. 1921; *RJ*, 1 Oct. 1921.　　　41 *RH*, 24 Dec. 1921.
42 *RJ*, 24, 31 Dec. 1921.　　　43 *Record of the rebellion*, p. 60; *RH*, 17 Dec. 1921.
44 *RH*, 17 Dec. 1921.　　　45 *DET*, 29 Dec. 1921; *RH*, 31 Dec. 1921.
46 Burke, *Athlone*, p. 218.
47 Pension claim of Patrick Madden (IMA, MSPC, 24SP7439); Pension claim of Francis Simons (IMA, MSPC, 24SP7402); Compensation claim of Dockery family (IMA, MSPC, W2D47); Pension claim of Thomas Lavin (IMA, MSPC 24SP2245).

48 *WFJ*, 24 Dec. 1921; Laurence Nugent (BMH WS 770, pp 259–62).

49 *FJ*, 27 Dec. 1921.

50 *TS*, *SDT*, 29 Dec. 1921; David Fitzpatrick, *Harry Boland's Irish revolution* (Cork, 2003), pp 255–8, 429.

51 *RJ*, 31 Dec. 1921.   **52** *RJ*, 11 Feb. 1922.

53 Laurence Nugent (BMH WS 770, p. 260).   **54** *RM*, 7 Jan. 1922.

55 *FJ*, 31 Jan., 2 Feb. 1922.   **56** *WFJ*, 14 Jan. 1922.

57 Cumann na mBan booklet (IMA, MSPC, CMB, 42); Cumann na mBan booklet (IMA, MSPC, CMB, 41); Pension claim of Kate Greene (IMA, MSPC, 34REF3921); Pension claim of Eileen O'Doherty (IMA, MSPC, 34REF39544); Pension claim of Teresa McDermott (IMA, MSPC, 34REF60035); *RM*, 11 Feb. 1922.

58 *FJ*, 9, 10 Jan. 1922.   **59** *RM*, 28 Jan. 1922; *WI*, 4 Feb. 1922.

60 *RH*, 8 Apr. 1922.   **61** Laurence Nugent (BMH WS 770, p. 262).

62 *BWT*, 14 Jan. 1922.   **63** *RH*, *RJ*, 14 Jan. 1922.   **64** *RH*, 23 Mar. 1922.

65 *WFJ*, *RM*, 14 Jan. 1922.   **66** *FJ*, 2 Feb. 1922.

67 *RJ*, 25 Feb., 1 Apr. 1922; *DJ*, 5 Apr. 1922.   **68** *FJ*, 15, 18 Mar. 1922.

69 *RH*, 1 Apr. 1922.   **70** *RJ*, *RM*, 1 Apr. 1922.

71 *Dáil Éireann debates*, 28 Feb. 1922.

72 *BWT*, 4 Mar. 1922; *RH*, 11 Mar., 8 Apr. 1922.

73 *RH*, 4, 11 Mar., 1 Apr. 1922; Donal J. O'Sullivan, *District Inspector John A. Kearney: the R.I.C. man who befriended Sir Roger Casement* (Bloomington, 2005), pp 136–51.

74 *RH*, 6 May 1922.   **75** *RJ*, 4 Mar. 1922.

76 *Record of the rebellion*, p. 58; From intelligence officer, South Roscommon IRA to IRA Director of Intelligence, 19 Nov. 1921 (IMA, Collins papers, A/076I).

77 *RH*, *RM*, 4, 11 Mar. 1922; *RJ*, 1 Apr. 1922.

78 *FJ*, 25 29 Mar. 1922; *RH*, *RJ*, 1 Apr. 1922.

79 *RH*, 23 Mar. 1922.   **80** *RH*, 8, 15 Apr. 1922.

81 *BNL*, 28 Mar. 1922; *WFJ*, 6 May 1922; *BWT*, 20 May 1922.

82 *FJ*, 3 Mar. 1921; *RM*, 11 Mar., 6, 13 May 1922; *RJ*, 29 Apr. 1922.

83 *NW*, 24 Apr. 1922; *WFJ*, 13 May 1922.

84 *DET*, 26 May 1922.   **85** *Sheffield Daily Telegraph (SDT)*, 9 June 1922.

86 *WFJ*, 17 June 1922.   **87** Foster, *Civil War*, pp 135–8.

88 *FJ*, 13 Apr. 1923; *WFJ*, 28 Apr. 1923.   **89** *FJ*, 6 Jan. 1923.

90 *RJ*, *RM*, *RH*, 1, 8 Apr. 1922.   **91** *RH*, 8 Apr. 1922.

92 *TS*, 2, 5 May 1922.

93 *FJ*, *DET*, 12 Apr. 1923; *DJ*, 13 Apr. 1923; *WFJ*, 21 Apr. 1923.

94 Irish Grants Committee claim of Henry Sampey, 5 Dec. 1928 (TNA CO 762/189/21).

95 *WFJ*, 3 June 1922.   **96** *DET*, 24 Feb. 1921.

97 OC North Roscommon Brigade IRA to IRA Adjutant General, 4 Feb. 1921 (IMA, Collins papers A/0760).

98 *RH*, *RJ*, 3 June 1922.   **99** *NW*, 29 May 1922.   **100** Burke, *Athlone*, p. 227–32.

101 *RH*, 8 Apr. 1922; Pension claim of Patrick Brennan (IMA, MSPC, 34REF29499); Michael Farry, *The aftermath of revolution: Sligo 1921–23* (Dublin, 2000), pp 54–5.

102 *RH*, 8 Apr. 1922.   **103** *RH*, 29 Apr., 6, 13 May 1922.

104 *YPLI*, 8 Apr. 1922.

105 *FJ*, 31 Dec. 1921; *WFJ*, 18 Feb. 1922; *RM*, 18 Mar. 1922.

106 *DJ*, 10 Apr. 1922; *BNL*, 12 Apr. 1922; *RJ*, 15 Apr. 1922.

107 *BNL*, 10 Apr. 1922; *RM*, 15 Apr. 1922.   **108** *BNL*, 3 May 1922.

109 *RM*, 22 Mar. 1922; *RJ*, 29 Apr. 1922; *WFJ*, 20, 27 May 1922; Report on post office robbery, Roscommon, 28 Apr. 1922 (NAI, Department of Finance papers, Fin 1/788).

110 *RH*, 26 Aug., 2, 30 Sept., 9 Dec. 1922, 10 Feb., 18 Apr. 1923.
111 *WFJ*, 13 May 1922; *FJ*, 16 Sept., 25 Nov. 1922, 29 Jan. 1923.
112 *RM*, 29 Apr., 6, 20 May 1922.
113 *SDT, DC*, 1 Apr. 1922; *RH*, 8, 15 Apr. 1922; Foster, *Civil War*, pp 123–8.
114 *RH*, 14, 21, 28 Oct., 9, 23 Dec. 1922; Compensation claim of James Edward Feely (IMA, MSPC, 24B926); *RJ*, 28 Apr. 1923.
115 *RJ*, 14, 28 Oct. 1922. **116** Foster, *Civil War*, pp 123–8.
117 *FJ, BNL*, 7 Nov. 1922; Vicky Conway, *Policing twentieth century Ireland: a history of an Garda Síochána* (Oxford, 2014), p. 37.
118 Operation report for Athlone Command, 5 Nov. 1922 (IMA, Athlone Command, CW/OPS/02); *BT*, 9 Nov. 1922.
119 *RJ*, 9, 30 Sept., 18, 25 Nov., 2, 30 Dec. 1922, 20 Jan. 1923.
120 Farry, *Aftermath*, p. 172.
121 *FJ*, 16 Jan., 7 Feb., 2 Apr. 1923; *DJ*, 17 Jan., 21 Feb. 1923; *RH*, 20 Jan., 24 Feb., 17 Mar. 1923; *NW*, 21 Feb. 1923; *DJ*, 2 Apr. 1923; *BT*, 6 Apr. 1923; Compensation claim of Francis O'Donohoe (IMA, MSPC, 2RB184); Compensation claim of John J. Moran (IMA, MSPC, 34SP768).
122 *RH*, 14 Apr. 1923. **123** *FJ*, 28 Apr. 1923.
124 Bill Kissane, *The politics of the Irish Civil War* (Oxford, 2005), p. 96.
125 *RH*, 8, 22 Apr. 1922. **126** *RM, RJ*, 22 Apr. 1922. **127** *RH*, 22, 29 Apr. 1922.
128 Ibid., 22, 29 Apr., 6, 13, 20 May 1922. **129** *RM*, 22, 29 Apr. 1922.
130 *RJ*, 23 Sept., 14 Oct. 1922; *FJ*, 3 Oct. 1922. **131** *RJ, RH*, 27 May 1922.
132 *RM*, 27 May 1922; *FJ*, 7 June 1922. **133** *RJ*, 3 June 1922; *FJ*, 8 June 1922.
134 Kissane, *Civil War*, pp 71–3. **135** *DJ*, 31 May 1922; *RH, RJ*, 3 June 1922.
136 *FJ*, 31 May, 2 June 1922; *RJ*, 3 June 1922. **137** *RJ*, 10 June 1922.
138 *DJ*, 5 June 1922; *FJ*, 15 June 1922; *RJ*, 24 June 1922.
139 Michael Gallagher, 'The pact general election of 1922', *Irish Historical Studies*, 21:84 (1981), 404–21.
140 *WFJ*, 10 June 1922. **141** Kissane, *Civil War*, p. 73.
142 *RH*, 17, 24 June 1922. **143** *RH*, 22 July 1922.
144 Pension claim of Patrick Brennan (IMA, MSPC, 34REF29499); Map of Boyle engagement by Patrick Brennan, Brigade activity report for the North Roscommon Brigade IRA (IMA, MSPC, A31/4/138).
145 Pension claim of Teresa McDermott (IMA, MSPC, 34REF60035).
146 *BT*, 8 July 1922; Pension claim of Patrick Brennan (IMA, MSPC, 34REF29499).
147 Pension claim of John Kelly (IMA, MSPC, 34REF29515).
148 *BNL*, 7 July 1922; Brigade activity report for the North Roscommon Brigade IRA (IMA, MSPC, A31/4).
149 *RH*, 22 July 1922. **150** *BT*, 7 July 1922; *RH*, 5 Aug. 1922.
151 *RH*, 29 July 1922.
152 *WI, BNL*, 8 July 1922; Pension claim of Patrick Brennan (IMA, MSPC, 34REF29499); Pension claim of Bridget Agnes Flynn (IMA, MSPC, 34REF41073); Pension claim of Joseph McGovern (IMA, MSPC, 34REF48819).
153 *RJ*, 1, 29 July 1922; *WFJ*, 15 July 1922; *YPLI*, 24 July 1922.
154 *RH*, 29 July, 5 Aug. 1922.
155 *RJ*, 1, 15 July 1922; *FJ*, 17 July 1922; *WFJ*, 12 Aug. 1922.
156 Brigade activity report for the South Roscommon Brigade IRA (IMA, MSPC, A/27).
157 *FJ*, 15 July 1922; *DJ*, 21 Aug. 1922; *Larne Times*, 18, 25 Nov. 1922.
158 *FJ*, 15 July 1922.
159 Booklet for South Roscommon Brigade IRA (IMA, MSPC, Booklet A27).

160 *Leeds Mercury*, 7 July 1922; Burke, *Athlone*, pp 240–1.
161 Michael Hopkinson, 'Civil War: the opening phase' in Crowley et al. (eds), *Atlas of the Irish Revolution*, p. 683.
162 *BT*, 8 July 1922; *WFJ*, 15 July 1922; *FJ*, 4 Aug. 1922.
163 *FJ*, 11 July 1922; *DJ*, 12 July 1922.   164 *RH*, 19 Aug. 1922.
165 *II*, 24 Aug. 1922.   166 *FJ*, 6 Sept. 1922.
167 Michael Hopkinson, *Green against green: the Irish Civil War* (Dublin, 1988), p. 212.
168 *FJ*, 20 July 1922; *RH*, 29 July 1922.
169 *FJ*, 22 July 1922; *LE*, 24, 27 July 1922.
170 Pension claim of Bridget Agnes Flynn (IMA, MSPC, 34REF41073).
171 Pension claim of Patrick Brennan (IMA, MSPC, 34REF29499).
172 *RH*, 26 Aug., 2, 16, 23, 30 Sept. 1922; Kissane, *Civil War*, p. 81.
173 *FJ*, 18 Aug. 1922; *RH*, 2, 9 Sept. 1922.
174 Shaun Costello to Officer Commanding No. 2 Brigade Castlerea ATIRA, 8 July 1922, 2nd Western Division II Brigade (Castlerea) (1/7/22), (IMA, MSPC, RO/260).
175 *FJ*, 12 July, 18 Aug., 7 Sept., 5, 17 Oct. 1922; *WFJ*, 22 July, 10 Mar. 1923; *RJ*, 22 July, 9 Sept. 1922; Brigade activity report for the South Roscommon Brigade IRA (IMA, A/27).
176 *FJ*, 18 Aug. 1922; *RJ*, 28 Aug. 1922.
177 *FJ*, 11 Nov. 1922; *RJ*, 2 Dec. 1922; *SDT*, 11 Dec. 1922; *DJ*, 29 Dec. 1922, 24 Jan. 1923; *RH*, 6, 13, 20, 27 Jan., 3 Feb. 1923; *DET*, 2 Mar. 1923; *BWT*, *RJ*, 10 Mar. 1923; Brigade activity report for the Athlone Brigade (IMA, MSPC, A68/2); Booklet for South Roscommon Brigade IRA (IMA, MSPC, Booklet A27); Michael Hopkinson, 'Railways: campaign of destruction' in Crowley, et al. (eds), *Atlas of the Irish Revolution*, pp 688–9.
178 *DET*, 9 Apr. 1923; *NW*, 23 Apr. 1923.
179 *BNL*, 15 Nov. 1922; *FJ*, 5 Mar. 1923; *DJ*, 16 Mar. 1923.
180 *DET*, 31 July 1922; *RH*, *RJ*, 5 Aug. 1922.   181 *RJ*, 12 Aug. 1922.
182 *FJ*, 11 Aug. 1922; *RJ*, *RH*, 12, 19 Aug. 1922; Kissane, *Civil War*, pp 143–4.
183 *FJ*, 12 Aug. 1922; *RJ*, 19 Aug. 1922.
184 *FJ*, 18 Aug. 1922; *RH*, 19, 26 Aug. 1922.   185 *LS*, 2 Sept. 1922.
186 *FJ*, 1 Sept. 1922; *RJ*, 2 Sept. 1922.
187 *NW*, 30 Aug. 1922; *FJ*, 1, 5, 7, 13, 21 Sept. 1922; Kissane, *Civil War*, p. 145.
188 *FJ*, 2 Sept. 1922.
189 *RJ*, 16 Sept. 1922; *BNL*, 26 Sept. 1922; *RH*, 25 Nov. 1922.
190 *RH*, 4 Nov., 16 Dec. 1922.
191 *RH*, 25 Nov. 1922, 27 Jan., 3, 17 Mar. 1923; Hopkinson, *Civil War*, p. 185.
192 *RJ*, 16, 30 Sept. 1922.   193 *Dáil Éireann debates*, 9 Sept. 1922.
194 *RH*, 30 Sept. 1922.   195 *RH*, 14 Oct. 1922.
196 *II*, 23 Nov. 1922; *FJ*, 1 Dec. 1922.   197 *RJ*, 4 Nov. 1922.
198 *RJ*, 16 Dec. 1922.   199 Burke, *Athlone*, p. 250.
200 *WI*, 27 Jan. 1923; Nollaig Ó Gadhra, *Civil War in Connacht, 1922–23* (Cork, 1999), pp 70–2.
201 Burke, *Athlone*, pp 238–9, 254; Compensation claim of Thomas Shannon (IMA, MSPC, DP24082).
202 *RH*, 2, 9, 16 Sept. 1922.
203 *RH*, 21, 28 Oct., 4 Nov. 1922; Pension claim of Joseph Edward O'Kelly (IMA, WMSP, 34REF56091); Compensation claim of Flannery family (IMA, MSPC, DP3523); *RJ*, *RH*, 6, 13 Jan. 1923.
204 *RH*, 4 Nov. 1922; Compensation claim of Mulrennan family (IMA, MSCP, 2RB588); Burke, *Athlone*, pp 248–9; Kissane, *Civil War*, p. 85.
205 *RH*, 23, 30 Sept., 14 Oct. 1922; Pension claim of Patrick Brennan (IMA, MSPC, 34REF29499).

206 *Dáil Éireann debates*, 7, 8 Feb. 1923.

207 *RH*, 17 Feb. 1923; Compensation claim of Callaghan family (IMA, MSPC, W3D134); Compensation claim of Cull family (IMA, MSPC, 2RB475).

208 *RH*, 3 Mar. 1923.   **209** *II*, 5 Mar. 1923.

210 *RH*, 31 Mar., 5, 12, 19 May 1923.

211 Brigade activity report for the Athlone Brigade (IMA, MSPC, A68/2); General Seán Mac Eoin to National army Chief of Staff, 24 Apr. 1923 (UCDA, Mac Eoin papers, P155/200).

212 General Seán Mac Eoin to National army Chief of Staff, 19 Apr. 1923 (UCDA, Mac Eoin papers, P155/220/52); Operation reports for Athlone Command, 6, 8, 23 Mar., 10 Apr. 1923 (IMA, Athlone Command papers, CW/OPS/02/03/02).

213 *RJ*, 17 Feb. 1923.

214 Foster, *Irish Civil War*, pp 33–4.   **215** Burke, *Athlone*, p. 254; *FJ*, 3 Mar. 1923.

216 *RJ*, 28 Apr. 1923.

217 *YPLI*, 1 May 1923; *BWT*, 12, 13 May 1923; Pension claim of Patrick Brennan (IMA, MSPC, 34REF29499).

218 *RJ*, 19 May 1923; *DET*, 23 May 1923.   **219** *RH*, 2 June 1923.

220 *RJ*, 2, 9 June 1923.

CHAPTER NINE *Revolution?*

1 Census of population, 1926 (10 vols, Dublin 1928–34), 3, table 9.

2 Marie Coleman 'Protestant depopulation in County Longford during the Irish Revolution', *English Historical Review*, 135:575 (2020), 931–77.

3 www.electionsireland.org (accessed 25 Apr. 2020).

4 *RM*, 3 Sept. 1927.

5 Ibid., 28 Jan. 1922.

Select bibliography

PRIMARY SOURCES

A. MANUSCRIPTS

Dublin
Irish Military Archives
Bureau of Military History
Brigade Activity reports
Civil War captured documents
Civil War operations and intelligence reports collection
Collins papers
Military Service Pensions Collection
Military Service Medal Applications
Truce liaison and evacuation papers

National Archives of Ireland
Ancient Order of Hibernians agenda book, 1912–81
Dáil Éireann Department of Local Government papers
Department of Finance
RIC Inspector General and County Inspector reports, 1903–1908

National Library of Ireland
Joseph Brennan papers
Irish National Aid and Volunteer Dependants' Fund papers
ITGWU List of branches in chronological order
General Sir John Maxwell papers
William O'Brien papers
Count Plunkett papers
John Redmond papers
Sinn Féin papers
United Irish League National Directory minute book

University College Dublin Archives
Seán Mac Eoin papers
Richard Mulcahy papers
Ernie O'Malley notebooks
Ernie O'Malley papers
Count Plunkett papers
Moss Twomey papers

London
The National Archives
Colonial Office records

Home Office records
War Office records

Parliamentary Archives, London
Lloyd George papers

B. OFFICAL RECORDS

Agricultural statistics of Ireland, with detailed report for the year 1915, House of Commons, 1916 (Cd. 8563).

Agricultural statistics of Ireland, with detailed report for the year 1916, House of Commons, 1917 (Cd. 112).

Agricultural statistics 1917, vol. LII. Part I. Acreage and livestock returns of England and Wales with summaries for the United Kingdom, House of Commons, 1918 (Cd. 9006).

Census of Ireland, 1911, Area, houses and population: also the ages, civil or conjugal condition, occupations, birthplaces, religion and education of the people.

Province of Connaught, County of Roscommon, House of Commons, 1912 (Cd. 6052-III).

Census of Ireland, part two: General report with tables and appendix, House of Commons, 1913 (Cd. 6663).

Dáil Éireann parliamentary debates.

Department of Agriculture and Technical Instruction for Ireland. Agricultural statistics of Ireland with detailed report for the year 1908, House of Commons, 1909 (Cd. 4940).

Department of Agriculture and Technical Instruction for Ireland. Agricultural statistics of Ireland with detailed report for the year 1912, House of Commons, 1913 (Cd. 6987).

Department of Agriculture and Technical Instruction for Ireland. Agricultural statistics of Ireland 1913. General abstracts showing the acreage under crops and the numbers and descriptions of livestock in each county and province 1912–13, House of Commons, 1913 (Cd. 7063).

Department of Agriculture and General Instruction for Ireland. Eighteenth Annual Report of the Department, 1917–18, House of Commons, 1918 (Cd. 106).

Department of Agriculture and General Instruction for Ireland. Agricultural statistics, Ireland, 1918. General abstracts showing the acreage under crops and the numbers and descriptions of livestock in each county and province 1916–7–8, House of Commons, 1919 (Cd. 113).

Emigration statistics for Ireland for the year 1912, reports and tables showing the numbers, ages, conjugal condition, and destinations of emigrants from each county and province in Ireland during the year 1912; also the occupations of the emigrants, and the number of emigrants who left each port in each month of the year, House of Commons, 1913 (Cd. 6727).

Emigration statistics of Ireland 1915, House of Commons, 1916 (Cd. 8230).

Hansard 5 (Commons) parliamentary debates.

Judicial statistics, Ireland, 1912. Part 1.– Criminal statistics: statistics relating to police-crime and its distribution-modes of procedure for punishment of crime-proceedings in criminal courts-persons under detention in prisons and other places of confinement-for the year 1912, House of Commons, 1913 (Cd. 7064).

Judicial statistics, Ireland, 1914. Part 1.– Criminal statistics: statistics relating to police-crime and its distribution-modes of procedure for punishment of crime-proceedings in criminal courts-persons under detention in prisons and other places of confinement-for the year 1914, House of Commons, 1915 (Cd. 8077).

Judicial statistics, 1915; Part I – Annual criminal statistics for the year 1915, House of Commons, 1916 (Cmd. 8636).

Report on recruiting in Ireland, 1914–16, House of Commons, 1916 (Cd. 8168).

Report of the Royal Commission on the rebellion in Ireland: minutes of evidence and appendix of documents, House of Commons, 1916 (Cd. 8311).

Report of the Royal Commission on the rebellion in Ireland. House of Commons, 1916 (Cd. 8279).

Report of the proceedings of the Irish Convention, House of Commons, 1918 (Cd. 9019).

Statement giving particulars of men of military age in Ireland, House of Commons, 1916 (Cd. 8390).

C. NEWSPAPERS AND PERIODICALS

Aberdeen Press and Journal
Army and Navy Gazette
Ballymena Weekly Telegraph
Belfast News Letter
Belfast Telegraph
Belfast Weekly News
Birmingham Daily Gazette
Birmingham Daily Post
Derby Daily Telegraph
Derry Journal
Drogheda Independent
Dublin Daily Express
Dublin Evening Mail
Dublin Evening Telegraph
Dundee Courier
Enniscorthy Guardian
Evening Despatch
Exeter and Plymouth Gazette
Freeman's Journal
Gloucestershire Echo
Illustrated Police News
Irish Bulletin
Irish Citizen
Irish Independent
Irish Times
Irish Volunteer
Kerry Evening Post
Larne Times
Leeds Mercury
Leitrim Advertiser
Liverpool Echo

Londonderry Sentinel
Manchester Courier and Lancashire General Advertiser
Manchester Evening News
Mid-Ulster Mail
Northern Whig
Nottingham Evening Post
Nottingham Journal
Pall Mall Gazette
Roscommon Herald
Roscommon Journal
Roscommon Messenger
Sheffield Daily Telegraph
Sheffield Independent
Sport
Strokestown Democrat
The Daily Herald
The Globe
The Leader
The People
The Scotsman
Thom's Directory, 1912–23
Weekly Freeman's Journal
Weekly Irish Times
Western Nationalist
Westmeath Independent
Wexford People
Wicklow News Letter and County Advertiser
Wicklow People
Yorkshire Post and Leeds Intelligencer

D. PRINTED PRIMARY MATERIAL

Mac Giolla Coille, Brendán, *Intelligence notes, 1913–16, preserved in the State Paper Office* (Dublin, 1966).

Martin, Hugh, *Insurrection in Ireland: an Englishman's record of fact* (London, 1921).

O'Malley, Ernie, *On another man's wound: a personal history of Ireland's War of Independence* (Dublin, 2002 [1936]).

——, *Raids and rallies* (Cork, 2011 [1982])

——, *Rising out* (Dublin, 2007).

——, Cormac O'Malley and Vincent Keane (eds), *The men will talk to me. Mayo interviews by Ernie O'Malley* (Cork, 2014).

SECONDARY SOURCES

E. PUBLISHED WORKS

Aalen, F.H.A., Kevin Whelan & Matthew Stout, *Atlas of the Irish rural landscape* (2nd ed. Cork, 2011 [1997]).

aan de Wiel, Jérôme, *The Catholic Church in Ireland, 1914–1918: war and politics* (Dublin, 2005).

Augusteijn, Joost, *From public defiance to guerilla warfare: the experience of ordinary Volunteers in the Irish War of Independence, 1916–1921* (Dublin, 1996).

——, 'Military conflict in the war of independence' in John Crowley, Donal Ó Drisceoil & Mike Murphy (eds), *Atlas of the Irish Revolution* (Cork, 2017), pp 348–57.

Behan, Cormac, *Citizen convict: prisoners, politics and the vote* (Manchester, 2014).

Bew, Paul, *Conflict and conciliation in Ireland, 1890–1910. Parnellites and radical agrarians* (New York, 1989).

——, *Ideology and the Irish question: Ulster unionism and Irish nationalism, 1912–1916* (New York, 1994).

Bligh, John, 'John Fitzgibbon of Castlerea: "A most mischievous and dangerous agitator"' in Brian Casey (ed.), *Defying the law of the land: agrarian radicals in Irish history* (Dublin, 2014), pp 201–19.

Borgonovo, John, *Spies, informers and the 'Anti-Sinn Féin Society': the intelligence war in Cork city, 1920–1921* (Dublin, 2007).

Bowman, Timothy, *Carson's army: the Ulster Volunteer Force, 1910–22* (Manchester, 2007).

Boyce, George & Alan O'Day, *Ireland in transition, 1867–1921* (London, 2004).

Breathnach, Diarmaid & Máire Ní Mhurchú, *Beathaisnéis a cúig* (Baile Átha Claith, 1997).

Brewer, John D., *The Royal Irish Constabulary: an oral history* (Belfast, 1990).

Buckland, Patrick, *Irish unionism. Vol. 1, The Anglo-Irish and the new Ireland, 1885–1922* (New York, 1974).

Burke, John, *Athlone, 1900–1923: politics, revolution and civil war* (Dublin, 2015).

Campbell, Fergus, *Land and revolution: nationalist politics in the west of Ireland, 1891–1921* (Oxford, 2005).

Carroll, Denis, *They have fooled you again: Michael O'Flanagan (1876–1942), priest, republican, social critic* (2nd ed., Dublin, 2016 [1993]).

Clark, Gemma, *Everyday violence in the Irish Civil War* (Cambridge, 2014).

Clark, Samuel & James S. Donnelly (eds), *Irish peasants, violence and political unrest, 1780–1914* (Manchester, 1983).

Coleman, Marie, *County Longford and the revolution* (Dublin, 2006).

——, 'Protestant depopulation in County Longford during the Irish Revolution', *English Historical Review*, 135:575 (2020), 931–77.

Collins, Peter (ed.), *Nationalism and unionism: conflict in Ireland, 1885–1921* (Belfast, 1994).

Conway, Vicky, *Policing twentieth-century Ireland: a history of an Garda Síochána* (Oxford, 2014).

Costello, Francis, *The Irish Revolution and its aftermath, 1916–1923: years of revolt* (Dublin, 2003).

Crowley, John, Donal Ó Drisceoil & Mike Murphy (eds), *Atlas of the Irish Revolution* (Cork, 2017).

Cullen, Seamus, *Kildare: the Irish Revolution, 1912–23* (Dublin, 2020).

Cunningham, John, *Labour in the west of Ireland: working life and struggle, 1890–1914* (Belfast, 1995).

Daly, Mary E., *Buffer state: the history of the Department of the Environment* (Dublin, 1997).

Dooley, Terence, *'The land for the people': the land question in independent Ireland* (Dublin, 2004).

Doughan, Christopher, *The voice of the provinces: the regional press in revolutionary Ireland* (Liverpool, 2019).

English, Richard, *Armed struggle: the history of the IRA* (New York, 2003).

Farrell, Richie, Kieran O'Conor & Matthew Potter, *Roscommon history and society: interdisciplinary essays on the history of an Irish county* (Dublin, 2019).

Farren, Seán, *The politics of education, 1920–65* (Belfast, 1995).

Farry, Michael, *The aftermath of revolution: Sligo 1921–23* (Dublin, 2000).

——, *Sligo: the Irish Revolution, 1912–23* (Dublin, 2012).

Feely, Barry, *They dared to challenge. The story of the troubles in the provincial town of Boyle, which included the old I.R.A., R.I.C. and the British army* (Boyle, 2016).

Ferriter, Diarmaid, *A nation and not a rabble: the Irish Revolution, 1913–23* (London, 2015).

Finnan, Joseph P., *John Redmond and Irish unity, 1912–1918* (Syracuse, 2004).

Fitzpatrick, David, *Politics and Irish life, 1913–21: provincial experiences of war and revolution* (2nd ed., Cork, 1998 [1977]).

——, 'The geography of Irish nationalism', *Past & Present*, 78 (1978), 113–44.

——, *Harry Boland's Irish Revolution* (Cork, 2003).

——, 'The geography of the War of Independence' in John Crowley, Donal Ó Drisceoil & Mike Murphy (eds), *Atlas of the Irish Revolution* (Cork, 2017), pp 534–43.

Flynn, Tomás, *Thomas J. Devine and the election of the snows: the North Roscommon by-election of 1917* (Carrick-on-Shannon, 2016).

Foley, Caitriona, *The last Irish plague: the great flu epidemic in Ireland, 1918–19* (Dublin, 2011).

Foster, Gavin M., *The Irish Civil War and society: politics, class, and conflict* (New York, 2015).

Foster, Roy, *Vivid faces: the revolutionary generation in Ireland, 1890–1923* (London, 2014).

Gallagher, Michael, 'The pact general election of 1922', *Irish Historical Studies*, 21:84 (1981), 404–21.

Garvin, Tom, *The evolution of Irish nationalist politics* (Dublin, 1981).

Greaves, C. Desmond, *The Irish Transport and General Workers' Union: the formative years, 1909–1923* (Dublin, 1982).

Hart, Peter, 'The geography of revolution in Ireland, 1917–1923', *Past & Present*, 155:1 (1997), 142–76.

——, *The IRA and its enemies: violence and community in Cork, 1916–23* (Oxford, 1998).

——, *The IRA at war, 1916–23* (Oxford, 2003).

Heffernan, Brian, *Freedom and the fifth commandment: Catholic priests and political violence in Ireland, 1919–21* (Manchester, 2014).

Hegarty-Thorne, Kathleen, '*They put the flag a-flyin': the Roscommon Volunteers, 1916–1923* (2nd ed., Oregon, 2007 [2005]).

Hennessy, Thomas, *Dividing Ireland: World War I and partition* (London, 1998).

Hepburn, A.C., *Catholic Belfast and nationalist Ireland in the era of Joe Devlin, 1872–1934* (Oxford, 2008).

Hopkinson, Michael, *Green against green: the Irish Civil War* (Dublin, 1988).

——, *The Irish War of Independence* (Dublin, 2002).

——, 'Civil War: the opening phase' in John Crowley, Donal Ó Drisceoil & Mike Murphy (eds), *Atlas of the Irish Revolution* (Cork, 2017), pp 675–87.

——, 'Railways: campaign of destruction' in John Crowley, Donal Ó Drisceoil & Mike Murphy (eds), *Atlas of the Irish Revolution* (Cork, 2017), pp 688–90.

Hughes, Brian, *Defying the IRA: intimidation, coercion, and communities during the Irish Revolution* (Liverpool, 2016).

Jackson, Alvin, *Home rule: an Irish history, 1800–2000* (Oxford, 2003).

——, *Ireland, 1798–1998: war, peace and beyond* (Chichester, 2010).

Jones, David Seth, *Graziers, land reform, and political conflict in Ireland* (Washington DC, 1995).

Kissane, Bill, *The politics of the Irish Civil War* (Oxford, 2005).

Kostick, Conor, *Revolution in Ireland: popular militancy, 1917–23* (London, 1996).

Laffan, Michael, 'The unification of Sinn Féin in 1917', *Irish Historical Studies*, 17:67 (1971), 353–79.

——, *The resurrection of Ireland: the Sinn Féin party, 1916–1923* (Cambridge, 1999).

Lee, J.J., *Ireland, 1912–1985, politics and society* (Cambridge, 1989).

Leeson, D.M., *The Black and Tans: British police and auxiliaries in the Irish War of Independence* (Oxford, 2012).

——, 'The Royal Irish Constabulary, Black and Tans and Auxiliaries' in John Crowley, Donal Ó Drisceoil & Mike Murphy (eds), *Atlas of the Irish Revolution* (Cork, 2017), pp 371–81.

Matthews, Ann, *Renegades: Irish republican women, 1900–1922* (Cork, 2010).

McArdle, Dorothy, *The Irish Republic* (4th ed., London, 1968 [1937]).

McCarthy, Cal, *Cumann na mBan and the Irish Revolution* (Dublin, 2014).

McCarthy, Pat, *Waterford: the Irish Revolution, 1912–23* (Dublin, 2015).

McConnel, James, *The Irish Parliamentary Party and the third home rule crisis* (Dublin, 2013).

McGarry, Fearghal, *The Rising: Ireland 1916* (2nd ed., Oxford, 2016 [2010]).

McGarty, Patrick, *Leitrim: the Irish Revolution, 1912–23* (Dublin, 2020).

McGee, Owen, *The IRB: The Irish Republican Brotherhood from the Land League to Sinn Féin* (Dublin, 2006).

McKenna, Joseph, *Guerrilla warfare in the Irish War of Independence, 1919–1921* (Jefferson, 2011).

McMahon, Timothy, *Grand opportunity: the Gaelic revival and Irish society, 1893–1910* (Syracuse, 2008).

McNamara, Conor, *War and revolution in the west of Ireland: Galway, 1913–1922* (Newbridge, 2018).

——, 'Connacht' in John Crowley, Donal Ó Drisceoil & Mike Murphy (eds), *Atlas of the Irish Revolution* (Cork, 2017), pp 600–7.

Meleady, Dermot, *John Redmond: the national leader* (Sallins, 2013).

Miller, David W., *Church, state and nation in Ireland, 1898–1921* (Dublin, 1971).

Miller, Ian, *Reforming food in post-famine Ireland: medicine, science and improvement, 1845–1922* (Manchester, 2014).

Milne, Ida, *Stacking the coffins: influenza, war and revolution in Ireland, 1918–19* (Manchester, 2018).

Mitchell, Arthur, *Labour in Irish politics, 1890–1930: the Irish labour movement in an age of revolution* (Dublin, 1974).

——, *Revolutionary government in Ireland: Dáil Éireann, 1919–22* (Dublin, 1995).

Moran, May, *Executed for Ireland: the Patrick Moran story* (Cork, 2010).

Mulvagh, Conor, *The Irish Parliamentary Party at Westminster, 1900–18* (Manchester, 2016).

Murphy, William, *Political imprisonment and the Irish, 1912–1921* (Oxford, 2014).

Murray, Patrick, *Oracles of God: the Roman Catholic Church and Irish politics, 1922–37* (Dublin, 2000).

Nolan, Michael, *The Parnell split in Westmeath: the bishop and the newspaper editor* (Dublin, 2018).

Ó Duibhir, Liam, *Prisoners of war: Ballykinlar, an Irish internment camp, 1920–1921* (Cork, 2013).

Ó Gadhra, Nollaig, *Civil War in Connacht, 1922–23* (Cork, 1999).

O'Callaghan, John, *Limerick: the Irish Revolution, 1912–23* (Dublin, 2018).

O'Callaghan, Michael, *For Ireland and freedom: Roscommon and the fight for independence, 1917–1921* (2nd ed., Cork, 2012 [1964]).

Ó Corráin, Daithí, 'J.J. O'Connell's memoir of the Irish Volunteers, 1914–16, 1917', *Analecta Hibernica*, 47 (2016), 1–102.

O'Day, Alan, *Irish home rule, 1867–1921* (Manchester, 1998).

O'Donoghue, Florence (ed.), *Sworn to be free: complete book of IRA jailbreaks, 1918–21* (Tralee, 1971).

O'Halpin, Eunan & Daithí Ó Corráin, *The dead of the Irish Revolution* (London & New Haven, 2020).

O'Leary, Cornelius & Patrick Maume, *Controversial issues in Anglo-Irish relations, 1910–1921* (Dublin, 2004).

O'Sullivan, Donal J., *The Irish constabularies, 1822–1922: a century of policing in Ireland* (Dingle, 1999).

——, *District Inspector John A. Kearney: the RIC man who befriended Sir Roger Casement* (Bloomington, 2005).

Ó Ruairc, Pádraig Óg, *Truce: murder, myth and the last days of the Irish War of Independence* (Cork, 2016).

——, '"Spies and informers beware?"': IRA execution of alleged civilian spies during the War of Independence' in John Crowley, Donal Ó Drisceoil & Mike Murphy (eds), *Atlas of the Irish Revolution* (Cork, 2017), pp 433–6.

Pašeta, Senia, *Irish nationalist women, 1900–1918* (Cambridge, 2013).

Pennell, Caitriona, *A kingdom united: popular response to the outbreak of the First World War* (Oxford, 2012).

Potter, Matthew, *The municipal revolution in Ireland. A handbook of urban government in Ireland since 1800* (Dublin, 2011).

Privilege, John, *Michael Logue and the Catholic Church in Ireland* (Manchester, 2008).

Regan, John M., *The Irish counter-revolution, 1921–1936: treatyite politics and settlement in independent Ireland* (Dublin, 1999).

Scholes, Andrew, *The Church of Ireland and the third home rule bill* (Dublin, 2010).

Shouldice, Frank, *Grandpa the sniper: the remarkable story of a 1916 volunteer* (Dublin, 2015).

Townshend, Charles, *Easter 1916, the Irish rebellion* (London, 2006).

——, *The Republic: the fight for Irish independence 1918–1923* (London, 2013).

Wheatley, Michael, *Nationalism and the Irish Party: provincial Ireland, 1910–1916* (Oxford, 2010).

F. THESES AND UNPUBLISHED WORK

Dyer Wolf, Daphne, 'Two windows: the tenants of the de Freyne rent strike, 1901–1903' (PhD, Drew University, New Jersey, 2019).

G. INTERNET SOURCES

Election results, 1922: https://www.electionsireland.org/results/general/03dail.cfm

Election results, 1923: https://www.electionsireland.org/results/general/04dail.cfm

Landed estates database: http://www.landedestates.ie

McGuire, James and James Quinn (eds), *Dictionary of Irish biography* (Cambridge, 2009) http://dib.cambridge.org

Ulster Covenant online, PRONI: http@//apps.proni.gov.uk/ulstercovenant/SearchResults.aspx

Index